Language-Based Approaches to Support Reading Comprehension

Language-Based Approaches to Support Reading Comprehension

Edited by Francine Falk-Ross

ROWMAN & LITTLEFIELD
Lanham • Boulder • New York • London

KH

Published by Rowman & Littlefield
A wholly owned subsidiary of The Rowman & Littlefield Publishing Group, Inc.
4501 Forbes Boulevard, Suite 200, Lanham, Maryland 20706
www.rowman.com

16 Carlisle Street, London W1D 3BT, United Kingdom

British Library Cataloguing in Publication Information Available

Library of Congress Cataloging-in-Publication Data
Language-based approaches to support reading comprehension / edited by Francine Falk-Ross.
    p. ; cm.
Includes bibliographical references and index.
ISBN 978-1-4422-2987-7 (cloth : alk. paper) — ISBN 978-1-4422-2988-4 (pbk. : alk. paper) — ISBN 978-1-4422-2989-1 (electronic) 1. Reading comprehension—Study and teaching. 2. Language experience approach in education. 3. English language—Study and teaching—Foreign speakers I. Falk-Ross, Francine C., editor.
    LB1050.45.L355 2015
    372.47—dc23
                                                                                    2014012129

∞™ The paper used in this publication meets the minimum requirements of American National Standard for Information Sciences—Permanence of Paper for Printed Library Materials, ANSI/NISO Z39.48-1992.

Printed in the United States of America

9/23/16

For my M & M girls whose models of unquenchable thirst for knowledge serve as inspiration to provide all students with equal access to learning through teachers' understanding of alternate perspectives.

Contents

Acknowledgments   ix

Part I: The Challenges for Literacy Development Across Disciplines

1   Overview of the Text   3
    Francine Falk-Ross

2   The Educational Issues Before Us   9
    Francine Falk-Ross

3   A Case Study to Consider Using Different Frames of Reference   13
    Francine Falk-Ross

Part II: Language as a Scaffold for Learning

4   The Mediating Role of Pedagogic Discourse   25
    Francine Falk-Ross

5   Providing Supportive Contexts for Young Children's Language to
    Develop Their Ideas and Opinions   51
    Shobana Musti-Rao and Lenwood Gibson

6   Looking at Literacy from the Family-School Frame of Reference   67
    Lee Shumow and Elena Lyutykh

7   Mathematics Talk: Literacy Development in a Mathematics Context   91
    Brian R. Evans

8   Literacy and the Arts: How Artistic Perspectives Enhance
    Literacy Learning   113
    Merryl Goldberg and Laurie Stowell

9   Promoting Agency, Access, and Acquisition Among Adolescent
    English Language Learners   143
    Kathleen A. J. Mohr, Michelle Flory, and Lois Ann Knezek

Part III: Talk and Textual Considerations

10 Multimodality in Children's School-Based Texts   167
    Roberta Linder

11 Addressing Adolescents' Need for Voice and Interaction   181
    Jill Lewis-Spector and Mary McGriff

12 From Resistance to Engagement—The Importance of the Digital
    Literacies for Struggling Readers and Writers   209
    Peter McDermott and Kathleen A. Gormley

13 Concluding Thoughts   237
    Francine Falk-Ross

Index   239

About the Contributors   243

About the Editor   247

Acknowledgments

I thank Susanne Caravan and Andrea Offdenkamp Kendrick for their patience and support in guiding the ideas in this text into print to share with educators of all levels. I thank the individual authors for their collaboration and interesting perspectives as they provided clear rationales for their various frames of reference and endeavored to provide educators with a view of students through their lenses. I thank Mario for his persistence to learn.

I

THE CHALLENGES FOR LITERACY DEVELOPMENT ACROSS DISCIPLINES

1

Overview of the Text

Francine Falk-Ross

At professional conferences and in university-school partnerships, my colleagues and I conversed about how to guide preservice and practicing teachers to support the individual needs of students marginalized by differences in learning and talking with positive approaches. We wanted to develop and share (i.e., transfer) empowering pedagogical strategies that highlighted students' strengths and not their perceived deficits. As we talked together, we acknowledged how each conversational member's perspective differed, and how each member's input changed the language we used and modified our proposed actions in proactive ways. This was especially true when we discussed students with linguistic and cultural differences. In fact, we each knew some information about alternate perspectives; however, when they were shared by experts in the area, it was explained in more detail and with insight we did not bring to the solution. We needed to hear one another's words and examples to further understand how to support the students' needs. For example, when considering students who were English language learners, teachers and teacher educators with knowledge of the second language learning process were able to specify their cultural and linguistic funds of knowledge (Moll, 1992) that we had not considered. Those educators with knowledge of critical discourse analysis (Gee and Handford, 2012) were able to deconstruct the language we used with the students to support learning and value their contributions. Those educators with knowledge of motivation and identity development for the students' age group were able to highlight the necessary elements for classroom environment and activity development. Educators with knowledge of the fine arts and new literacies were able to share alternative approaches to teaching that match learning styles and personal intelligences (Gardner, 2011). These conversations among educators were both informative and uplifting. Those past collaborations inspired the invitations for expert contributions in this text focusing on specific perspectives, or frames of reference, and the common case study of one middle-grade second-language learner that serves to replicate a common focus.

This set of interactive conversations of educators set a model for how preservice teachers can learn their instructional craft and how practicing teachers can gain professional development to inform their assessment and instruction. Preservice and practicing teachers require new information and new lenses for developing their critical thinking about educating students so they can adapt instruction for students' specific strengths and challenges in fair and just ways. There are many sources for this information, yet they often remain discrete from one another as coursework and professional development opportunities frequently focus on one topic separated from the larger considerations that impact students' education (i.e., with little context). There is a popular old story of seven blind men and an elephant, and all its variations. The tale relates the story of seven blind men explaining what they think an elephant looks like; since each only touch one part of the elephant, such as the trunk or the tail or the ear, and each can only provide a correct description for one part. In short, without seeing all the parts, they cannot understand the whole. The same is true in education. In our case, the story relates to a theme of informed decision-making including many perspectives so teachers may consider the full complexity of teaching.

Although we feel that the information presented in this text may be applied to all students since they all bring varied personal, cultural, linguistic, historical, and cognitive needs to all learning experiences, this text is focused on students who are frequently marginalized by language differences in the classroom, whether by teachers' oversight or lack of information. The contributing authors offer their perspectives on supporting English language learners (ELLs) through specific strategies for assessment and instruction. A short case study is presented to further focus the readers' attention on a young adolescent, Mario, for whom Spanish is a language that surrounds home experiences and outside-of-school interactions, and which influences his language and cultural orientation to learning in his school classrooms and literacy events.

Each chapter presents a specific issue and challenge, supportive research and updated information, classroom implications and strategies, and case study applications relating to the particular perspective of literacy development for ELLs of middle-level ages. The authors focus on approaches to building and supporting literacy through the frames of pedagogical discourse that facilitate comprehension, multimodality that bridges textual resources, digital media that pervades childhood and adolescent cultures, and culturally responsive educational approaches that acknowledge a diverse population of students.

This text will help educators recognize key elements in critical literacy approaches that distinguish different reading instruction programs. Specifically, emphases will be on the following topics:

- to introduce and explain language-based and discourse-focused literacy strategies to support a variety of multicultural literature, media resources, and non-print

materials suitable for middle-level students and matched to their interests, consistent with professional standards and recent national standards (e.g., Common Core Learning Standards for students' competencies and International Reading Association's Standards for Reading Professionals for classroom teachers' perspectives) for reading, writing, listening, speaking for building content knowledge;
- to provide research-based reading strategies to help a diverse student population and develop critical thinking and comprehension activities for content area reading through development of oral discussion and questioning routines;
- to present highlight the centrality of supportive pedagogic discourse and appropriate language modifications for implementation of literacy activities for young adolescent students.

Each chapter contributes with its own perspective, or frame of reference, to a deeper understanding of the various frames of reference for educators to impact students' learning.

Chapter 2 provides review of theoretical and educational issues that is intended to contextualize the need for this text and the importance of the organization of theory-into-practice contributed by each author. The main themes of the chapter development focus on teachers' (re)consideration of the cultural and linguistic diversity of the student population, the development of learning standards by professional organizations and state initiatives, technological innovations that affect students' learning and may not be accessible, and approaches to professional development of teachers for 21st-century approaches to teaching and learning. This chapter sets the stage for the deeper development of each topic by contributing authors.

Chapter 3 provides an excerpt of a literacy lesson in Mario's classroom. Background information about Mario and the learning lesson is offered to provide a working context. The learning event is a mixture of conversation generated when the teacher conducts an assessment of Mario's motivation to read (Pitcher et al., 2007) and a running record of his read-aloud of a passage. The background information he provides for the teacher and readers of this excerpt serve as a focus for all contributing authors to suggest instructional approaches, aligned with the Common Core Learning Standards (2012) adopted by the majority of states in the United States.

In Chapter 4, "The Mediating Role of Pedagogic Discourse," Francine Falk-Ross reviews the research on discourse analysis and develops applications for using expanded forms of pedagogic discourse to mediate learning in content area learning. Using the frame of discourse specialists, an extension of these suggestions is the process for critiquing teachers' language routines. A more critical analysis of these routines sets the stage for use of expanded questioning and comments to guide teachers' comments in the classroom. Educators are encouraged to consider if and how they offer equal access to learning to all students, and to minimize the marginalization of some cultural groups.

In Chapter 5, "Providing Supportive Contexts for Young Children's Language to Develop Their Ideas and Opinions," Shobana Musti-Rao and Lenwood Gibson provide a frame of reference focused on how teachers can provide supportive contexts to develop students' language as it relates to literacy instruction. The authors review the theories of language acquisition, including Skinner's Behaviorist theory (1957), Chomsky's (1957) Innatist theory (1957), and Hymes' Interactionist theory (1972), to understand the interconnectedness of language and literacy. Then, they discuss ways in which teachers and adults can provide supportive contexts to facilitate language development in students in the classroom setting, including the use of new literacies for language and literacy development.

Chapter 6, "Looking at Literacy from the Family-School Frame of Reference," Lee Shumow and Elena Lyutykh highlight the importance of partnerships between educators and parents in supporting literacy development of children from diverse backgrounds. Using a socio-cultural perspective on literacy, such as Lee and Bowen (2006), and Moll, Amanti, and Neff (1992), the authors describe a multitude of ways in which ethnic minority, immigrant, and multilingual families support literacy development at home. These efforts are often unrecognized by schools and the advantages of bilingualism are often clouded by struggles that students like Mario often experience performing on standardized tests. The authors call for closer connections between schools and families and suggest novel approaches for partnerships that can capitalize on home and community literacy practices and strengthen families' involvement, confidence, and competence in literacy.

In chapter 7, "Mathematics Talk: Literacy Development in a Mathematics Context, " Brian Evans seeks to provide the reader with current research-based practical information on how to implement reading and writing strategies into the mathematics classroom. In particular, this chapter is grounded on current standards both from the National Council of Teachers of Mathematics and the Common Core. Problem solving is critically important in how students best learn mathematics, and this chapter seeks to help teachers help students become better problem solvers through strong literacy skills. The chapter is organized to first orient the reader to the issue of reading and writing in mathematics. Next, connections to Mario's case study are made. The chapter includes strategy suggestions with an appendix of children's literature to use in mathematics class.

In chapter 8, "Literacy and the Arts: How Artistic Perspectives Enhance Literacy Learning," Merryl Goldberg and Laurie Stowell describe study of the arts as both *products*, such as finished paintings, poems, dances, plays, songs, as well as a *process* through which individuals communicate and express information, ideas, and emotions. They remind teachers that the arts can provide access to information through alternative modes for all learners. They emphasize that the arts provide a vehicle for individuals, communities, and cultures to explore their own world and journey to new ones, thus enriching their understanding of varied topics. From Goldberg and Stowell's frame of reference, art-infused pedagogy melds the process of creating art with specific classroom content. To develop this theme, they detail their development of an approach referred to as DREAM: Developing Reading Education with Arts Methods, and they align their approach with the Common Core standards in the areas of English language arts for reading, writing, speaking and listening, and language/vocabulary conventions, as well as for mathematics standards.

In chapter 9's "Promoting Agency, Access, and Acquisition Among Adolescent English Language Learners," Kathleen A. J. Mohr, Michelle Flory, and Lois Ann Knezek challenge teachers to consider a new frame of reference for English language learners (ELLs) like Mario in grades 4–9 classrooms. Using social cognitive theory, the authors encourage teachers to serve as learning-life coaches in support of ELLs who are acquiring English while encountering grade-level academic content. The authors promote the use of language and literature to model a more hopeful and proactive perspective. A positive view of ELL middle schoolers and their learning trajectories influence the talk and text that teachers share with their students. As noted, if teachers broaden their role to include that of learning-life coach, they can upgrade their instruction in ways that promote agency, access, and accelerated learning that could contribute to students' hopeful, life-long success. While acknowledging reading comprehension as a critical skill, chapter 9 broadens the role of literacy teachers and expands their view of students' potentials.

In chapter 10, "Multimodality in Children's School-Based Texts," Roberta Linder emphasizes the centrality of design to an individual's production of or participation with multimodal texts. In their participation with multimodal texts, readers use different approaches to navigate through and interpret these print and non-print texts; they are *designers*, actively constructing meaning as they engage with the texts. Although multimodal texts may be highly motivating to students and dominate their out-of-school reading, teachers should be aware of the difficulties they may present to struggling readers such as the case study student, Mario. The chapter presents literature that aligns comprehension strategies for print texts with comprehension strategies needed to derive meaning from texts and frameworks for analyzing and comprehending multimodal literacy material. In addition, recommended classroom materials and professional resources for classroom instruction are provided.

In chapter 11, "Addressing Young Adolescents' Need for Voice and Interaction," Jill Lewis-Spector and Mary McGriff focus on the identity challenges of adolescence, and emphasize that as the school population becomes more diverse, teachers need to be mindful of their own ethnic and cultural norms that they bring to their educational interactions with students. They highlight the fact that teachers through these interactions can dramatically impact the process of adolescent identity formation, and they provide suggestions for critical consideration on these experiences through their frame of reference. They consider cross-cultural, psycho-social, and sociocultural perspectives as they examine the adolescent experience in classrooms and align their suggestions with the Common Core standards.

In chapter 12, "From Resistance to Engagement—The Importance of the New Literacies for Struggling Readers and Writers," Peter McDermott and Kathleen Gormley focus on the newer aspects of literacy education. After defining and reviewing the digital literacies, this chapter explores how technology can engage learners, specifically students struggling and/or resistant to traditional literacy activities, and also improve their traditional and digital reading and writing. Common Core State Standards as well as communication in the 21st century require that students become purposeful, savvy viewers, readers, and communicators with technology. Within the categories of podcasts, graphic organizers, digital drawings, and media productions (audio, video, text, image) and screencasts, several free web tools and apps are suggested for use in classrooms. They offer specific ideas of how these can be utilized as a starting point for educators. Finally, they showcase how these tools might improve Mario's engagement and progress in literacy.

REFERENCES

Common Core State Standards Initiative. (2012). *Common Core State Standards.* Washington, DC: National Governors Association Center for Best Practices and Council of Chief State School Officers. Retrieved from http://www.corestandards.org/ELA-Literacy.

Gardner, H. (2011). *Frames of mind: The theory of multiple intelligences,* 3rd edition. NY: Basic Books.

Gee, J. P., & Handford, M. (2012). Introduction. *The Routledge handbook of discourse analysis,* pp. 1–6. Pondicherry, India: Integra Softrware Services.

Moll, L. (1992). Funds of knowledge for teaching: Using a qualitative approach to connect homes and classrooms, *Theory into Practice, 31*(2), 132–41.

Pitcher, S. M., Albright, L. K., DeLaney, C. J., Walker, N. T., Seunarinesingh, K., Mogge, S., Headly, K. N., Ridgeway, V. G., Peck, S., Hunt, R., & Dunston, P. (2007). Assessing adolescent motivation to read. *Journal of Adolescent and Adult Literacy, 50*(5), 378–96.

2

The Educational Issues Before Us

Francine Falk-Ross

In increasing numbers and statistical variations, schools have become environments rich in diversity (U.S. Department of Education, 2012, 2013), and the challenges for educators to meet students' needs have become more complex. The students in our school populations have both benefitted from and been challenged by the increased mobility and participation of families in school environments, the more inclusive nature of classrooms involving students of different cognitive and learning levels, and a larger variety of cultural and linguistic characteristics that individualize students' needs. However, with these developments in mind, there's a growing consensus in research circles focused on the need for further development and consideration of approaches to provide access to these participatory environments for marginalized populations with challenges in language learning, culture, and identity, to note just a few issues (Moje, Overby, Tysvaer, & Morris, 2008).

In an effort to focus educators' attention toward meeting these mounting needs and to increase accountability in teaching responsibilities, national and state initiatives in the form of standards' development have been supplied as guidelines for instruction and assessment for teachers and students. For example, the International Reading Association (2010) has set standards for classroom teachers and literacy coaches at each educational level in their work developing areas of foundational knowledge, instructional and assessment practices, diversity accommodations, literate environment, and professional resource development and participation. A national movement began recently toward more rigorous and higher achievement expectations for students' learning in the classroom. In a consideration of all students' college and career preparedness, state officials have chosen to adopt standards to strengthen students' use of academic language in content literacy activities and discourse. These standards for students' competencies have been provided by a collaboration between the Council of Chief State School Officers (CCSSO) and the

National Governors Association (NGA) (2010). At the writing of this text, all but four of the United States (i.e., the exceptions being Texas, Nebraska, Virginia, and Alaska) have adopted the Common Core Learning Initiative's standards, which set benchmarks for instruction in the English language arts and content area learning experiences for all students. The Common Core Learning Standards have gained recognition by educators, and professional development information is provided for teachers in books (Calkins, Ehrenworth, & Lehman, 2012; Kendall, 2011) journals (Brunner, 2013), and online sites (ReadWriteThink, 2012, http://www. readwritethink.org/) for their specificity and the range of experiences that students are required to master in their classrooms. The competencies that are listed include categories for reading and writing, listening and talking, use of print and nonprint resources, language, mathematics, history, and science behaviors. In each category, the standards mandate that we consider students' individual learning needs that stem from cultural and linguistic diversity.

Teacher education programs are often at a disadvantage in providing the depth of knowledge in this area that teachers need to work toward in schools (Anderson & Stillman, 2013). For example, researchers interested in the diversity of student populations and evolution of technological tools have focused on the advantages of matching learning styles to assignments (Armstrong, 2009; Gardner, 2011) and the development of non-print aspects of learning (i.e., technology and media) (Coiro, Knobel, Lankshear, & Leu, 2008; Alvermann & Hagood, 2000). Teachers may not be familiar or comfortable with the use of new literacies to mediate new literacy learning which have been shown to be effective with all students, especially young adolescents (Sternberg, Kaplan, & Borck, 2007). Another example is the necessity of teachers' deep knowledge of the differences in language learning and vocabulary instruction among the students in classrooms due to cultural and linguistic backgrounds. As a third example, teachers often find themselves in a "catch-22" when they need to reach out to parents, hoping to gain information and not offend or appear to stereotype cultural groups. Research in this area indicates the insight and importance of school-home connections (Heath, 2013).

In addition, it has been suggested that changing teachers' practices may not be about teaching new information and strategies, but about teaching them why they need these new perspectives (Boling, 2008). Recent research publications call for resources and instruction as part of teacher education initiatives for the last ten years to persuade teachers to reflect on their work with the expanding diversity of student populations in schools today (e.g., Anderson & Davis, 2012; Anderson & Stillman, 2013; O'Hara & Pritchard, 2008; Sobel, Gutierrez, Zion, & Blanchett, 2011). Yet, in multicultural school environments, a large percentage of teachers report that they feel unsure of their competencies teaching such a diverse population of students (Futrell, Gomez, & Bedden, 2003). To gather the knowledge to meet these challenges, teachers reach out to administrators for organizational options, to universities for professional development, to educational specialists for strategic approaches, to colleagues for collaboration, and to parents for contextual information. However, the use of reciprocal talk with students, the primary stakeholders, to communicate their needs and understandings, and to inquire about misunderstandings, is not as frequent as might be necessary. According to research studies, the foundational element of classroom talk is often not given the attention it deserves (Alvermann, 1995; Nystrand, 2006). Using a balance of resource information from multiple sources of expertise as well as students' own language from discourse provides a more informed knowledge base for instruction. Studies of students' language-into-literacy needs will provide necessary information for teachers and teacher educators focused on how programs can transition into more inclusive classroom organizations and face challenges that may lead to lags in literacy achievement and content area reading despite progress in other disciplinary areas; new research projects for promising new approaches are necessary.

In the following chapters, authors with perspectives from varied disciplines offer models for conceptualizing the issues that confront educators. Taken as a whole, they combine multidisciplinary interests and research (i.e., language development, second language learners, literacy education, middle level) that will benefit teachers and teacher educators. They provide an examination of context and literacy practices appropriate for young adolescent students conducted from several unique research perspectives with the purpose of expanding the view of interpreting text for literacy development and content area instruction. Using research reviews and practical applications for developing literacy in general, they also offer specific suggestions for supporting one middle-level student in particular with the purpose of expanding the view of interpreting text for literacy development and content area instruction. Individual chapters will provide important information and case studies of new trends in integrating increased language/vocabulary development and pedagogic knowledge into teacher education and professional development programs in content area reading education. We have much to learn from their varied frames of reference.

REFERENCES

Alvermann, D. E. (1995). *Talking is something we're pretty deprived of at school: Middle school students speak out.* Paper presented at the annual conference of the American Educational Research Association, San Francisco.

Alvermann, D. E., & Hagood, M. C. (2000). Critical media literacy: Research, theory, and practice in "new times." *Journal of Educational Research, 91*(3), 193–205.

Anderson, K. L, & Davis, B. M. (2012). Creating culturally considerate schools: Education without bias, Thousand Oaks, CA: Corwin Press.

Anderson, L. & Stillman, J. A. (2013). Student teaching's contribution to preservice teacher development: A review of research focused on the preparation of teachers for urban and high-needs contexts, *Review of Educational Research, 83*(1), 3–69.

Armstrong, T. (2009). *Multiple intelligences in the classroom,* 3rd ed. Alexandria, VA: Association for Supervision and Curricular Development.

Boling, E. (2008). "Learning from teachers' conceptions of technology integration: What do blogs, instant messages, and 3D chat rooms have to do with it?" *Research in the Teaching of English, 43*(1), 74–100.

Brunner, J. (2013). Academic rigor: The Core of the Core, *Principal Leadership,* 13(6), 24–28.

Calkins, L., Ehrenworth, M., & Lehman, C. (2012). *Pathways to the Common Core: Accelerating achievement,* Portsmouth, NH: Heinemann.

Coiro, J., Knobel, M., Lankshear, C., & Leu, D. J. (2008). *Handbook of research on new literacies.* New York: Erlbaum.

Falk-Ross, F. C. (2007). Language factors in literacy achievement of young adolescents. In S. Mertens, V. Anfara, & M. Caskey (Eds.), *The young adolescent and the middle school,* Vol. 6 of the Handbook of Research in Middle Level Education (pp. 73–89). Westerville, OH: National Middle School Association.

Futrell, M., Gomez, J., & Bedden, D. (2003). Teaching the children of a new America. *Phi Delta Kappan, 84*(5), 381–85.Gee, J. P. (2001). Reading as situated language: A sociocognitive perspective. *Journal of Adult and Adolescent Language, 44*(8), 714–25.

Gardner, H. (2011). *Frames of mind: The theory of multiple intelligences,* 3rd ed. NY: Basic Books.

Heath, S. B. (2013). *Ways with words: Language, life and work in communities and classrooms,* Cambridge, UK: Cambridge University Press.

International Reading Association (2010). *Standards for reading professionals.* Newark, DE: Author.

Kendall, J. S. (2011). *Understanding Common Core State Standards.* Alexandria, VA: Association for Supervision and Curriculum Development.

Moje, E. B., Overby, M., Tysvaer, N., & Morris, K. (2008). The complex world of adolescent literacy: Myths, motivations, and mysteries. *Harvard Educational Review, 78,* 107–54.

National Governors Association (2010). *Common Core State Standards.* National Governors Association Center for Best Practices, Council of Chief State School Officers, Washington, D.C. Available at http://www.corestandards.org/.

Nystrand, M. (2006). Research on the role of classroom discourse as it affects reading comprehension. *Research in the Teaching of English, 40*(4), 392–412.

O'Hara, S., & Pritchard, R. H. (2008). Meeting the challenge of diversity: Professional development for teacher educators, *Teacher Education Quarterly,* 35(1), 43–61.

Sobel, D. M., Gutierrez, C., Zion, S., & Blanchett, W. (2011). Deepening culturally responsive understandings within a teacher preparation program: It's a process, *Teacher Development,* 15(4), 435–52.

U.S. Department of Education, National Center for Education Statistics (2012). *Digest of Education Statistics, 2011* (NCES 2012-001), Inclusion.

U.S. Department of Education, National Center for Education Statistics (2013). *The Condition of Education 2013* (NCES 2013-037), English Language Learners.

3

A Case Study to Consider Using Different Frames of Reference

Francine Falk-Ross

Mario Ramos is a sixth-grade student in a middle school located in a semi-urban city. He has lived in the United States since he was a young child and has one older brother and one younger sister. Hs struggles in all his content area classes, and inconsistently scores two to three years below his grade level in reading activities. Mario's writing competencies are below grade level, as well. Although not classified as having a learning disability, Mario receives special reading help in a resource room each day for forty minutes. Mario was asked to complete the Adolescent Motivation to Read Profile (AMRP) (Pitcher, et al., 2007) and to complete a running record of a fifth-grade narrative reading passage (*Analytical Reading Inventory,* Wood & Moe, 2000). He first completed the reading survey on his own (see the attached survey). His responses were read and written by himself; however, he began talking out loud to the interviewer, who joined in with the question/answer responses beginning as he began to converse on question 8 and continue talking for the interview. The written questions and responses to questions 1–8 in the AMRP are listed, followed by Mario's and the interviewer's comments.

Key

- ABC: Capitalization represents read aloud comments of the questions in the survey and for Mario's reading aloud from the Running Record passage.
- [..]: represents author's interpretation of wording
- (..): represents comments about context

Results of the Profile

- *[Silent/subvocal reading and written choices]*
- I AM IN . . . sixth grade.
- I AM . . . male.
- MY RACE/ETHNICITY IS . . . Hispanic.
- MY FRIENDS THINK I AM . . . an OK reader.
- READING A BOOK IS SOMETHING I LIKE TO DO . . . not very often.
- I READ . . . not as well as my friends.
- MY BEST FRIENDS THINK READING IS . . . no fun at all.
- WHEN I COME TO A WORD I DON'T KNOW, I CAN . . . almost never figure it out.
- I TELL MY FRIENDS ABOUT GOOD BOOKS I READ . . . I almost never do this.
- WHEN I AM READING BY MYSELF, I UNDERSTAND . . . some of what I read.
- PEOPLE WHO READ A LOT ARE . . . not very interesting.

- *[Mario starts talking out loud.]*

Mario: —doesn't really hate them but—

Teacher: Wait—who does?

Mario: My family doesn't read very often and a lot of people I know that read books are not very interested [either]. We would just mainly read ____ and when we are at friends' [houses], we just go inside because the other person is reading.

Teacher: Okay, okay Mario. Let's see. What is that last choice?

Mario: I AM A POOR READER.

Teacher: Oh, you think so? Okay.

Mario: I'm not very good at reading.

Teacher: Well, okay. You can always get better. I THINK MY WORRIES ARE—

Mario: ____ yeah, it's always quiet for science.

Teacher: Yeah? Okay. And I WORRY ABOUT WHAT OTHER KIDS THINK ABOUT MY READING. EVERY DAY OR ALMOST EVERY DAY? ONCE? *(His selection is "never").* Oh, never. Okay. KNOWING HOW TO READ WELL IS NOT VERY IMPORTANT? VERY IMPORTANT? *(His selection is "very important").*

Mario: Well, it depends. If you are doing math, you don't really need reading. You just need to know how to be able to read the math problem. But other than that, you are going to have to read papers and stuff so to me, it's very important because almost everything I do is reading. I play lots of video games with ____ and all of them; I have to read what they say. And when I am texting my friends on my PS3, when I'm online signed in, I have to read what they are saying and I have to spell out the word I am going to tell them back.

Teacher: That's true. So is that hard?

Mario: Well, not very hard. It's just we really don't use very big words. We might be sometimes lazy. Sometimes we are lazy so instead of putting like the word because, we put 'cos.

Teacher: I've seen that.

Mario: My cousin, we just put CUZ. And why, we just put the letter Y.

Teacher: Oh, and are, you just put the letter R? Okay. WHEN MY TEACHER ASKS ME A QUESTION ABOUT WHAT I HAVE READ, I CAN NEVER THINK OF AN ANSWER OR I HAVE TROUBLE THINKING OF AN ANSWER OR I SOMETIMES THINK OF AN ANSWER? *(His selection is "sometimes think of an answer").* Okay. I THINK READING IS A BORING WAY TO SPEND TIME, AN OKAY WAY TO SPEND TIME, AN INTERESTING WAY TO SPEND TIME—*(His selection is "a boring way to spend time").*

Mario: It depends. Most likely it's boring.

Teacher: Oh, no. Okay. READING IS VERY EASY FOR ME, KIND OF EASY, KIND OF HARD, VERY HARD. *(His selection is "kind of hard for me").* Okay. AS AN ADULT, I WILL SPEND NONE OF MY TIME OR SOME OF MY TIME. *(His selection is "a lot of my time").* Okay . . . a lot of my time. WHEN I AM IN A GROUP TALKING ABOUT READING, I ALMOST NEVER TALK ABOUT MY IDEAS, SOMETIMES TALK ABOUT MY IDEAS, ALWAYS TALK ABOUT MY IDEAS. *(His selection is "always talk about my ideas").* Okay. I WOULD LIKE MY TEACHER TO READ ALOUD IN MY CLASSES EVERY DAY OR ALMOST EVERY DAY? *(His selection is "once in a while").* Okay. WHEN I READ OUT LOUD, I AM A POOR READER, AN OKAY READER, A GOOD READER? *(His selection is "poor reader").* Okay. And WHEN SOMEONE GIVES ME A BOOK FOR A PRESENT, I AM VERY HAPPY, SORT OF HAPPY. *(His selection is "sort of happy").* Okay. Good for you.

Mario: It depends if it's the kind of books I read because I most likely like comics.

Teacher: Oh yeah? You like them?

Mario: It's very interesting how they—because in books you have to think about the idea and the person but comics always has the picture and they always help you out with the picture to understand stuff. So it's simple and not very simple.

Teacher: Yeah, that's hard to know. Can I ask you something? Do you speak another language fluently?

Mario: Not fluently. I don't speak Spanish that well. Next year I'm going to take Chinese because both of my parents know how to speak Spanish so I just get good teaching lessons from them 24/7. And in ___ just in China ___ schooldays, because you don't always stay in school, you get months off. But if you are getting teached by your parents, every day you get teached no matter if there's no school or school.

Teacher: Well, do you speak at home all the time in Spanish?

Mario: English.

Teacher: When you are at home you speak English?

Mario: Yeah, except when my dad's friends come back. We speak Spanish to some of them.

Teacher: Okay, so here's another thing. Let's see, I will ask these questions. Tell me about a book that you have read recently that you think is really good.

Mario: Well, I like animations so I am guessing possibly my favorite book I like to read is this animation that I downloaded for free. I forgot the title but it's on my PSP. It's like this magical boy and this book, the most recent one I liked was *The Return of King* I forgot his name but it's *The Return of King*—

Teacher: Okay, and where did you read that?

Mario: At the library. I checked it out.

Teacher: This library?

Mario: Mmm-hmm.

Teacher: And how did you find it?

Mario: I looked in the fantasy space, so yeah.

Teacher: So you looked it up for it, you went looking for one.

Mario: Yeah, and each time I read a fantasy book, it's kind of like giving me thousands of ideas in my mind.

Teacher: Oh, that's good. Okay. And it was interesting to you because you liked the—

Mario: I like reading fantasy books that make my ideas faster and faster so if I ever write a book, I know how to write a book like that.

Teacher: Okay, do you ever talk about the books you read with your friends?

Mario: No, we just talk about—well, we don't really gossip or anything. We just talk about facts about us. Like we might sometimes say that we have lots of homework that we have in first period.

Teacher: Okay, I meant like about books. Like your fantasy books. Do you talk about that with your friends?

Mario: They are not really interested in fantasy books. They are interested in books that are not real but our normal. But my friend Pablo, he read a book that was called *A Kid for President* and yeah, that kind of book.

Teacher: So he talked about his book and you talked about yours?

Mario: No, he is a comedy guy so we talk about that stuff.

Teacher: Okay, I see. Well, good to know. Do you discuss them with your family?

Mario: Yes, I do discuss them.

Teacher: Okay. The other thing I need to ask you is how many other people speak Spanish. Do you have any brothers and sisters?

Mario: Yeah, a younger brother and a younger sister.

Teacher: And they all speak, too? Can they write it?

Mario: No, but my baby sister can speak more Spanish than us and she's only four.

Teacher: Really? How do you like that because she's the youngest.

Mario: She's only four and my dad only speaks to her in Spanish. And we help out most of the time. Like (speaks Spanish) as in do you want this or this? So yeah.

Teacher: Oh, I see. Well, that's nice of you. So do you have a computer of your own?

Mario: Well, yes but it's in mine and my brother's room. We share a room and _____.

Teacher: So you share a computer?

Mario: But we mostly play the PS3 (PlayStation 3 System).

Teacher: Okay, but what do you do on the computer?

Mario: We just go on games. Well, I go on YouTube most of my time and look for videos that I like like *Pokey Fables* but the bad part is not only the books I read or not all of the videos I watch are appropriate for my little brother and sister as in they will have curse words from time to time.

Teacher: Oh, you shouldn't be listening either then right?

Mario: Well, not really. I have a limit of curse words but it's only a few curse words I can say.

Teacher: Okay. Well, here's my question. Do you read on the Internet? Like do you go to—?

Mario: Yeah, lots of reading.

Teacher: What kind of reading?

Mario: Well, on Pokey Fables, there's like this guy who speaks in a random language and on the bottom, he says his English in a funky, like sometimes he will have words together. And so then I have to think of it in my head and read it.

Teacher: Okay, good to know. Do you ever look it up for information like if you wanted to know how to do something?

Mario: Mmm-hmm.

Teacher: Okay.

Mario: Well, lots of people like looking up cheat codes. I don't do that to my PS3 (PlayStation3) games because I want to play it fairly but I do it to my PSP (PlayStation Portable System) Go games. Just important stuff like how to get health, how to get armor.

Teacher: I see. So do you do anything else? Do you write e-mails or letters to people?

Mario: My phone just broke the other day. I always send a text message, not calling.

Teacher: Okay, well, that's good. So then you are spelling. What else do you know? Like for example, have you learned anything brand-new from reading something new? Something in the newspaper or in a magazine or something at school that was brand-new information?

Mario: The magazine that I read is called *Game Informer* which informs me about games that are recently coming soon. Or games and their rankings and a few months ago, because it comes once a month, that *Game Informer* instead of being a normal *Game Informer*, it was a special *Game Informer* that only comes once a year. The special *Game Informer* talks about the ranking of games. The best ranking game was I forgot what it was called. The second for shooting was Black Ops which I have at my house. Call of Duty: Black Ops.

Teacher: Okay, here's another question. What class do you read the most in school? What class do you read the most?

Mario: Reading lab.

Teacher: Reading lab, okay. And which is the most difficult class for reading? It could be like social studies or math or science.

Mario: English because we are reading big books.

Teacher: Because you are reading hard books? Okay. Do you have any books you are reading now?

Mario: Well, I got these books that Ms. ___ gave me that I have to read all 12 of them for a grade of 95.

Teacher: Okay. What's one of them? Do you know? What's the one you are reading now?

Mario: Well, the one I am reading now is *Sports* and I'm in the middle of the page, the middle of the book. It's just sports. It has many sports stories in it.

Teacher: Okay. Do you have anything in your locker that you are reading? Any other kind of book that you brought from home or something?

Mario: No, I only read one book at a time.

Teacher: Okay. Do you think you have a favorite author?

Mario: Well, when I was younger it was Dr. Seuss and I didn't know that he was dead. So then when I found out, I was mad because I wanted to get his autograph.

Teacher: Oh, that would have been nice. Well, he's a good writer. He's a good writer.

Mario: Well my favorite author, there's this book called *The Girl Who Could Fly*. The main character is Piper McCloud. I have the book and the author only wrote one book but I really like that book. Piper McCloud has the ability to fly and then they introduce Conrad in the beginning of the story he is rude but actually he is the nicest kid there. He is planning an escape for everybody. And the place is called Insane for people who have powers like Piper and Conrad and other people. Conrad has a special ability, he gets really mad that he knows anything in a flash. He's the smartest kid there, too.

Teacher: Oh, so that is a good author. You do like that author. You like that book.

Mario: And there's this other kid, and the people from Insane try to make them lose their powers. They've been doing it for a long time and the owner of Insane, she can fly, too. But the reason why she started that was that one day she ran away with her sister and they were flying and they went into a cloud and it was raining, and they let go of each other and her sister couldn't fly so then, yeah.

Teacher: Wow, you remember a lot about that book. Okay. Here's another question. One more. What else do you think you could do to improve your reading?

Mario: Read harder books little by little.

Teacher: Harder books little by little. So you take them bit by bit. Okay, that's good. So you are in sixth grade, right? So let's see. Now what we're going to do is we are going to read something. And here's something, I'll tell you which one we are going to read.

Mario: Wait—is this from *Homeward Bound?*

Teacher: No, this is from something else. Some of the books are taken from stories that you may know. I don't know. Let's see. Okay, here we go. This one is called *The Bicycle Race.* Okay? Let's see how this one goes. Okay?

Mario: I'm not very good with names.

Teacher: Oh, I can help you with the name, that's okay. This person's name is Sheila.

Mario: Sheila?

Teacher: So you will know that. Because you don't have to know the name. That's kind of an interesting word. Okay. So why don't you read about *The Bicycle Race,* okay?

Mario: Okay.

Teacher: Take your time. Okay.

Mario: When should I—should I start right now?

Teacher: Yes, okay?

Mario: Look out, Sheila yelled. ___ as she saw her challenger's bicycle come too close. Watch out or you will foul me. At the (that) moment, a horrible thing happened as she bumped by another racer at 40 mph. Stacy's—

Teacher: Sheila's.

Mario: SHEILA'S BIKE CRASHED AND SHE SKIDDED ON THE SURFACE OF THE TRACK. FOR THE WRECK, SHE RECEIVED A 9-INCH GASH ON HER HEAD. THE JUDGE RULED THAT THE RACE SHOULD RUN AGAIN SINCE A FOUL HAD BEEN MADE. SHEILA WOULDN'T HAVE ENOUGH TIME TO GET HER WOUNDS DITCHED. STILL, SHE DIDN'T WANT TO QUIT THE RACE BECAUSE SHE COULDN'T (COULD) ONLY THINK OF WINNING. SHE'S STOMPED THE CUT TOGETHER TO BANDAGE IT, SHE TOLD THE DOCTOR. I WISH TO RUN THE RACE. THE DOCTOR DID AS SHEILA ASKED—SHE STOOD IN SILENCE WHILE THEY TREATED (HER),

TEARS ROLLED DOWN HER FACE FROM THE INSTANT PAIN. THEN WITH BLOOD STIRRING—

Teacher: Stained. That's a hard one.

Mario: STAINED BLANCHED (BLOOD) ON HER FOREHEAD, SHE PUSHED ON TO AMAZE THE CROWD WITH A SIGNIFICANT VICTORY AND A GOLD MEDAL.

Teacher: Okay, that was a hard one but you got through it. Very good. Okay. Let's ask some questions. Who was the main character?

Mario: Sheila.

Teacher: Yes, that's right. And now you remember her name right? That was a hard one. And what was the problem?

Mario: That in the first race, a boy fouled her I think and she got bandages and she got back in the race and won.

Teacher: Okay, yeah. What do you know about the word *challenge*? Challenger?

Mario: A rival? A person who was on the same thing that you are but they want to do it better than you.

Teacher: Very good. And how do you know that the crash was dangerous?

Mario: Because it said that she needed staples on her forehead and bandages.

Teacher: Okay. Why didn't Sheila want to quit the race?

Mario: Because she wanted to win.

Teacher: That's exactly right. And what about the phrase *intense pain*?

Mario: Horrible pain that a normal person can't handle as easily as a—a stronger person can handle as easily as a weaker person.

Teacher: Okay, that's good. And in your opinion, how important was this race to Sheila?

Mario: Very important. If she was training for three years.

Teacher: Yeah, she had been training for it. Okay, that's it. Thank you very much. You were very, very patient. And we got all of our work done. And what I'm going to do is I am going to give you this because this is to help you figure out words if you have trouble with the word, okay?

Mario: Yeah, I've been through lots of things like this.

Teacher: Yeah, but it's good to have one that deals with every part of the word and find word parts and that would really help you, don't you think maybe?

Mario: ___ candy.

Teacher: Yeah, see? But it just shows you how to do it. Find a word part. It would help you with a longer word like in the word candy. So they use an easy example.

[End of Audio]

Results of the Running Record

Word Recognition: Very Low Instructional Level/Frustration Level
The/that
Horrible/horrifying
Bile/bicycle
For/from
Judge/judges
Wound/wounds
Ditched/stitched
She/just
Stomped/stapled
To/and
Wish/want
Run/win
The/this
They/being
Rolling/rolled
Instant/intense
Stirring/stained
Bleached/bandage
-/throbbing
Significant/sensational

Comprehension: Independent Level

Fluency: Repeated words and phrases because he was self-monitoring the meaning

II

LANGUAGE AS A
SCAFFOLD FOR LEARNING

4

The Mediating Role of Pedagogic Discourse

Francine Falk-Ross

"Spoken language is the medium by which much teaching takes place, and in which students demonstrate to teachers much of what they have learned. As Barnes [1974]. . . says so profoundly, through the actual curriculum enacted between teacher and students, 'speech unites the cognitive and the social.'" (Courtney Cazden, 2001, p. 2)

When we engage in conversation, whether it is to question a teacher for more information, to comment to a friend about an observation, persuade a parent or vendor to change his mind, or to share a new poem or summary of a book at a gathering, we are engaging in what is referred to as discourse. The forms and meanings of each of the previous examples, however, are very different, and complicate the definition of discourse. A significant characteristic of discourse is the shared contextual nature of the language used by the speakers. Speakers share common experiences, mutual needs, and physical surroundings that define the particular nature of the context constructed during their conversations (Bloome & Clark, 2006; Bloome & Willis, 2013). Seminal research has proposed that all discourse events are further defined by how they are historically situated (Bakhtin, 1981), and this social-historical directly impacts learning (Vygotsky, 1978). So the text (i.e., language) of discourse, or functional language, needs to be considered as both a process of an ongoing series of semantic choices, and also as a product of the result of those choices (Halliday & Hasan, 1989).

In order to understand the role of pedagogic discourse, defined generally as the language routines used in educational environments to mediate learning, it is necessary to learn about what researchers know about the nature of discourse, and how this knowledge can provide opportunities for teaching and learning during literacy events.

DISCOURSE PROCESSES

The study of discourse processes is based on a social constructivist perspective of language interaction. In their seminal studies on this topic, Vygotsky (1978) explains the uses of language for gaining knowledge, and Bakhtin (1986; Wertsch, 1998, Holquist 1990) explains the contexts for sharing information. In more recent explanations, Gee (2001, 2011) also refers to the situated context of language, and Bloome and Willis (2013) prefer to describe the interaction as *discoursing* to refer to its constant flow. Since we use discourse processes to communicate in and out of educational settings, it is important to understand the characteristics and nature of language and interaction as they affect pedagogic discourse.

Discourse as a Mediator of the Social Processes and Practices of Language and Literacy

A social perspective of language requires insight into interpretation of linguistic organization. Language is not just what is presently said, but may reflect an understanding of what is unsaid but shared between participants. Looking more critically at the elements of language and shared interactions supports a deeper understanding of discourse. Researchers, specifically, psychologists, anthropologists, and learning theorists, have set many of the original definitions and explanations that guide the path for understanding and interpreting discourse.

The nature and purposes of language interaction. Language is considered the primary cognitive, or thinking, tool through which children and adults learn from one another as they invite and receive feedback from family, friends, and more knowledgeable peers (Vygotsky, 1978). Language in the form of social interaction is important for the development of knowledge (Chapman, 2003). Piaget (2001) originally proposed that the construction of knowledge is facilitated through language in cooperative as opposed to constraining relationships. Halliday (1975) describes the seven basic purposes of language for communication as they are used by young children; however, these categories describe purposes for all ages: *instrumental:* to express their needs; *regulatory:* to tell others what to do; *interactional:* to make contact with others and form relationships; *personal:* to express feelings, opinions, and individual identity; *heuristic:* to gain knowledge about the environment; *imaginative:* to tell stories and to create an imaginary environment; and *representational:* to convey facts and information.

In short, knowing more about the banter between speakers provides scaffolds for understanding and clues for revising our ideas and communication; however, the process is complex in that what is said may be interpreted by others in ways we may not have intended (Halliday & Hasan, 1989) and the rules may not always be transparent (Edwards & Mercer, 1987).

This example serves as a clue to understanding that when considered carefully, language is assumed to be created, shaped, constrained, and given meaning by the specific *context of situation* in which is it socially, culturally, and historically situated. Malinowski (1923) first introduced this term to indicate that it is not just the words before and after what we say that is important, but the *total environment* of the text (Halliday & Hasan, 1989). In a reciprocal manner, language form and content also affect the speaker's social environment. Bakhtin (1986) noted that in deciphering and understanding language in discourse, language and context share a *dynamic, symbiotic relationship* and the social and linguistic characteristics of language are seen to be inseparable. Underlying theories of discourse use and analysis (Fairclough, 2003; Gee, 2001) support these views of the seminal nature of language for literacy development and social practices.

Dell Hymes (1974; Cazden, 2011) described discourse as the major medium of teaching and learning all new knowledge. To explain the concepts more clearly, he developed an acronym that is useful to current teachers and researchers to remember the intersecting factors in the context of situation, SPEAKING, to represent **s**etting/scene, **p**articipants, **e**nds, **a**ct sequence, **k**ey, **i**nstrumentalities, **n**orm, and **g**enre. These are further explained in Table 4.1.

From these definitions of the characteristics of language and language interaction, linguists and theorists have made it clear that discourse, including classroom discourse in the context of literacy development, is never value-free (Green, 1983), never neutral (Bakhtin, 1986; Luke, 1988), and never autonomous (Street, 1984); instead, the process is *fluid*. Discourse, or discoursing (Bloome & Willis, 2013), is a flow of ideological processes and a mix of social practices.

The forms and formats of discourse. The characteristics of language interaction described above "play out" in different forms and formats in the multiple environments, or communities, in which people engage. Gee (1990, 2010) describes two distinct forms of language interaction: discourse and Discourse. He theorizes that *discourse* ("little d") refers to language-in-use, while Discourse refers to a combination of a series of social practices that occur together, and that would be considered a Discourse Community. In Gee's words:

> . . . at any moment we are using language we must say or write the right thing in the right way while playing the right social role and (appearing) to hold the right values, beliefs and attitudes. What is important is not language, and surely not grammar, but saying (writing)-doing-being-valuing-believing combinations. These combinations I will refer to as "Discourses," with a capital "D" ("discourse") with a little "d," I will use for connected stretches of language that make sense, like conversations, stories, reports, arguments, essays; "discourse" is part of "Discourse"—("Discourse" with a big "D" is always more than just language). Discourses are ways of being in the world, or forms of life which integrate words, acts, values, beliefs, attitudes, social identities, as well as gestures, glances, body positions and clothes. (Gee, 2000, p. 142)

The reference to use of Discourse also implies use of social language practices that include membership in a specific social community . . . or not. This differentiation between the types of interaction "packages" is important when speakers engage in

Table 4.1. Factors in Context of Situation

Setting and Scene. Setting refers to the time and place in which interaction takes place: June 15th, 1998, 10 a.m. in the largest space in the town hall of a small town in north-west Europe, for example. Scene refers to the psychological setting; that is, participants' understanding of what sort of event is taking place. Thus in that north-western European town hall there might be some kind of legal proceedings, a neighborhood mediation meeting, an awards ceremony, a lecture or a party. People's understandings of scene, and what sort of behavior is appropriate to each type of event, can vary quite widely (especially cross-culturally) and these divergences can act as triggers for (increased) conflict.

Participants. Participants include the speaker and the audience, the latter including the addressee(s) and any others present. In conflict negotiations, these "other" categories may be of great importance—observers who are there to see fair play, etc.

Ends. Ends refers to both outcomes (the assumed purpose of an activity or event) and goals (the purposes of the individuals involved). Defining what these are in the case of mediation can of course be difficult and generic. "Resolution" requires more detailed examination in particular cases to determine what in fact will be accepted by parties to conflict.

Act Sequence. The different parts of a communicative event are referred to by "act sequence." They would include, for example, opening remarks, formal and less formal turns by participants, and closing remarks. In informal situations (such as arguments leading to conflicts) the sequence may not be agreed and may not be coherent. This will lead to a lot of overlaps and interruptions and possibly to unfinished or cut-off communications.

Key. The key of an utterance or speech event is determined by cues that indicate its tone or spirit. This can, of course, be different for different speakers. Thus, one speaker may indicate through choice of words that s/he is going to be aggressive and uncompromising whilst another may give cues that s/he is behaving light-heartedly or playfully. Mismatches of this kind can of course cause—or perpetuate—offence.

Instrumentalities. Instrumentalities refers to two aspects. One is the forms and styles of speech used by participants. Thus, the choice of whether to use a strong or weak version of a dialect or accent, or whether to use one language rather than another, might indicate the speaker's view of the interaction that is taking place and demonstrate intimacy, respect (or disrespect), formality, etc. The other aspect of instrumentalities is channel. Obviously, many of the other aspects of context of situation, and what can and cannot be communicated, are influenced by whether communication takes place face-to-face, by Skype, by conventional written messages, or some other means.

Norms. This refers to any socially accepted conventions regarding when people can speak, what kinds of things they can say and who they can say it to. Some norms, such as how soon someone is expected to speak, relate to conversation generally in a community. Others pertain to specific, relatively formal events such as court proceedings or job interviews. When participants do not share the same norms, there can be undesirable consequences. As regards the more general norms, for instance, someone who expects a clear gap after one person has spoken before s/he starts speaking is never going to get a word in when faced with someone who expects the next speaker to start talking before s/he has even finished and finds any silence uncomfortable. Norms for specific events can also raise questions of power and control. Thus, a victim of war crimes giving evidence in a trial may be at a disadvantage when cross-questioned by the defensecounsel if s/he is not very well briefed about what is and is not acceptable communicativebehavior.

Genre. Genre is not just used to refer to literary works (poem, novel. Etc.) but also to the kind of communication that is taking place. This could include testimony in court (a kind of co-produced story-telling) but also includes interviews, speeches, joke-telling etc.

(From http://www.languageinconflict.org/how-language-works/context-of-situation.html). Source: Hymes, 1974.

conversation, listening to one another's contributions and often evaluating the speaking partner, as in classroom discourse/Discourse (Edwards & Mercer, 1987).

Another approach to specifying the type of interaction uses a more individualized and focused view of a language interaction by documenting the combination of three central features of context (Halliday, 1989). The first is the *field of discourse*, which refers to "what is happening, to the nature of the social action that is taking place" (p. 12). The second feature is the *tenor of discourse*, which refers to "who is taking part, to the nature of the participants, their statuses and roles" (p. 12) including their relationships to one another and their roles in the discourse. The third feature is the *mode of discourse*, which refers to "what part the language is playing, . . . the symbolic organization of the text, the status that it has, . . . including the channel (is it spoken or written) . . . and what is being achieved" (p. 12). As the field, tenor, and mode change, so do the meanings of the text/language created. In short, these three constructs define the social situation of context. These features are used to classify the social interactions in the large variety of language events under study.

As is noted in Halliday's and Gee's classifications, discourse may occur between speakers in formats other than oral language. Writing and several of the new literacies (or nonprint) formats also are developed around social and cultural practices, and serve as *situated language* using new and different semiotic domains (Gee, 2008). The *new literacies* serve for interaction in all environments; however, this is never more obvious than in educational environments and classroom discourse (Lankshear & Knobel, 2003).

Classroom Discourse as a Means to Hear Students' Individual and Collective Voices

Talk in the classroom has been shown to be an important contributor toward literacy through dialogic interactions (Ganske & Jocius, 2013). Meaning is constructed and signaled through the specific communicative interactions between teachers and students, students and peers, and the teacher and the class (Bloome & Theodorou, 1988). As these routines become ritualized over time, a subtle predictability develops that defines communication in the classroom, and a procedural knowledge guides them through everyday activities (Bloome & Theodorou, 1988; Edwards & Mercer, 1987; Mercer, 2000). Knowing the specific elements that benefit or challenge students will help teachers to build environments rich in supportive classroom discourse.

Characteristics of classroom discourse. Following a seminal classroom research study of the verbal interactions between teachers and students, Cazden (2001) identified a specific regularity to the discourse that was common in most classrooms. She noted that the flow of discourse revolved around shared knowledge about the structure of turn allocation and contingent participatory moves in classroom routines. In general, being able to participate in the classroom tasks was actually a matter of mastering the necessary linguistic routines in which the teacher presented the material. In most classrooms, these routines consisted of discourse that was initiated and controlled by the teacher following a familiar IRE/IRF pattern: the teacher *initiated* a question or direction to the student(s), the nominated student *responded* with an answer or comment, and then the teacher provided *evaluation,* or *feedback,* for the student's response with an acknowledgment or judgmental comment (Cazden, 2001; Wells, 1999). For example, a teacher might engage in a routine with the students in the class using the following interaction:

- **Teacher initiation**: Who was the first president of the United States?
- **Student's response**: Lincoln.
- **Teacher evaluation/feedback**: That's not right. Would someone else want to try?

This interaction is typical of most in that the student responds to the usually literal question with a one-word response. This traditional IRE pattern is still observed in many middle-level classrooms (Ganske & Jocius, 2013). These instructional language patterns focus primarily on what is referred to as *academic language,* or discourse focused on building students' competencies using discipline-specific vocabulary and content area literacy conventions (Cummins, 2000, 2001). They provide a context that influences learning and literacy development (Gutierrez, 1995; Brown & Kennedy, 2011). When used to include all students' participation, talk in the classroom should meet the developmental, academic, and cultural needs of students (Howell, Thomas, & Ardasheva, 2011; Johnston, Ivey, & Faulkner, 2011).

The need for developing students' academic language has gained attention for its infusion in the Common Core Standards (O'Hara, Pritchard, & Zwiers, 2012), and the focus on second language learners who may require specific vocabulary support to achieve at grade levels in school (Anstrom et al., 2010; Echevarria, Vogt, & Short, 2004).

In addition, in each classroom, common linguistic patterns within specific activity structures are identifiable. These language "registers" are referred to as "curriculum genres" (Christie, 2005; Pappas, Kiefer, & Levstik, 2005). They set up specific language and rules for verbal interactions within disciplinary discussions that are expected to be followed (Cazden 2001; Michaels & Cazden, 2012; Michaels, O'Connor, & Resnick, 2008). Michaels' (2006) research with students revealed that students' format for discourse style in their narrative presentations often varied with cultural backgrounds. She observed that her study,

> . . . was centrally informed by work in interactional sociolinguistics, pioneered by John Gumperz and Jenny Cook-Gumperz, which emphasized the systematic resources speakers from diverse cultural groups used to signal intent and interpretation of intent in managing conversational inference in face-to-face encounters. Taken together, all of this work has come to be looked at as supporting a cultural or linguistic "mismatch" or "difference" hypothesis—emphasizing difference rather than deficiency in linguistic and sociocultural tools for interaction, and the ways these differences influence access to instruction and evaluation of competence in academic settings. (p. 110–11)

Edwards and Mercer (1987) noted that these categories of language routines become *common knowledge* to all participants if they are to succeed. However, their research showed how classroom communications take place against a background of implicit understanding, some of which is never made explicit to pupils. Students often struggle to meet these expectations (Fisher & Larkin, 2008). This has been problematic for students who are marginalized by cultural, linguistic, or cognitive differences. *Equity factors in classroom discourse.* A person's communicative competence is defined by his or her ability to use language appropriately to convey an idea, understanding, or question in a variety of meaningful social ways (Halliday, 1975; Hymes, 1974). It has been suggested that the content, dialogue, and flow of traditional classroom discourse have been influenced by the mainstream cultural norms, often limiting the type and form of communications, and limiting equal access to school knowledge (Freebody, Luke, & Gilbert, 1991). Cummins (2001) recognized that a student's communicative competence often refers to his or her cultural and linguistic competence. Teachers' consideration (and tolerance) for the richness of other languages—the lilts, tones, rhythms, and sounds—in literature and voices in the classroom varies. These differences from more dominant Discourses (Gee, 1990), or languages of power (Delpit, 1988) may be misinterpreted as a lack of mastery of discourse approaches. Understanding these differences and accommodating them in verbal exchanges can increase learning and success in school for marginalized students (Heath, 1995; Gee, 2004).

In their studies on this topic, O'Brian, Beach, and Scharber (2007) found that students were more likely to express opinions or judgments in classroom discourse in which they were granted some power or agency. Similar findings were found for the positive effects of using expanded discourse routines to support non-traditional language users' communication competence (Cazden, 2011; Falk-Ross, 2001; Fecho & Botzakis, 2007), for discussion in diverse middle and secondary schools (Falk-Ross, 2007; Nystrand, 2006; Smart & Marshall, 2013), for discourse in urban settings (Collins, 1995; de los Rios, 2013), and for second language and struggling learners (Buxton, et al., 2013; Falk-Ross & Carrier, 2005; Kibler, 2011). Aukerman and Pandya (2013) raise the question about what is considered *fruitful discourse* and suggest that unless educators are careful to consider students' backgrounds, this might be privileged in classrooms. Cummins' (2000, 2001) work supports the need for developing students' cognitive academic language proficiency, and academic language.

In an effort to learn more about students, we seem to be leaning a bit too heavily on more formal assessments without the balance of the students' voices. Future teachers may need to dig deep into their educational tool boxes to develop unifying elements using collaborative efforts that help students to communicate their knowledge more clearly to drive our instruction. Identifying students' individual strengths for learning through tests alone may not be communicating to us all the necessary information. We need to learn and consider students' contexts and cultures of learning. Insight into their competencies can come from the students' voices and we can interpret their needs more personally in classroom discourse in small groups (Almasi, 2003), and individually (Atwell, 1997; Falk-Ross, 2014) so they can ask questions, share understandings,

and learn new information. In short, we need to develop their communicative competence through pedagogic discourse in educational forums and formats.

Godley and Minnici (2008) have suggested three issues that may affect teachers' negotiation of students' contributions to classroom talk: resistance to dialect
diversity, issues of language, identity and power, and knowledge of pedagogical applications of research on language variation. Understanding the nature of pedagogic
discourse and the effects of changes in language routines for all students within
educational interactions is an important endeavor for teacher educators and for pre-
service and practicing teachers. Although it is important to show value for students'
socially situated speech forms, the difficulties that some students experience require
that we teach the different genres using both explicit and immersion approaches
to allow access to talk across disciplines. In short, teachers need to be patient with
students' contributions within classroom talk and in our own interactions because
our approaches and language forms have influences on their sense of self and identity
(Gee, 2000; Young, 2008). Educators, as the main mediators of school-based learning, can integrate new and necessary information to support students' achievement
and positive self-images using a few basic language-into-literacy strategies.

CLASSROOM OPPORTUNITIES TO DEVELOP
LITERACY THROUGH CLASSROOM DISCOURSE

The goals of these suggested interventions are to open up conversation for students
to participate in discourse routines, for teachers for more student comments and
questions rather than dominate conversation, and for teachers to consider how their
comments and questions can be more responsive to and supportive of students'
sociocultural differences. These goals are at the heart of the Common Core Learning Standards (CCSS) (National Governors Association, 2010). For example, one
standard that aligns with these discourse opportunities is CCLS ELA standard in the
area of Speaking and Listening 5.1 that requires students (specifically at the middle
grade level), to engage effectively in a range of collaborative discussions (one-on-one,
in groups, and teacher-led) with diverse partners on grade [level] topics and texts,
building on others' ideas and expressing their own clearly. In order to meet this standard, teachers can change their routines and open/expand conversation simply by
modifying their form of comments and questions (Just & Carpener, 1987) to give
students a greater role in the conversations. It can draw students into literacy discussions and co-construction of knowledge (Falk-Ross, 2001; Nystrand, Wu, Gamoran,
Zeiser, & Long, 2003). Teachers who use more supportive language can encourage
deep conversation, promote critical literacy, and boost students' confidence about the
significance of their own experiences (Johnston, 2004). The following interventions,
each of which consists of a combination of research-based strategies, are offered to
help educators support all students' literacy through the use of classroom-based discourse. These build on the concepts explained earlier in this chapter focused on the
elements of pedagogic discourse. Each is aligned with Common Core Standards for
classroom applications, as is summarized in Table 4.2. The intention is to provide

Table 4.2. Literacy Interventions and Common Core Learning Standard Alignment

Literacy Intervention and Strategy Description	Common Core Learning Standard(s) Alignment
All Classroom Discourse Events	CCSS.ELA-Literacy.SL.5.1 Engage effectively in a range of collaborative discussions (one-on-one, in groups, and teacher-led) with diverse partners on grade [level] topics and texts, building on others' ideas and expressing their own clearly.
Table Talk Student-focused, student-directed, individual conferences to ascertain levels of literacy competencies and infuse new content or strategy information. *Set goals:* *Learn for assessment:* *Word identification:* *Reading comprehension:* *Text structure:*	CCSS.ELA-Literacy.SL.5.1d Review the key ideas expressed and draw conclusions in light of information and knowledge gained from the discussions. CCSS.ELA-Literacy.RF.5.3a Use combined knowledge of all letter-sound correspondences, syllabication patterns, and morphology (e.g., roots and affixes) to read accurately unfamiliar multisyllabic words in context and out of context.
Expanded Language Routines Approaches to extend language interaction time for higher quantity and quality of interaction. *Open-ended:* *Question uptake:*	CCSS.ELA-Literacy.L.5.6 Acquire and use accurately grade-appropriate general academic and domain-specific words and phrases, including those that signal contrast, addition, and other logical relationships (e.g., *however, although, nevertheless, similarly, moreover, in addition*). CCSS.ELA-Literacy.RI.5.2 Determine two or more main ideas of a text and explain how they are supported by key details; summarize the text. CCSS.ELA-Literacy.RI.5.1 Quote accurately from a text when explaining what the text says explicitly and when drawing inferences from the text.

(continued)

Table 4.2. (Continued)

Literacy Intervention and Strategy Description	Common Core Learning Standard(s) Alignment
Online Learning Communities Student-led online discussions following an initial teacher prompt for reading response.	CCSS.ELA-Literacy.RL.5.9 Compare and contrast stories in the same genre (e.g., mysteries and adventure stories) on their approaches to similar themes and topics.
Asynchronous discussions: *Synchronous discussions:*	CCSS.ELA-Literacy.W.5.6 With some guidance and support from adults, use technology, including the Internet, to produce and publish writing as well as to interact and collaborate with others; demonstrate sufficient command of keyboarding skills to type a minimum of two pages in a single sitting.
(Modified) Critical Discourse Consideration of unjust practices in communication between teacher and students.	CCSS.ELA-Literacy.L.5.5 Demonstrate understanding of figurative language, word relationships, and nuances in word meanings.
Transcribe or listen back to the discourse communication: *Think about what information you need to "fill in" to make sense of the members' communication:* *Ask yourself why you think the person chose to say what he or she did in just that way:* *Consider the intonation and emphases of the language in the communication:* *Consider the language of the communication for its genre of interacting, the type-/mode of discourse, and the interpersonal relationships among the speakers:*	CCSS.ELA-Literacy.W.5.6 With some guidance and support from adults, use technology, including the Internet, to produce and publish writing as well as to interact and collaborate with others; demonstrate sufficient command of keyboarding skills to type a minimum of two pages in a single sitting.

starter sets of experiences that educators can adapt to their own needs to increase the quality and quantity of discourse opportunities in their classrooms.

Expanded Language Routines

Why it works. The IRE/F system of teacher-student academic interaction serves as the most frequent model for teaching/learning; however, it has some limitations. In many cases, teachers set up questions for students in this way allowing for minimal, one-word or yes/no responses. The teacher may have one answer in mind, and there is the expectation that the student will provide that response. In expanded language routines, the questions do not usually have prespecified answers, and whether an answer is considered correct or not may be considered more carefully. In fact, the talk that occurs in classrooms is often dominated by about two-thirds via teacher-directed questions and directives (Cazden, 2001: Fisher & Larkin, 2008; Nystrand, 2006), and is most often dominated by evaluative comments and corrections rather than construction of knowledge (Wells, 2006). The goal of classroom discourse is to provide opportunities for more student participation. These routines are at the heart of the CCLS ELA standards in the areas of vocabulary development and reading comprehension of narrative and expository text: L.5.6, RI.5.2, and RI.5.1.

It has been suggested that in order to invite (really empower) more students to join the conversations, the use of more open-ended (and higher level) questions to replace the direct (and usually literal and lower level) questions would be a more inclusive approach (Ganske & Jocius, 2013; Gutierrez, 1995) allowing for students of differing cultural, linguistic, and cognitive backgrounds to participate. Responses would then hopefully be longer and more complex and would allow for new knowledge to be owned by students. These expanded language routines would also give teachers the opportunity to infuse new information into lessons (Lapp, Fisher, & Frey, 2013).

How it works. The main purpose of using expanded language routines is twofold: to increase the complexity of students' responses and to increase the number of students' (compared to the teacher's) responses/comments/questions. This requires some patience and wait-time on the part of teachers who learned from teachers using the IRE system. Many educators have noted that it takes a conscious effort to initiate, but that once they tried it, they could not go back to what seemed then to be the limited interactional routine.

Open versus closed questioning. Rather than asking a closed, one-word response question, this variation requires more information from the class on the same topic. It represents a Teacher-Student-Student-Student discourse organization. These variations allow for many students to respond in a row, often to each other, and sets up a larger number of facts for students to build background knowledge. This open questioning also allows students to receive positive responses since they are able to draw upon a wider set of options and be successful in answering with an acceptable response. For example:

Example 1

- Closed question: Who was the first president of the US?
- Vs.
- Open question: What can you tell me (i.e., what do you know) about the first president of the US?

Example 2

- Closed question: Is the word *unique* an adjective or an adverb?
- Closed question: What are the functions of an adjective in a sentence?
- Vs.
- Open question: How would I know if the word *unique* is an adjective or an adverb in this sentence?

Question uptake. This variation on expanded discourse opportunities requires the student to further explain his or her response using some background knowledge or evidence from a previous reading source (Cummins, 2000). This usually raises the level of the discourse in substantive ways, lengthens the student's response, provides opportunities for self-revision/explanation, and often pulls other students into the discussion, if the teacher agrees, to assist the student who is speaking. This variation represents a Teacher-Student-Teacher-Student organization but raises the analytic level of the responses. An example might be:

Example 1

- Closed question: Who was the most important character in the book?
- Vs.
- Uptake question: Explain why you chose that character over others. (textual evidence; inference)
- Vs.
- Uptake question: How does that character compare to one from another book or resource? (intertexuality)

Example 2

- Open question: Describe for the class who was your favorite character in the book.
- Vs.
- Uptake question: Give us some examples about what s/he did that you enjoyed? (textual evidence; personal connections)

- Vs.
- Uptake question: Why do you think the author included that character? (critical thinking, author connections)

Collaborative student responses. This variation on questioning has also been referred to as negotiated meanings (Wells, 1999), and represents a collective set of responses that are shared by several students. This is most appropriate for a content area class discussion, and is appropriate for developing student-constructed definitions. The teacher or another student can sum up the collaboration for class use. This variation on expanded routines takes a Teacher-Student-Student-Student-Teacher/Student organization. An example is:

Example 1

- Student response: Using your ideas and those of others from the jigsaw (or biography literature circle) activity, how would you describe the main themes of the [historical event] we just studied?

Example 2

- Teacher response: Everyone in the class shared a different feature of an oemeba. . . . Let me sum up all of your contributions for a class definition.

Table Talk

Why it works. Table talk consists of conversational interviews and student-directed instruction with middle-level students. Not all students who have challenges to their learning perceive these difficulties as limiting, and many are unaware of, or unwilling to engage in, behaviors that will improve their literacy development. This is especially true for young adolescent students in the middle grades. These set of strategies is at the heart of the CCLS ELA standard for Speaking and Listening 5.1d which requires that teachers help students to review the key ideas expressed and draw conclusions in light of information and knowledge gained from the discussions. A second CCLS standard met in this activity set is for building students' Reading Foundations, by helping them to use the combined knowledge of all letter-sound correspondences, syllabication patterns, and morphology (e.g., roots and affixes) to read accurately unfamiliar multisyllabic words in context and out of context.

Individual conferences with struggling students can be revealing related to their perceptions of their language and literacy strengths and knowledge. This can help educators pinpoint which areas of literacy competencies are strongest and which are most challenging for marginalized middle grade students. Marginalized students experience word identification challenges (important for decoding new content words, or academic language), disinterest in school and in reading (important for motivation to achieve), a lack of knowledge and practice with technology (important for involvement with new literacies and a comment on access issues), and confusions with content vocabulary (that is important for reading comprehension) (Falk-Ross, in press). These findings pull together previous research on vocabulary challenges in the increasing number of schools in which language difference is a factor in learning (Brown 2007; Garcia, Jensen, & Scribner, 2009), and that the link between students' motivation to read in and out of school and achievement has been established and supported over the years (Guthrie, Coddington, & Wigfield, 2009; Logan, Medford, & Hughes, 2011; Rasinski & Padak, 2011). Also important in this chapter as focused on discourse is that individual conferences consisting of open-ended questions often elicit more information than would normally be shared in class discussions, since these students are often marginalized in the quick pace of the question-answer formats (e.g., IRE, Cazden 2001) of classroom discourse. For example, through the use of individual conferences and semi-structured interviews, teachers may learn about the students' self-expressed understanding of their competencies and their perceived challenges (Atwell, 1997; Pitcher et al., 2007).

The purpose of this conferencing intervention is to use this special time to determine marginalized students' engagement and use of literacy activities, and to infuse new ideas and new competencies for literacy during these teachable moments. Table talk provides opportunities to re-energize and re-position students' attitudes toward reading with teacher feedback, mini-lessons, and suggested matched reading material. Through one-on-one interactions, teachers may receive much-needed discourse samples to evaluate students' understandings and explanations of their language and literacy knowledge and use.

How it works. Optimally, 10–20 minutes of time is assigned to the intervention, at least once per week. The steps for Table Talk include the following activities; however, due to its individualized nature, the strategies within each step are negotiated by the student and teacher working closely together.

Student-directed statement of goals for discussion (needs/questions). The student is asked to bring or explain a list of literacy challenges or goals that he or she chooses to inform completion of a class assignment of a project or to help with independent work, such as reading or writing. For example, a student in your ELA class might find that his difficulty reading the words in the novel assigned in class is slowing down his completion of the response activity. He finds that he is also having difficulty understanding the storyline, as well. He explains these as his goals. Another example could be that the student is having challenges with the vocabulary in a content area class, with both reading and writing. For her goal, she wants to learn how to decode/decipher these words so she can following along in class.

Shared (teacher/student) informal assessment of literacy challenges. This step is used to help both student and teacher learn the extent of the challenge and set a more specific objective for the rest of the talk/conferencing at the table. If this is a first meeting for the year/quarter, an informal set of interests and needs profile questions may be used to position the student's challenge in a larger context (e.g., *the Adolescent Motivation to Read Profile;* Pitcher et al., 2007), a running record of the reading that is a challenge, and a summary of the findings to set the specific nature of the support that will be needed, such as a Retrospective Miscue Analysis (Goodman, 1996). This set of assessments would be appropriate for both examples noted in the first step.

Teacher-led infusion of necessary information (e.g., vocabulary/word identification, text organization, reading comprehension) with guided practice. In this step, teachers can match the student with a much-needed strategy or focused information aligned with the set goal. In the example of the ELA student, following a discussion of the running record, specific words can be chosen to re-teach for word identification, probably morphemic analysis, for the immediate and future applications of word attack for multisyllabic words or for meaningful parts that will be used for reading and writing for the responsive assignment. For the example of the student with content area class challenges, following a review of the results of the running record of his reading of that material, specific academic vocabulary can be listed by the teachers and reviewed for reading. This list may serve as a personal "word wall" for writing work, which was also noted as a goal. Introduction to a graphic organizer may be introduced as helpful for the organization of information while reading (such as for themes or sequence of events or cause/effect relationships). In both cases, a guided practice using the new information would be used. For example, the first paragraph of the challenging reading could be re-read and then interpreted after learning the vocabulary, or the content could be graphed for specific events or elements in the student's own interpretation.

Student questions or comments or summary for closure. This step may be used for an independent application of the new information by the student, or for a retell statement collectively by the teacher and/or the student.

Online Learning Communities

Why it works. Most students have had access to computers by the time they reach middle level classrooms either from their homes or from school libraries; however, they have not all had experience with academic discourse using this format. The lessons that derive from using these activities are at the heart of the CCLS ELA RL.5.9 and W.5.6 standards in the areas of reading comprehension and writing as they focus on interpreting and sharing themes in text and using technology to interact and collaborate with peers. An advantage of using online learning communities is that they provide ". . . equitable opportunities to share their thoughts and voice their opinions about literature" (Larson, 2009, p. 638) and other topics. Leu (2002) noted that the new literacies include more of a social component for literacy development than traditional means and invite social interaction. Additionally, online learning communities provide all students equal access since all comments and questions are posted. The online format also empowers students who struggle in classroom discourse for a variety of reasons, including self-image, language mastery, and the fast-paced competitive nature of in-class interactions. Larson's study of an asynchronous project among students revealed that the fifth-grade students were motivated to seek extra information from the teacher about how to construct useful questions with higher level inquiry focused on experiential knowledge, aesthetic knowledge, interpretive knowledge, clarification of information, and cognitive thinking.

How this works. Educators may ask the school for access to a safe and private message forum for students to engage in online discussions that the teacher can follow. Optimally, parents' permission will be secured even if the communication occurs in schools.

Asynchronous messaging. This method allows students to prepare their responses clearly prior to posting for the other classroom members. For students with language or learning differences, this affords them a chance to edit and revise responses at their own pace, and successfully participate. Teachers may help students individually to develop the language and written conventions that are needed to succeed on a needs-based schedule. Opportunities for cueing and clueing by teachers may support special-needs students to develop stronger responses and develop academic language. Rules for engagement, such as appropriate and inappropriate language and tone, will need to be developed prior to the discussions. The teacher can then post a series of initial prompts at different levels, and the threads that students develop will guide the students' discourse. For example (based on Larson, 2009):

Initial prompts by teacher for a literary selection:

- What event in the text so far was most surprising and why did you feel this way?
- What do you predict will occur next in the book?
- Does this story remind you of any other book that you have read?

Synchronous online messaging. This version may occur as a workshop activity for a class in a school's computer laboratory or between two of the same grade level classes in their own rooms, or among five students within one room during a literacy center time activity. This version is a bit more fast-paced, and the requirements for editing and revisions are not as high; however, students have equal access to being included in the discussions. Often, in my experiences, students have voiced their opinions that it is easier to respond freely when they are in an online format than in person-to-person interactions. The same teacher-prompted questions may be posted initially as in the asynchronous discussions.

(Modified) Critical Discourse Analysis for Revisions in the Language of Literacy Teaching

Why it works. Critical literacy theory derives from the work of Paulo Freire (1970), who described the importance of "reading the world." Much of the theory and work in this area are focused on four main applications, as described by Lewison, Flint, and Van Sluys (2002) including disrupting a common understanding to gain perspective, examining multiple viewpoints, thinking about power relationships between people, and promoting social justice. These applications need to be included in the literacy activities of adolescent reading events. Clearly, the characteristics of students' inquisitive nature and academic needs require different approaches to literacy instruction than elementary students. As a group with access to a wide range of text through multiple literacies within a global community, students today require focused instruction in developing their critical thinking. Therefore, discussions of context, and immersing students in context considerations is an important first step. Johnson & Freedman (2006) discuss how context colors life, and students need to consider context of a situation whether it is created by their society, family, or their own thoughts. Context provides a view into places from which to view the world and learn the lesson offered by the reading.

Critical discourse analysis is an evaluative approach toward considering the interactions and relationships of language, power, and identities (Fairclough, 2003, 2011; Rodgers & Wetzel, 2014). This builds on the work of Gee (2006, 2011) and Young (1992, 2008) as it closely considers that complex influences on the pedagogical language we use when interacting with students in classrooms. The results of critical discourse analysis inform educators so that teaching literacy can occur in socially-just ways in classrooms (Dozier, Johnston, & Rodgers, 2006; Lewison, Leland, & Harste, 2007, Rogers & Wetzel, 2014). As noted earlier, Halliday developed three contextual influences on language that assist in analyzing the communication: mode, tenor, and field. Fairclough (2011) developed parallel organizers for analysis: ways of interacting or genre of the discourse (i.e., the mode), ways of representing or discourse (i.e., the field), and ways of being or interpersonal relationship (i.e., the tenor). This process by nature is a complex process and involves layers of critical thinking about the language of communication. In a modified version, using these guidelines for consideration, teachers can try to catch their assumptions and restructure their own discourse as models to students, as well. For example, teachers can begin to generate more respectful, caring, interactional relationships, and understand and confront learning histories; students can learn to make connections with previous learning and be willing to engage in new practices and conversations (Dozier, Johnston, and Rogers, 2006). The suggested steps for critically considering teachers' and students' language during interactions are supported indirectly by the CCLS ELA standards L.5.5 and W.5.6 in the areas of reading and writing as they focus on supporting students' communications about content text.

How this works.

Transcribe or listen back to the discourse communication. The dialogue can be transcribed separating out and identifying each speaker with specific comments listed on different lines or as a flow of language for each speaker's turn (the latter is the format for the case study in chapter 3). As you read for the following considerations, notations can be made with letters (e.g., FI for fill-in, CH for choices of wording, and IE for intonation and emphases) and/or markers so that trends in necessary interpretations can be determined for future communications.

Think about what information you need to "fill in" to make sense of the members' communication. Specifically, think and notate any assumptions you may have made, and what other information you or another class member might need before interpreting that comment or question.

Ask yourself why you think the person chose to say what he or she did in just that way. Consider what biases might you or another member have brought to the conversation. How could you have introduced that topic or responded differently? Specifically, make the communication seem "strange" to you so you consider a different perspective. Consider how that way of asking or commenting affected you (or a class member) and your response.

Consider the intonation and emphases of the language in the communication. The intonation and emphases on words can affect the whole meaning. For example, asking in different ways has different meanings to listeners: "How did you complete that essay question? How *did* you complete that essay question? How did *you* complete that essay question?

Consider the language of the communication for its genre of interacting, the type/mode of discourse, and the interpersonal relationships among the speakers. Would the conversation be interpreted differently if it was conducted via email or asynchronous online format versus in person? How different would it be if a comment was "passed" to you or a class member as a note or with an oral response? How does the difference between teacher-student versus student-student affect the communication?

APPLICATIONS OF DISCOURSE APPROACHES USING MARIO'S CASE STUDY

Mario was not described by his teachers as being very talkative in school; in fact, they noted that he took a marginalized stance in content area classrooms; however, in this individual conference event, he offered a good deal of information about his literacy habits and his family background. It is proposed that some of the expanded responses to questions were derived from the more relaxed conference format, some from the teacher's prompts using question uptake neutral response evaluations, and some from Mario's own motivation to share his "story" with a listener. Each of these areas can be discussed in more detail using the instructional discourse suggestions from above and a modified critical discourse analysis. When the discourse between Mario and the teacher are considered carefully, there were several opportunities for the teacher to expand and revise the language used, as suggested from educational applications described earlier in this chapter.

For example, one of the early excerpts from the transcription of Mario's meeting with his teacher can be used to point out possible interventions.

Key:

Capitalization represents read-aloud comments.

[..] represents author's interpretation about wording

(..) represents comments about context

Mario (subvocally): PEOPLE WHO READ A LOT ARE . . . not very interesting.

[Mario starts talking out loud.]

Mario: —doesn't really hate them but—

Teacher: Wait—who does?

Mario: My family doesn't read very often and a lot of people I know that read books are not very interested [either]. We would just mainly read ____ and when we are at friends' [houses], we just go inside because the other person is reading.

Teacher: Okay, okay Mario.

In this short interaction, Mario pauses on his own to revise his written response with an oral comment explaining about people who read a lot (i.e., a change in the way of representing, or mode). From his response (i.e., ". . . doesn't really hate them") it is not completely clear whether he is referring to people hating people who do not read or if he means that he or his family don't really hate the books. The question uptake ("wait . . . who does?") was assumptive by the teacher of the first possible meaning, that *someone* doesn't like them. Mario responds by describing his family's and friends' reading habits; however, the true reference was missed, and might have changed the meaning from one assumed to be about people to one about the books, possibly a further reference to the types of books that are available for the family and friends to read. This difference in interpretation might lead to different actions on the part of the teacher following the interaction, such as introducing new books to take home to share if the latter meaning was intended by Mario. The teacher followed Mario's response with a neutral word for feedback, "okay," that allowed for an acceptance of the comment for whatever reason it was intended, which opened the conversation for additional explanation if Mario chose to share more information, which he did. A better language move, or turn, by the teacher might have been to encourage more discussion on this topic to learn more about what might be "missing" from what the teacher needs to know (i.e., what can be "filled in") for further literacy education. A simple comment such as "Tell me more about what you mean" would encourage Mario to provide more specific and useful information for further discussion and a possible teachable moment.

A second example would focus on Mario's background as a second language learner:

Teacher: Yeah, that's hard to know. Can I ask you something? Do you speak another language fluently?

Mario: Not fluently. I don't speak Spanish that well. Next year I'm going to take Chinese because both of my parents know how to speak Spanish so I just get good teaching lessons from them 24/7. And in ____ just in China ____ schooldays, because you don't always stay in school, you get months off. But if you are getting teached by your parents, every day you get teached no matter if there's no school or school.

Teacher: Well, do you speak at home all the time in Spanish?

Mario: English.

Teacher: When you are at home you speak English?

Mario: Yeah, except when my dad's friends come back. We speak Spanish to some of them.

Teacher: Okay, so here's another thing.

In this excerpt, although the teacher started the discussion with a closed question, requiring only a one-word or short answer without an explanation, Mario continued to supply more information as a qualification. The use of the word *fluently* might have limited the response further; however, this was not the case. Mario's extended response may have been due to the informal organization of the conference format (or "table talk") and that Mario appreciated having a patient listener for conversation with fewer evaluative comments than in the usual classroom discourse (i.e., a more even social or interpersonal relationship, or tenor). He was aware that the basic goal of the meeting was for assessment (i.e., the field or topic being represented) by the teacher and for self-assessment by himself, and was motivated to reflect about his competencies honestly. His communication suggests that his parents may be try- ing to teach him Spanish and that he is still learning this language. A more critical analysis for missing information reveals that probably the teacher does not know if Mario can read or write in Spanish, suggesting that he is not literate in this language, and that this may or may not have been his first language. This is important for the teacher to learn now that Mario has offered this information because our knowledge of building second language proficiency is best developed if students can build on the literacy behaviors of the first language by mapping lexical knowledge of one language to another; however, Mario may have been building semantic and syntactic knowledge of both languages simultaneously, which is important information for the teacher to pursue for the purpose of Mario's further literacy development.

The teacher's second question focused only on Mario's use of Spanish in the home as a primary language, which seemed assumptive; however, the uptake question con- tinued the discussion and provided more information about dual language use in the home. Further questioning by the teacher in open-ended format, such as "That all sounds interesting. . . . I would like to know more about how and what your parents teach you and your brother and sister about Spanish" would clarify the extent of use of both languages, the parents' purposeful attention to language development, and the culture of the home environment.

CONCLUSIONS

Drawing on sociocultural perspectives, this chapter was intended to show that expectations of talk are grounded in particular sociocultural values that represent hegemonic interpretations of the quality of talk and classroom discourse. From research on this topic and by observation in classroom, it appears that both pupils' and teachers' expectations are guided more by their own perceptions of an ideal state than by pedagogic or heuristic motives. Disrupting the commonplace, in this case the IRE/F format for pedagogic routines, by using more frequent individual conferences, by expanding language routines to include students' comments and questions, by expanding the formats for interacting about content topics, and by self-checking knowledge assumptions and language choices, teachers can use pedagogic discourse that strengthen students' learning and self-esteem in positive ways. As important as is the knowledge of content that educators transfer to their students, the flexible format and appropriate/just language of this teaching/learning through effective classroom discourse that students and teachers is the stuff that mediates learning.

QUESTIONS FOR THOUGHT

1. In your experiences, how you observed that teachers gain knowledge of students' funds of knowledge and language strengths? What approaches or assessments have you used? Have these assessments included a student interview or students' self-assessment?
2. What are the different formats in which you have observed teachers engaging students in classroom discourse? Have they used a variety of formats to balance students' response, such as one-on-one conferencing, small-group interactions among students, online postings for deeper reflection and more prepared responses? How often do they allow for classroom discourse opportunities and form what purposes?
3. Look back to the case study of Mario, and brainstorm various questions you might ask him and comments you might make to him about his reading habits. Consider the form of your questions (e.g., open or closed for details in his response? fair and supportive or focused on deficits?) using discourse examples. What would you change in the way that you interacted with Mario using language?

REFERENCES

Almasi, J. F. (2003). *Teaching strategic processes in reading*, New York, NY: Guilford Press.

Alvermann, D. E. (1995). *Talking is something we're pretty deprived of at school: Middle school students speak out.* Paper presented at the annual conference of the American Educational Research Association, San Francisco.

Anstrom, K., DiCerbo, P., Butler, F., Katz, A., Millet, J., & Rivera, C. (2010). *A review of the literature on academic language: Implications for K–12 English language learners.* Arlington, VA: George Washington University Center for Equity and Excellence in Education.

Atwell, N. (1997). *In the middle: New understandings about writing, reading, and learning.* Portsmouth, NH: Heinemann.

Aukerman & Pandya (2013) Rethinking common answers to critical questions about classroom discourse, *Language Arts, 91*(1), 41–47.

Bakhtin, M. M. (1981). *The dialogic imagination: Four essays by M. M. Bakhtin.* Austin, TX: University of Texas Press.

Bakhtin, M. M. (1986). *Speech genres and other late essays.* Austin, TX: University of Texas Press.

Bloome, D., & Clark, C. (2006). Discourse-in-use. In J. L. Green, G. Camilli, & P. B. Elmore (Eds.), *Handbook of complementary methods in education research* (pp. 227–42), Mahwah, NJ: Lawrence Erlbaum.

Bloome, D., & Theodorou, E. (1988). *Analyzing teacher-student and student-student discourse.* In J. Green, J. Harker, & C. Wallet (Eds.), Multiple perspective analyses of classroom discourse. Norwood, NJ: Ablex Publishing Corp.

Bloome, D., & Willis, A. I. (2013, September). Conversation currents: On discourse and language learning, *Language Arts, 91*(1), 61–67.

Brown, D. H. (2007). *Principles of language learning and teaching,* Boston, MA: Longman Publishing Group.

Brown, K. & Kennedy, H. (2011). Learning through conversation: Exploring and extending teacher and children's involvement in classroom talk, *School Psychology International, 32*(4), 377–96.

Buxton, C. A., Allexsaht-Snider, M., Suriel, R., Kayumova, S, Choi, Y., Bouton, B, & Baker, M. (2013). Using educative assessments to support science teaching for middle school English-language learners, *Journal of Science Teacher Education, 24*(2), 347–66.

Cazden, C. B. (2011). Dell Hymes's Construct of "Communicative Competence," *Anthropology & Education Quarterly, 42*(4), 364–69.

Cazden, Courtney (2001). *Classroom discourse* (2nd edition). Portsmouth, NH: Heinemann.

Chapman, R. S. (2003). Children's language learning: An interactionist perspective, Journal of *Child Psychology and Psychiatry, 41*(1) 33–54.

Christie, F. (2005). *Classroom discourse analysis.* London, UK: Bloomsbury Academic.

Collins, J. (1995). *Discourse and resistance in urban elementary classrooms: A poststructuralist perspective.* Paper presentation for the American Educational Research Association, San Francisco, CA, April 22, 1995.

Cummins, J. (2000) *Language, power and pedagogy: Bilingual children in the crossfire.* Clevedon: Multilingual Matters.

Cummins, J. (2001). Bilingual children's mother tongue: Why is it important for education? *Sprogforum NR, 19,* 1–20. [Electronic version] Retrieved from: http://www.fiplv.org/Issues/CumminsENG.pdf.

de los Rios, C. V. (2013). A curriculum of the Borderlands: High school Chicana/o-Latina/o studies as "Sitios y Lengua," *Urban Review: Issues and Ideas in Public Education, 45*(1), 58–73.

Delpit, L. D. (1988). *The silenced dialogue: Power and pedagogy in educating other people's children,* Harvard Educational Review, 58(3), 280–98.

Dozier, C., Johnston, P. H., & Rodgers, R. (2005). *Critical literacy/critical teaching: Tools for preparing responsive teachers.* New York, NY: Random House.

Echevarria, J., Vogt, M. E. & Short, D. (2004). *Making content comprehensible for English language learners: The SIOP model* (2nd ed.). Boston: Allyn & Bacon.

Edwards, D., & Mercer, N. (1987). *Common knowledge: The development of understanding in the classroom.* New York: Taylor and Francis.

Fairclough, N. (2003). *Analyzing discourse: Textual analysis for social research*. New York: Routledge.

Fairclough, N. (2011). Semiotic aspects of social transformation and learning. In Rodgers, R. (Ed.), *An introduction to critical discourse analysis in education* (2nd ed.), (pp. 119–26), New York, Routledge.

Falk-Ross, F. C. (2001). Classroom discourse routines: Changing the rules. American Reading Forum Yearbook, 21, 243–53.

Falk-Ross, F. C., & Carrier, K. (2005). Transitions from Spanish to English: Supporting students' language and literacy constructions in the classroom. *Illinois Reading Council Journal, 33*(4), 9–20.

Falk-Ross, F. C. (2007). Language factors in literacy achievement of young adolescents. In S. Mertens, V. Anfara, & M. Caskey (Eds.), *The young adolescent and the middle school,* Vol. 6 of the Handbook of Research in Middle Level Education (pp.73–89). Westerville, OH: National Middle School Association.

Falk-Ross, F. C. (in press). Table talk: Conversational interviews with middle-level students focused on attitudes about reading, *The International Journal of Learner Diversity and Identities.*

Falk-Ross, F. C. (2007). Language factors in literacy achievement of young adolescents. In S. Mertens, V. Anfara, & M. Caskey (Eds.), *The young adolescent and the middle school,* Vol. 6 of the Handbook of Research in Middle Level Education (pp.73–89). Westerville, OH: National Middle School Association.

Fecho, B., & Botzakis, S. (2007). Feasts of becoming: Imagining a literacy classroom based on dialogic beliefs. *Journal of Adolescent & Adult Literacy, 50*(7), 548–58.

Fisher, R., & Larkin, S. (2008). Pedagogy or ideological struggle? An examination of pupils' and teachers' expectations for talk in the classroom, *Language and Education, 22*(1), 1–16.

Freebody, P., Luke, A., & Gilbert, P. (1991). Reading positions and practices in the classroom, *Curriculum Inquiry, 21,* 435–57.

Freire, P. (1970). Pedagogy of the oppressed. New York: Continuum.

Ganske, K., & Jocius, R. (2013). Small-group word study: Instructional conversations or mini-interrogations? *Language Arts, 91*(1), 23–40.

Garcia, E. E., Jensen, B., and Cuellar, D. (2006). Early academic achievement of Hispanics in the United States: Implications for teacher preparation, *New Educator* 2(2), 123–47.

Gee, J. P. (1990). *Social linguistics and literacies: Ideology in discourses. Critical perspectives on literacy and education.* London: Falmer Press.

Gee, J. P. (2000). Identity as an analytic lens for research in education. *Review of Research in Education, 25,* 99-125.

Gee, J. P. (2001). Reading as situated language: A sociocognitive perspective, *Journal of Adolescent and Adult Literacy, 44*(8), 714–25.

Gee. J. P. (2004). *Situated language and learning: A critique of traditional schooling.* London: Routledge.

Gee, J. P. (2006). *An introduction to discourse analysis: Theory and method* (2nd Ed.), New York: NY: Routledge.

Gee, J. P. (2008). *What video games have to teach us about learning and literacy,* revised and updated, pg. 18. Basingstoke: Palgrave Macmillan.

Gee, J. P. (2010). *An introduction to discourse analysis: Theory and method.* Taylor & Francis.

Gee, J. P. (2011). *How to do discourse analysis: A toolkit,* New York, NY: Routledge.

Godley, A. J., & Minnici, A. (2008). Critical language pedagogy in an urban high school English class, *Urban Education, 43*, 319–46.

Goodman, Yetta M. (1996). "Revaluing readers while readers revalue themselves: Retrospective miscue analysis." *The Reading Teacher* 49(8): 600–609.

Green, J. L. (1983). Exploring classroom discourse: Linguistic perspectives on teaching-learning processes, *Educational Psychologist, 18*(3), 180–99.

Guthrie, J. T., Coddington, C. S., & Wigfield, A. (2009). Profiles of motivation for reading among African American and Caucasian students, *Journal of Literacy Research, 41*(3), 317–53.

Gutierrez, K. (1995). Unpacking academic discourse, *Discourse Processes, 19*, 21–27.

Halliday, M. A. K. (1975). *Learning how to mean*, London, Edward Arnold.

Halliday, M. A. K., and Hasan, R. (1989). *Language, context, and text: Aspects of language in a social-semiotic perspective*. Oxford University Press.

Heath, S. B. (2013). *Ways with words: Language, life and work in communities and classrooms*, Cambridge, UK: Cambridge University Press.

Holquist, M. (1990). *Dialogism: Bakhtin and his world*, New York, NY: Routledge.

Howell, P. B., Thomas, S. , & Ardasheva, Y. (2011). Talk in the classroom: Meeting the developmental, academic, and cultural needs of middle school students, *Middle Grades Research Journal, 6*(1), 47–63.

Hymes, D. (1974). *Foundations of sociolinguistics: An ethnographic approach*. Philadelphia: University of Pennsylvania.

Johnson, H., & Freedman, L. (2006). Developing critical awareness at the middle level: Using texts as tools for critique and pleasure. Newark, DE: International Reading Association.

Johnston, P. H. (2004). *Choice words: How our language affects children's learning*. Portland, ME: Stenhouse.

Johnston, P. H., Ivey, G., & Faulkner, A. (2011). Talking in class: Remembering what is important about classroom talk. *Reading Teacher, 65*(4), 232–37.

Kibler, A. (2011). Understanding the "mmhm": Dilemmas in talk between teachers and adolescent emergent bilingual students, *Linguistics and Education: An International Research Journal, 22*(3), 213–32.

Lankshear, C., & Knobel, M. (2003). *New literacies: Changing knowledge and classroom learning*, Buckingham, UK: Open University Press.

Lapp, D., Fisher, D., & Frey, N. (2013). It's not impossible to acquire and expand classroom language: Instruction matters. *Voices from the Middle, 20*(4), 7–9.

Larson, L. C. (2009). Reader response meets new literacies: Empowering readings in online learning environments, *The Reading Teacher, 62*(8), 638–48.

Leu, D. J. (2002). The new literacies: Research on reading instruction with the Internet and other digital technologies. In A. E. Farstrup & S. J. Samuels (Eds.), *What research has to say about reading instruction* (3rd ed., pp. 310–36). Newark, DE: International Reading Association.

Lewison, M., Flint, A. S., & Van Sluys, K. (2002). Taking on critical literacy: the journey of newcomers and novices. *Language Arts, 79* (5), 382–92.

Lewison, M., Leland, C., & Harste, J. (2007). *Creating critical classrooms: K-8 reading and writing with an edge*. New York, NY: Taylor & Francis Group.

Logan, S., Medford, E., & Hughes, N. (2011). The importance of intrinsic motivation for high and low ability readers' reading comprehension performance. *Learning and Individual Differences, 21*, 124–28

Luke, A. (1988)). The non-neutrality of literacy instruction: a critical introduction. *Australian Journal of Reading, 11*(2), 79–83.

Malinowski, B. (1923). *The problem of meaning in primitive languages.* In C. K. Ogden and I. A. Richards (Eds.), The meaning of meaning: A study of influence of language upon thought and of the science of symbolism (pp. 296–336). New York: Harcourt, Brace and World.

Mercer, N. (2000). *Words and minds: How we use language to think together.* New York, NY: Routledge.

Michaels, S. & Cazden, C. (2012) Reading comprehension in class discussions. In, *Literacy Standards for the Middle Grades.* Pittsburgh, PA: New Standards and the University of Pittsburgh Press.

Michaels, S. (2006). Narrative presentations: An oral preparation for literacy with first graders. In J. Cook-Gumperz (Ed.), *The Social Construction of Literacy,* 2nd Ed., pp. 94–116. New York: Cambridge University Press.

Michaels, S., O'Connor, C., & Resnick, L. (2008). Deliberate discourse idealized and realized: Accountable talk in the classroom and in civic life, *Studies in Philosophy and Education, 27,* 283–97.

National Governors Association (2010). *Common Core State Standards.* National Governors Association Center for Best Practices, Council of Chief State School Officers, Washington, D.C. Available at http://www.corestandards.org/.

Nystrand, M. (2006). Research on the role of classroom discourse as it affects reading comprehension. *Research in the Teaching of English, 40*(4), 392–412.

Nystrand, M., Wu, L. L., Gamoran, A., Zeiser, S., & Long, D. A. (2003). Questions in time: Investigating the structure and dynamics of unfolding classroom discourse, *Discourse Processes, 35*(2), 135–98.

O'Brian, D., Beach, R., & Scharber, C. (2007). "Struggling" middle schoolers: Engagement and literate competence in a reading writing intervention class, *Reading Psychology, 28,* 51–73.

O'Hara, S., Pritchard, R., & Zwiers, J. (2012). Identifying academic language demands in support of the Common Core Standards. ASCD Express, 7/17, retrieved from http://wwwascd.org/ascd-express/vol7/717-ohara.aspx.

Pappas, C. C., Kiefer, B. Z., & Levstik, L. S. (2005). *An integrated language perspective in the elementary school: An action approach* (4th Ed.), Boston: Pearson.

Piaget, J. (2001). *The language and thought of the child,* New York, NY: Routledge.

Pitcher, S.M., Albright, L. K., DeLaney, C. J., Walker, N. T., Seunarinesingh, K., Mogge, S., Headly, K. N., Ridgeway, . G., Peck, S., Hunt, R., & Dunston, P. (2007). "Assessing adolescent motivation to read." *Journal of Adolescent and Adult Literacy, 50*(5): 378–96.

Rasinski, T. V., & Padak, N. (2011). "Who Wants to Be a (Reading) Millionaire?" *The Reading Teacher, 64*(7): 553–55.

Rogers, R., & Wetzel, M. M. (2014). *Designing critical literacy education through critical discourse analysis: Pedagogical and research tools for teacher researchers,* New York, NY: Routledge.

Smart, J. B., & Marshall, J. C. (2013).Interactions between classroom discourse, teacher questioning, and student cognitive engagement in middle school science, *Journal of Science Teacher Education, 24*(2), 249–67.

Street, B. (1984). *Literacy in theory and practice.* New York, NY: Cambridge University Press.

Vygotsky, L. S. (1978). *Mind in society: The development of higher psychological processes.* Cambridge, MA: Harvard University Press.

Wells, G. (1999). *Dialogic inquiry: Towards a sociocultural practice and theory of education,* New York, NY: Cambridge University Press.

Wells, G. (2006). The language experience of children at home and at school. In J. Cook-Gumperz (Ed.), *The Social Construction of Literacy*, 2nd ed., pp. 76–109. New York: Cambridge University Press.

Wertsch, J. V. (1998). *Mind as action.* New York: Oxford University Press.

Young, R. (1992). *Critical theory and classroom talk.* Philadelphia, PA: Multilingual Matters.

Young, R. F. (2008). *Language and interaction: An advanced resource book.* New York: Routledge.

5

Providing Supportive Contexts for Young Children's Language to Develop Their Ideas and Opinions

Shobana Musti-Rao and Lenwood Gibson

Mario Ramos belongs to the fastest growing ethnic group attending schools in the United States, namely, the Hispanic population. Students who speak Spanish are often referred to as English Language Learners or language-minority students. However, Goodrich, Lonigan, & Farver (2013) draw a distinction between the two terms: English language learner is used in reference to students who have limited English proficiency; whereas, language minority is used in reference to students who are exposed to a language other than English regardless of their English proficiency skills. For the purpose of this chapter, we will use the term English Language Learner (ELL) to refer to the children and youth who speak a language other than English at their homes, and enter school with English as their second language. Language is an integral part and unique characteristic of a student's culture; however, it is important to understand that students like Mario have a linguistic difference and not a linguistic deficiency (Obiakor, 2007). The danger of labeling ELLs as having a linguistic deficiency is that it can easily lead to issues of overrepresentation of culturally and linguistically diverse students in special education programs, further marginalizing these students from the general education environment. Although Mario was not identified with a learning disability, he was receiving instructional supports in the resource room each day for forty minutes. With appropriate multicultural education and support, Mario's language differences can be supported in the general education classroom.

There are about five million school-going ELLs who come from 400 different language backgrounds. Approximately 80 percent of these students are from Spanish-speaking households (Teale, 2009). The ELLs enter school with different levels of English language proficiency, and face the unique challenge of having to learn to speak and read English at the same time (Fry & Kress, 2006). The language and literacy skills that each ELL brings to the learning context span the gamut anywhere from a learner who does not speak a word of English but is literate in the native language to a learner who can speak some conversational English but is not literate in the native language, or anything in between (Goldenberg, 2008). As a result, ELLs are at an inherent disadvantage entering school and are at risk for academic failure. Results from the National Assessment for Educational Progress (2011) revealed that fourth-grade ELLs score thirty-six points below non-ELLs in reading. Although the tests were administered in English, the reasons for the low performance were not captured in these test results. For example, there is no way to know if students scored poorly due to their limited English proficiency, lack of content knowledge, or a combination of both (Goldenberg). The inability to read and write proficiently in English has a debilitating effect on ELLs' ability to participate fully in schools, workplace, and society.

In an effort to better educate and support ELLs in schools, the U.S. Department of Education's Institute of Educational Studies (IES) commissioned the National Literacy Panel (August & Shanahan, 2006), a group of experts in the fields of reading, language, bilingualism, research methods, and education, to identify, assess, and synthesize research on the literacy instruction of language-minority children and youth. According to the NLP report, literacy instruction that focuses on the five areas of reading as identified by the National Reading Panel (NICHHD, 2000)—phonemic awareness, phonics, fluency, vocabulary, and comprehension—can benefit ELLs. A finding that is key to improving literacy instruction for ELLs is the importance of oral English skills during the early years. Research evidence suggests that although emphasis is placed on word-level skills in literacy such as word recognition, decoding, and spelling, little emphasis is placed on text-level skills such as comprehension and writing. Thus, ELLs lag behind their native English-speaking peers when the instructional focus is at the text-level. By contrast, well-developed English proficiency *is* associated with better comprehension and writing skills for ELLs. The need for early, systematic, and intensive instruction to develop oral English proficiency (in both reading and writing) is warranted in order to improve literacy outcomes for students from culturally and linguistically diverse backgrounds. In an era of educational accountability, educators and teaching professionals need to make connections among curriculum, instruction, and assessment and align them with the Common Core State Standards (CCSS) (McLaughlin & Overturf, 2012). Referred to as the Common Core, the CCSS consists of English Language Arts and Mathematics standards that are aligned with college and work expectations to prepare students for being successful in the global society. The Common Core standards are organized according to the College and Career Readiness (CCR) standards and include benchmarks for each grade level.

Statewide assessments are conducted to assess students' English language skills and determine the level of instructional support needed for students less proficient in English. For example, the New York State English as a Second Language Achievement Test (NYSESLAT) is administered to all English language learners in Grades K–12 on an annual basis. Based on NYSESLAT results, a student's English proficiency is classified as beginner, intermediate, advanced, or proficient. Those students classified as beginner, intermediate, or advanced receive English as a Second Language (ESL) services as outlined by the Department of Education. Students will no longer be eligible for ESL services when they score at the proficient level in both the Listening and Speaking and the Reading and Writing components of the test. Given the importance of oral proficiency in literacy instruction, students like Mario need instruction in oral language development that is very closely aligned with the high-quality literacy instruction. In this chapter, we will provide a frame of reference on how teachers can provide supportive contexts to develop students' language as it relates to literacy instruction. First, we will review the theories of language acquisition to understand the interconnectedness of language and literacy. Then, we will discuss ways in which teachers and adults can provide supportive contexts to facilitate language development in students as they formulate their own ideas and opinions and link this new vocabulary to their learning in the classroom. We will also emphasize the use of new literacies in the classroom for language and literacy development.

THEORETICAL FRAMEWORK FOR LANGUAGE ACQUISITION

Before discussing effective strategies to promote language development, it is important to understand the theoretical underpinnings of many of these strategies. The three most popular theories of language acquisition have been Skinner's (1957) Behaviorist theory, Chomsky's (1957) Innatist theory, and Hymes' (1972) Interactionist theory. Skinner believed that a verbal community was required to provide meaning to the language, verbal practices, and events that take place in the environment. He treated language (i.e., verbal behavior) like any other behavior that is learned and maintained by natural contingencies of reinforcement in the environment. According to this theory, language can be learned with modeling, imitation, repetition, and pattern drills (Dolati, 2012). Chomsky (1957), on the other hand, believed that humans were equipped with a language acquisition device (LAD) which gives us an innate ability to process linguistic rules. Samples of language (i.e., input) are needed to trigger the LAD to discover grammatical rules and produce language (Dolati, 2012). The interactionist theory takes into account the experiences that children bring to the learning environment, and the interactions that take place in learner-centered contexts. The interactional modifications that take place in the process of communication is essential for children to gain *communicative competence* or become proficient in a language (Conteh-Morgan, 2002; Dolati, 2012). Strategies that are based on the interactionist theory emphasize the use of real-life, authentic interactions situated within the natural learning environment that provide meaning for the teacher-student interactions. Such interactions push students to acquire and use language beyond their current linguistic abilities (McNeil, 2012). For example, there is evidence to suggest that teachers' use of referential questions results in longer and more complex responses on the part of the students. The scaffolding provided by teachers in the communication process is vital in expanding the communicative competence of students. Therefore, many of the strategies discussed in this chapter will focus on the rich interactions between teacher and student to facilitate and promote language acquisition.

COMPONENTS OF HIGH-QUALITY LITERACY INSTRUCTION

Literacy instruction is the foundation for success in a student's school career and further on in life. Students who gain access to high-quality literacy instruction from a young age are more likely to perform well in school. Specific strategies have been developed and used to support language acquisition and literacy for all students but can be particularly beneficial for struggling students and/or ELLs. These strategies include cooperative learning, comprehension strategies, language objectives, oral language practice, and academic vocabulary development (Goodrich, Lonigan, & Farver, 2013). The alignment of each of these strategies with the Common Core State Standards (CCSS) is presented in Table 5.1. Each of these strategies can be used to support ELL students like Mario.

Cooperative learning. Cooperative learning strategies involve small groups of students working together to complete a common task or assignment. The arrangement of these groups can take on various forms such as same ability or mixed ability groupings. By working in a small group setting students have an opportunity to express their thoughts, ideas, and knowledge in a less threatening setting (Calderon, Slavin, & Sánchez, 2011). This may be particularly important for ELLs because they could be more reluctant to share their ideas and express their understanding due to their language deficits. One of the reasons for this reluctance may be issues with pronunciation and mastery of oral communication. In order to improve pronunciation skills, ELLs need to engage in activities that focus on phonological awareness (Chen & Goswami, 2011).

In a study by Chen and Goswami (2011) cooperative learning groups were used to improve the pronunciation of 19 ELLs. Students in the cooperative learning groups engaged in learning strategies designed to improve their skills pronouncing words in English. The cooperative learning groups utilized a "jigsaw" strategy in which each group member mastered specific word pronunciations and then shared them with their home group. The idea was to have students work together to master multiple pronunciations. The results of this study demonstrated that students in the cooperative learning group significantly improved their pronunciation of English words.

Another specific cooperative learning strategy used for literacy skills is Peer Assisted Learning Strategies (PALS). The PALS program is a variation of classwide peer tutoring in which students are paired together to engage in a series of literacy activities. For students in early primary grades (i.e., kindergarten and first grade)

Table 5.1. Sample of Instructional Strategies and Alignment with the Common Core State Standards

Strategy	New York Common Core State Standards (CCSS)–English Language Arts (ELA)

Cooperative Learning:
• Jigsaw Strategy
• Peer Assisted Learning Strategy
	Reading Standards: Foundational Skills (K–5)
	4. Read with sufficient accuracy and fluency to support comprehension.
	  a. Read grade-level text with purpose and understanding.
	  b. Read grade-level prose and poetry orally with accuracy, appropriate rate, and expression on successive readings.
	  c. Use context to confirm or self-correct word recognition and understanding, rereading as necessary.

Oral Language Practice:
• Print Rich Environment
• Word Walls
	Speaking and Listening Standards K–5:
	1. Engage effectively in a range of collaborative discussions (one-on-one, in groups, and teacher-led) with diverse partners on grade 3 topics and texts, building on others' ideas and expressing their own clearly.
	  a. Come to discussions prepared, having read or studied required material; explicitly draw on that preparation and other information known about the topic to explore ideas under discussion.
	  b. Follow agreed-upon rules for discussions (e.g., gaining the floor in respectful ways, listening to others with care, speaking one at a time about the topics and texts under discussion).
	  c. Ask questions to check understanding of information presented, stay on topic, and link their comments to the remarks of others.
	  d. Explain their own ideas and understanding in light of the discussion.
	  e. Seek to understand and communicate with individuals from different cultural backgrounds.

(continued)

Table 5.1. *(Continued)*

Strategy	New York Common Core State Standards (CCSS)–English Language Arts (ELA)

Academic Vocabulary Development:
• Explicit Vocabulary Instruction
• Subject Specific Vocabulary (Technical Words)
	Language Standards K–5: Vocabulary Acquisition and Use
	5. Demonstrate understanding of word relationships and nuances in word meanings.
	  a. Distinguish the literal and nonliteral meanings of words and phrases in context (e.g., take steps).
	  b. Identify real-life connections between words and their use (e.g., describe people who are friendly or helpful).
	  c. Distinguish shades of meaning among related words that describe states of mind or degrees of certainty (e.g., knew, believed, suspected, heard, wondered).
	6. Acquire and use accurately grade-appropriate conversational, general academic, and domain-specific words and phrases, including those that signal spatial and temporal relationships (e.g., After dinner that night we went looking for them).

Comprehension Strategies: • Text-based Questioning • Self-Questioning • Graphic Organizers	**Reading Standards for Informational Text K–5: Key Ideas and Details** 1. Ask and answer questions to demonstrate understanding of a text, referring explicitly to the text as the basis for the answers. 2. Determine the main idea of a text; recount the key details and explain how they support the main idea. 3. Describe the relationship between a series of historical events, scientific ideas or concepts, or steps in technical procedures in a text, using language that pertains to time, sequence, and cause/effect. 4. Determine the meaning of general academic and domain-specific words and phrases in a text relevant to a *grade 3 topic or subject area*.

there are skills such as phonological awareness, phonological recoding, and reading fluency (Mathes, Howard, Allen, & Fuchs, 1998) and other activities such as paired readings and stories. Although the PALS program has proven effective for various types of students, specific attention has also been given to how this program works with ELLs. Several studies have been conducted using the PALS literacy program with young ELLs (Sáenz, Fuchs, & Fuchs, 2005; Calhoon, Otaiba, Cihak, King, & Avalos, 2007). For example, Sáenz et al. used PALS with a group of low achieving Spanish speaking students. These students were paired with average and high achieving students and as per PALS protocol each student spent time as both the tutor and the tutee. Students engaged in the following literacy activities: partner reading with story retell, paragraph shrinking, and prediction relay. These activities were designed to strengthen literacy skills and promote an enriched learning environment. The results of this study demonstrated that PALS was effective in improving the reading and comprehension skills of the low achieving ELLs.

An additional benefit of using cooperative strategies such as PALS is the socialization that is required by the students who engage in the learning activities. By working together as a team or in small groups, students can improve their social standing and therefore feel more comfortable in the classroom environment. In a study conducted by Fuchs, Fuchs, Mathes, and Martinez (2002) students with disabilities who engaged in fifteen weeks of PALS were able to enjoy same social standings as their non-disabled counterparts. Although this study was conducted with students with learning disabilities, the potential social benefits for Mario can be projected.

Oral language practice. One way to help ELLs become more comfortable with expressing their ideas and opinions in a second language is to give them numerous opportunities to practice using this language. Research supports the use of oral language practice for ELLs and there is evidence to suggest a positive correlation with increased oral language practice and improvements in literacy (Saunders, Foorman, & Carlson, 2006). Children who are explicitly taught how to use and improve their oral language in the classroom do better in listening, speaking, reading, and writing in English Language Arts (Kirkland & Patterson, 2005). Due to the positive impact on literacy, oral language practice should occur throughout the school day especially for young children and ELLs. This practice can range from having casual conversations between classmates to creating academic assignments that require the use of English (e.g., reading aloud during a class assignment). Although having casual conversations with classmates is important and can help with literacy development it is far more important to provide ELLs opportunities to speak about academic topics throughout the day (Soto-Hinman, 2011).

There are several ways to help students become more proficient in academic language during the school day. The first and probably simplest way to promote language practice is to organize and arrange the classroom environment to be print rich (Kirkland & Patterson, 2005). An example of one strategy to make the environment more print rich is by using word walls for various academic topics. By posting a list of vocabulary words around the classroom, ELLs have more of a chance to visualize and therefore use these words in their conversations with their peers. Jackson, Tripp, and Cox (2001) described the use of interactive word walls to improve science instruction for a group of middle school students. The classroom teacher used high frequency science words to help support the understanding of all students but indicated that it was particularly helpful for ELLs.

Another way to help students practice their oral language is by scheduling activities that allow students to discuss various classroom assignments. As discussed previously, the use of small groups provide a safe and supportive environment for ELLs to participate in assignments. Student groupings should vary throughout the day and the composition of the groups can be adjusted depending on student needs. For example, ELLs who are new to the classroom or struggle with a particular subject can be placed in a group with students who are proficient in both languages. In this situation, the new student can elicit information in their native language from the more proficient student without fear of being embarrassed. Additionally, as the ELL improves the more proficient student can explain some academic concepts in English as well as Spanish.

Academic vocabulary development. A crucial component to the success of ELLs in their academics is the development of a strong vocabulary. Many times these students struggle across subjects because they lack the needed academic vocabulary to understand the material. It is noted that even though ELLs may perform adequately with conversational vocabulary, they may continue to struggle with academic vocabulary (Sibold, 2011). This will not only impact their ability to perform well within their academics but also their willingness to participate in the group activities that foster strong ideas and opinions. Therefore the focus on improving academic vocabulary becomes important to the success of ELLs like Mario.

Although teaching vocabulary to students might seem like an easy endeavor, it can present challenges particularly for ELLs. This is mostly due to the type of vocabulary words that best support academic success. Beck, McKeown, and Kucan (2002) developed a three-tier model that illustrates the different types and levels of vocabulary words. Tier 1 consists of words that are commonly used in everyday conversations. While tier 2 and 3 are vocabulary words that are directly related to academics, tier 2 words are used across subjects and tier 3 are content specific vocabulary. It is important to make these distinctions when providing vocabulary instruction so specific strategies can be used to improve vocabulary at tiers 2 and 3. These technical words need to be explicitly taught to ensure ELLs understand and can use these words appropriately.

There is research evidence that ELLs who are involved in explicit vocabulary instruction perform better on literacy tasks (Filippini, Gerber, & Leafstedt, 2012; Kim & Linan-Thompson, 2013; Lesaux, Kieffer, Faller, & Kelley, 2010). In a study by Lesaux and colleagues (2010) the researchers used an explicit teaching strategy named Academic Language Instruction for All Students (ALIAS) to improve the academic vocabulary of students including ELLs. The ALIAS program consisted of eight two-week lessons that used selected academic vocabulary in a variety of lesson activities. Each lesson was delivered in a whole group, small group, or individual format depending on the type of activity being performed. Activities were designed to provide students with repeated opportunities to use the academic vocabulary in listening, speaking, reading, and writing. The results of this study demonstrated the use of explicit instruction to improve students' academic vocabulary and reading comprehension skills. This study along with other studies lends credibility to the use of vocabulary instruction to help improve the literacy skills of ELLs.

Comprehension strategies. The ultimate goal of reading is comprehension and therefore teaching comprehension strategies is a major focus of literacy instruction. Reading comprehension is the product of all the other reading skills combined. In order for students to be effective in understanding what they read, they need to master phonemic/phonological awareness, have a strong vocabulary, and read with speed and accuracy (i.e., fluency). All of these skills contribute to making meaning of what is read, and allow students to formulate and express their ideas and opinions in the classroom. Although many students will naturally have good comprehension skills, there are some that need explicit instruction using comprehension strategies.

There are several strategies that have proven effective in improving the reading comprehension of ELLs. These include using text-based questioning (Taboada, Bianco, & Bowerman, 2012), self-questioning (Berkeley, Marshak, Mastropieri, & Scruggs (2011), and graphic organizers (Pang, 2013). Teachers can use these strategies in isolation or combine with other strategies to help improve student comprehension. Taboada and colleagues (2012) taught ELLs to use text-based questioning when trying to improve comprehension. In this study the authors used a scaffolding technique that gradually taught a small group in ELLs to formulate their own questions about a science topic. The teacher initially used modeling to guide the students on how to formulate appropriate questions regarding what they are reading. She provided a context for student to create their own questions and share them with the group where she provided feedback. This instruction took place every day for a total of six weeks. The results of this instruction demonstrated that the ELLs in this study were able to improve their questioning skills and in turn their comprehension of science material.

Another questioning strategy was explored by Berkeley and colleagues (2011). In this study the authors trained the teachers to provide instruction to students on how to use self-questioning to better understand social studies material. In the treatment group the teacher provided three scripted lessons that consisted of modeling, guided practice, and independent practice. The lessons focused on teaching students how to develop effective self-questions based on the social studies topics in the textbook. The results of this study indicated that the self-questioning strategy was effective in improving both multiple choice and open-ended post-tests. Although this study did not single out instruction for ELLs, 13 percent of the participants were identified as English as a Second Language (ESL) students.

Providing Supportive Contexts for Mario Using New Literacies

With the continuous advancements in technology and wide-reaching capability of the World Wide Internet, the concept of literacy is expanding and evolving to include the new literacies of twenty-first century technologies. New literacies include the Internet and other information and communication technologies (ICTs) that our students engage with in their daily lives. These can include but not limited to search engines, webpages, WebQuests, email, instant messaging, blogs, wikis, e-books, podcasts, and YouTube. There is general consensus among professionals in the field of literacy instruction that it is the responsibility of educators and teachers to effectively incorporate these new literacies in their reading and writing instruction. Our twenty-first century learners need to be proficient in the use of these new literacies for "successful civic participation in a global environment" (International Reading Association, 2009).

In addition to high-quality literacy instruction, students like Mario need instruction in supportive contexts that increase the scope and sequences of their oral language skills. These oral language skills will enhance their participation and understanding with other literacy-related activities. In this section, we will look at how we can incorporate both elements of the high-quality literacy instruction discussed earlier in the chapter and new literacies to provide Mario with a supportive context for language and literacy development. Although Mario indicated that he does not worry about what other students think about his reading skills, he admitted that knowing how to read well is a "very important" skill.

> *Mario:* Well, it depends. If you are doing math, you don't really need reading. You just need to know how to be able to read the math problem. But other than that, you are going to have to read papers and stuff so to me, it's very important because almost everything I do is reading. I play lots of video games with ____ and all of them; I have to read what they say.

Mario is able to clearly articulate the different uses and necessity of reading. Later in the interview he admits that reading can be a boring way to spend time and that he considers himself a poor reader. It is not uncommon for students struggling with reading to have low confidence and self-esteem on their reading skills. Teachers can easily leverage on students' interests and make reading more engaging. For example, Mario indicated that he likes fantasy books. Using new literacies, teachers can create online reading groups and forums in which students have the opportunity to read books of their choice and engage in online discussions with other members on the Internet. Participating in book clubs and reading groups can further encourage students like Mario to read along with peers having similar interests. When paired up with another student who also enjoys fantasy books, Mario and his partner can engage in Peer Assisted Learning Strategies (PALS), taking turns playing the role of coach and reader. Completing steps in the PALS protocol (e.g., partner reading, paragraph shrinking, and retelling) will facilitate both reading fluency and comprehension skills.

Students are more likely to learn vocabulary words when embedded in meaningful contexts. Mario indicated that he likes comics because of "*the picture to understand stuff.*" The visual representation of the concepts can be a powerful tool to aid in comprehension. One form of comic popular among twenty-first century learners is *Manga*, a style that originated in Japan. There are several online applications and software available with easy user-interface, allowing students to create their own comics. For example, the popular Disney˚ Company has its own online *Manga Comic Creator* where Mario can create a story with sound and animation and share with the online community. When students become producers of work, they are more likely to be engaged and invested.

Writing, for the twenty-first century digital natives, has taken on new meaning and roles in the way students socialize and communicate with others. Instant messaging or text messaging has gained popularity as a way of communicating and relaying information. However, the writing in these messages seldom follows traditional conventions (Sweeney, 2010); instead, the writing includes a form of short-hand and abbreviations. Mario is all too familiar with this writing style, commonly referred to as *Text Speak* or *Text Talk*, when describing how he texts his friends.

Mario: And when I am texting my friends on my PS3, when I'm online signed in, I have to read what they are saying and I have to spell out the word I am going to tell them back.

Teacher: That's true. So is that hard?

Mario: Well, not very hard. It's just we really don't use very big words. We might be sometimes lazy. Sometimes we are lazy so instead of putting like the word because, we put 'cos.

Teacher: I've seen that.

Mario: My cousin, we just put CUZ. And why, we just put the letter Y.

Teachers can leverage students' fluency in Text Speak by infusing these skills in their classroom instruction. For students who do not have access to mobile phones, texting is still possible by using websites that are free. In some cases, teachers who may have reservations to give out their personal mobile phone numbers to students can use the websites for texting purposes. It will be important for teachers to establish ground rules on acceptable language used in texting to prevent any possible misuse of the strategy. See Table 5.2 for more information on these websites. Some ideas for using texting in the classroom are as follows:

- ***Motivating hook.*** Teachers can send a thought-provoking question as a text message to students prior to the start of the new unit or lesson. Students will be required to think about the question, research the Internet, and come prepared to class to share their responses. Alternatively, students can text their responses back to the teacher who can then collate the responses in preparation for class.

Table 5.2.   Resources for Using New Literacies in the Classroom

Resource	Description
Manga Comic Creator http://disney.go.com/create/apps/ comiccreator/manga	Online application to create comic stories with sounds and animation.
Remind 101 https://www.remind101.com	A free and safe way for teachers to text students and parents using the website.
KikuText https://kikutext.com/	A safe way for teachers to communicate with parents. The service includes a fee.
Reminder Guru http://reminderguru.com/	Teachers and students can send reminders to any email or phone for free. Particularly useful for students who need reminders to complete specific homework tasks or to bring items to school.
Polleverywhere http://www.polleverywhere.com/	Allows teachers to create polls and uses texting or online responses to teacher-posed questions.

- *Comprehension.* Sweeney (2010) shares an example of a teacher who asked students to read a passage of text and summarize the main ideas of the passage using a text message. The short nature of the message was appropriate and a suitable form of response for this purpose. Using texting to respond in class can be an effective means of engaging the learner and checking for understanding.
- *Brainstorming ideas.* The teacher can also assign students to brainstorm ideas on a topic and text their ideas to each other. In class, the students can convert these text messages to conventional sentences and submit their responses. The popular social networking site *Twitter* can also be used for this purpose.
- *Responding to quizzes.* In order to increase student participation in class, teachers can create review questions with selected choice responses, and students can respond by texting their answers. Websites such as *Polleverywhere.com* enable students to use texting options for assessment/survey purposes.

As mentioned earlier, teachers should work towards providing Mario with supportive contexts to practice his oral language skills and build an academic vocabulary. In the interview, Mario was able to read the passage and answer questions, but not without the prompting from the teacher. What do you notice about the following interaction between the teacher and Mario as she asks him questions about the passage that they read?

Mario: That in the first race, a boy fouled her I think and she got bandages and she got back in the race and won.

Teacher: Okay, yeah. What do you know about the word challenge? Challenger?

Mario: A rival? A person who was on the same thing that you are but they want to do it better than you.

Teacher: Very good. And how do you know that the crash was dangerous?

Mario: Because it said that she needed staples on her for head and bandages.

Teacher: Okay. Why didn't Sheila want to quit the race?

Mario: Because she wanted to win.

Teacher: That's exactly right. And what about the phrase intense pain?

The teacher in this example is providing immediate feedback to Mario's responses, showing him that he is adding value and contributing to the exercise. She follows each feedback statement with a prompt that requires Mario to elaborate on his responses. In a sense, the teacher is tactfully eliciting the responses from Mario. In order to allow students to demonstrate their understanding, teachers need to provide students like Mario access to competent speakers who are able to value contributions and prompt further elaborations (Manyak, 2007).

As educators we need to be cognizant of students' cultural and linguistic experiences that they bring to school. Vasquez, Pease-Alvarez, and Shannon (1994) noted the intercultural transactions that ELLs make outside of school by way of serving as translators for their parents in the community (e.g., doctor's visit). Teachers who recognize these cultural experiences can incorporate the student's strengths during classroom conversations by drawing upon student's experiences and relating it to classroom discussions. In another example, Dworin (2006) describes how students were required to interview their family members and create family memoirs to share in class. Again, with new literacies, such a project can become engaging for the student. The students can video record or audio record the interview, take pictures of various culture-specific artifacts to include in their memoirs.

Strategies to provide students with meaningful and supportive contexts for language and literacy development are endless. It is important for teachers to gain a thorough understanding of students in this population and then arrange their learning environments to support and encourage oral language practice and literacy development.

REFERENCES

August, D. and Shanahan, T. (2006). *Developing literacy in second-language learners: Report of the National Literacy Panel on Language-Minority Children and Youth.* Center for Applied Linguistics, Lawrence Erlbaum Associates: Mahwah, NJ.

Beck, I. L., McKeown, M. G., & Kucan, L. (2013). *Bringing words to life: Robust vocabulary instruction* (2nd Ed.). New York: The Guilford Press.

Berkeley, S., Marshak, L., Mastropieri, M. A., & Scruggs, T. E. (2011). Improving student comprehension of social studies text: A self-questioning strategy for inclusive middle school classes. *Remedial and Special Education, 32*(2), 105–13.

Calderón, M., Slavin, R., & Sánchez, M. (2011). Effective instruction for English Learners. *Future of Children, 21*(1), 103–27.

Calhoon, M., Al Otaiba, S., Cihak, D., King, A., & Avalos, A. (2007). Effects of a peer-mediated program on reading skill acquisition for two-way bilingual first-grade classrooms. *Learning Disability Quarterly, 30*(3), 169–84.

Chen, H., & Goswami, J. (2011). Structuring cooperative learning in teaching English pronunciation. *English Language Teaching, 4*(3), 26–32.

Chomsky, N. (1957). *Syntactic structures.* The Hague: Mouton.

Conteh-Morgan, M. (2002). Connecting the dots: Limited English proficiency, second language learning theories, and information literacy instruction. *The Journal of Academic Librarianship, 28*(4), 191–96.

Dolati, R. (2012). Overview on three core theories of second language acquisition and criticism. *Advances in Nature and Applied Sciences, 6*(6), 752–62.

Dworin, J. (2006). The Family Stories Project: Using funds of knowledge for writing. *The Reading Teacher, 33,* 934–45.

Filippini, A. L., Gerber, M. M., & Leafstedt, J. M. (2012). A vocabulary-added reading intervention for English learners at-risk of reading difficulties. *International Journal of Special Education, 27*(3), 14–26.

Fry, E. B., Ph.D. & Kress, J. E. (2006). *The Reading Teacher's Book of Lists,* 5th Ed. San Francisco, CA: Jossey Bass.

Fuchs, D. D., Fuchs, L. S., Mathes, P. G., & Martinez, E. A. (2002). Preliminary evidence on the social standing of students with learning disabilities in PALS and No–PALS classrooms. *Learning Disabilities Research & Practice, 17*(4), 205–15.

Goldenberg, C. (2008). Teaching English language learners: What the research does—and does not say. *American Educator, Summer,* 8–44.

Goodrich, J. M., Lonigan, C. J., & Farver, J. A. M. (2013). Do early literacy skills in children's first language promote development of skills in their second language? An experimental evaluation of transfer. *Journal of Educational Psychology, 105*(2), 414–26.

Hymes, D. (1972). On communicative competence. In J. B. Pride & J. Holmes (Eds.), *Sociolinguistics* (pp. 269–93). England: Penguin.

Jackson, J., Tripp, S., & Cox, K. (2011). Interactive word walls: Transforming content vocabulary instruction. *Science Scope, 35*(3), 45–49.

Kim, W., & Linan-Thompson, S. (2013). The effects of self-regulation on science vocabulary acquisition of English Language Learners with learning difficulties. *Remedial & Special Education, 34*(4), 225–36.

Kirkland, L. D., & Patterson, J. (2005). Developing oral language in primary classrooms. *Early Childhood Education Journal, 32*(6), 391–95.

Lesaux, N. K., Kieffer, M. J., Faller, S. E., & Kelley, J. G. (2010). The effectiveness and ease of implementation of an academic vocabulary intervention for linguistically diverse students in urban middle schools. *Reading Research Quarterly, 45*(2), 196–228.

Manyak, P. C. (2007). A framework for robust literacy instruction for English learners. *The Reading Teacher, 6*(12), 197–99. DOI: 10.1598/RT.61.2.10

Mathes, P. G., Howard, J. K., Allen, S. H., & Fuchs, D. (1998). Peer-assisted learning strategies for first-grade readers: Responding to the needs of diverse learners. *Reading Research Quarterly, 33*(1), 62.

McLaughlin, M., & Overturf, B. J. (2012). The common core: Insights into the K–5 standards. *The Reading Teacher, 66,* 153–64.

McNeil, L. (2012). Using talk to scaffold referential questions for English language learners. *Teaching and Teacher Education, 28,* 395–404.

National Institute of Child Health and Human Development (2000). *Report of the National Reading Panel. Teaching children to read: An evidence-based assessment of the scientific research literature on reading and its implications for reading instruction* (NIH Publication No. 00-4769). Washington, D.C.: U.S. Government Printing Office.

Obiakor, F. (2007). Multicultural special education: Effective intervention for today's schools. *Intervention in School and Clinic, 42,* 148–55.

Pang, Y. (2013). Graphic organizers and other visual strategies to improve young ELLs' reading comprehension. *New England Reading Association Journal, 48*(2), 52–58.

Sáenz, L. M., Fuchs, L. S., & Fuchs, D. (2005). Peer-assisted learning strategies for English Language Learners with learning disabilities. *Exceptional Children, 71*(3), 231–47.

Saunders, W. M., Foorman, B. R., & Carlson, C. D. (2006). Is a separate block of time for oral English language development in programs for English Learners needed? *Elementary School Journal, 107*(2), 181–98.

Sibold, C. (2011). Building English Language Learners' academic vocabulary: Strategies and tips. *Multicultural Education, 18*(2), 24–28.

Skinner, B. F. (1957). *Verbal Behavior.* New York: Appleton-Century.

Soto-Hinman, I. (2011). Increasing academic oral language development using English language learner shadowing in classrooms. *Multicultural Education, 18*(2), 20–23.

Sweeney, S. M. (2010). Writing for the instant messaging and text messaging generation: Using new literacies to support writing instruction. *Journal of Adolescent & Adult Literacy, 54*(2), 121–30.

Taboada, A., Bianco, S., & Bowerman, V. (2012). Text-based questioning: A comprehension strategy to build English language learners' content knowledge. *Literacy Research and Instruction, 51*(2), 87–109.

Teale, W. H. (2009). Student learning English and their literacy instruction in urban schools. *The Reading Teacher, 62*(8), 699–703. DOI: 10.1598/RT.62.8.9

Vasquez, S., Pease-Alvarez, L., & Shannon, S. M. (1994). *Pushing boundaries: Language and culture in a Mexicano community.* New York: Cambridge University Press.

6

Looking at Literacy from the Family-School Frame of Reference

Lee Shumow and Elena Lyutykh

Literacy—a discourse in and around the written language—is a complex interactive and interpretive process, situated in a particular social and cultural context, in particular ways and for particular purposes. From a socio-cultural perspective, learning to read and write well involves mastery of a particular set of cultural tools, which are used and highly valued in school and in other important settings such as families and communities. Within the socio-cultural perspective tools refer to systems of written language as well as the devices (e.g., books, computers) that convey language. Children master the tools of literacy when they communicate purposefully as they co-participate in culturally meaningful practices of their lives (Lee & Smagorinsky, 2000; Rogoff, 1990; Vygotsky, 1986). Thus, in order to succeed in learning to read and write, children must find literacy-rich cultural practices meaningful, must participate in these practices (often scaffolded by competent others), and, through this participation, must internalize culturally preferred ways of using literacy tools and the value of reading and writing.

HOW IS LITERACY MEANINGFUL IN MARIO'S LIFE?

Mario ascribes high value to literacy. In fact, he claims that almost everything he does is reading. He has a favorite book, reads the *Game Informer* magazine regularly, and is able to recall a great deal of information from readings that interested him. There appears to be a disconnect between the tools of literacy that he uses at school and those that he uses to do activities with his family and friends that are meaningful to them. Like many other middle-school boys, Mario enjoys playing video games and communicates in abbreviated language with his peers about these activities. He is far more successful with literacy within these "meaningful to him" practices than with literacy at school, a phenomenon that has been observed with other adolescent males (Steinkuehler, 2011).

Bronfenbrenner's (1993) ecological systems perspective overlaps with the socio cultural perspective in several ways helpful to understanding literacy development. Both conceptualize learning and development as a transactional process between a person and the environment—in other words, people both change and are changed by their environments. Both (Bronfenbrenner, 1979, 2005; Vygotsky, 1978) explain learning and development as arising from an interaction between personal character istics and the activities and relationships the individual routinely engages in within the immediate settings, like homes and schools, in which they spend their time. According to Bronfenbrenner, personal characteristics like age, gender, personality, and abilities are especially influential. In Mario's case, this would mean that the literacy activities available to him and his relationship with others about literacy are likely to be partially determined by being a young adolescent male who has struggled with reading. In turn, those activities impact the rate and extent of his literacy learning. Importantly, learning may be related to but is not explained by an individual's "social address" (e.g. class, race). Rather, it is the processes (doing activities, playing roles, relating to others) engaged in during daily life that explain or cause learning.

Like the sociocultural perspective, an ecological systems perspective also highlights the considerable importance of consistency between the immediate settings that children frequent, such as their home and school. So, for example, the adjustment of younger children, like Mario's sister, to starting school and their success with meeting classroom expectations in literacy will depend on how often they have been read to and how much they have participated in language interactions similar to those they will encounter at school (Neuman, Koh, & Dwyer, 2008). We will next focus on parents, schools, and the interaction between them and discuss how different types of engage ment within those overlapping settings contribute to the development of reading and writing. As you are reading, notice how the themes from the sociocultural and ecologi cal systems perspectives recur throughout the remainder of this chapter.

PARENTAL ENGAGEMENT WITH CHILDREN'S LITERACY

The importance of parental involvement in their children's literacy development is widely recognized. The research literature demonstrates that parents contribute to their children's literacy performance at all grade levels. A review of studies focusing on elementary school children identified parents as a strong influence on children's reading skill and enjoyment during the elementary school years (Caspe, Lopez, & Wolos, 2006, 2007). The extent of parental engagement decreases as students transi tion to middle and high school and the type of parent engagement that is develop mentally appropriate changes as well (Hoover-Dempsey, Ice, & Whitaker, 2009), yet evidence from a number of studies suggests that some types of parental engagement are beneficial for achievement related to language arts skills across grade levels.

TYPES OF PARENTAL ENGAGEMENT WITH SCHOOL

Parent engagement with school is multidimensional. Many scholars have identified parental engagement at-home and at-school as separate dimensions (Jeynes, 2007). Parental engagement at-home includes: (a) socializing children, (b) establishing rules and routines at home conducive to school success, (c) participating in or arranging for informal educational activities and resources, (d) directly teaching skills, and (e) providing help, monitoring, or extending homework from the child's formal school setting. Parental engagement at-school includes communicating and interacting with teachers as well as attending or participating in events or organizations at school (Hill & Craft, 2003). Educators tend to be most aware of how parents are involved at school, because that involvement is visible to them. Yet many parents who rarely or never communicate with or come to school often deeply care about their children's education and are involved at home (Hill, Tyson, & Bromell, 2009; Shumow & Miller, 2001).

As predicted by ecocultural theory, the extent to which parents engage in these different activities tends to vary by their personal characteristics. Parents who are native born, white and have more income and education are more likely to be engaged at school, but not at home (Hill & Taylor, 2004; Shumow & Lyutykh, 2011). Native born and better-educated parents are likely to have greater knowledge of how the U.S. school system works and use their cultural capital to navigate at-school involvement (Valdes, 1996). African American parents often are more involved at home than at school, whereas Euro-American parents often are more involved in the actual school setting

Figure 6.1. Parent Involvement at Home.

than at home (Eccles & Harold, 1996). This tendency to be more involved at home than at school is also typical of ethnic minorities whose primary language is not English (Garcia Coll & Pachter, 2002). Many immigrant parents have high expectations (Goldenberg, Gallimore, Reese, & Garnier, 2001) and are deeply involved at home trying to foster and encourage academic success (Strickland & Shumow, 2008), even though they tend to be minimally involved at school (Turney & Kao, 2009). Some immigrants understand their role differently than what U.S. teachers typically expect. For example, Mexican-American parents believe that it is their primary responsibility to socialize their children to be *bien educado* or respectful, well-mannered, and responsible (Carger, 1997; Goldenberg et al., 2001) rather than to be good readers, a job they see as the teacher's. So what does this mean for Mario?

Mario is a first-generation immigrant from a Mexican-American family whose parents speak English as a second language. His parents are not highly visible at school, even though Mario has had difficulties in language arts. Mario's teachers might be puzzled at why the parents are not more actively involved in Mario's learning and may even think that they are not involved at home and do not care about his education. Is that true?

Mario tells us that he discusses what he is reading with his parents. Further, he implies that his parents "teach" him Spanish all the time and that learning from parents never stops regardless of what is going on in school. This indicates that his parents are engaged with their son's education, even though they may not know how to help Mario with school-based reading and writing or may not consider it their place to do so.

Knowledge about how parent engagement influences literacy development can serve as a basis for the specific activities on which educators might focus parent partnership. What is known about the impact of parental engagement on literacy practices is presented next.

INFLUENCE OF AT-HOME
PARENT ENGAGEMENT ON LITERACY

Socialization at-home. Parents socialize their children about what is valued and important through how they live and who they are (Taylor, Clayton, & Rowley, 2004). Children pick up attitudes toward reading, writing, and school through the feelings and attitudes their parents model. Parent's own literacy and school experiences are one important source of their feelings and attitudes (Finders & Lewis, 1994). Mothers with higher educational attainment have usually had positive literacy experiences and consequently read to their children more often (Barton & Coley, 2007). Parents who showed positive affect while reading picture books with their kindergartners enhanced their children's motivation to read in first grade (Sonnenschein & Munsterman, 2002). In a literature review, Baker (2003) concluded that parents of struggling readers who establish a literacy supportive home environment can contribute to increased reading achievement by motivating their children to do more voluntary reading. While not focused on reading and writing skills per se, studies with both middle and high school students have found that parents' expectations and at home engagement impact students' school orientation and their motivation in school (Shumow, 2003; Shumow, Lyutykh, & Schmidt, 2011).

Rules and routines. The extent to which parents establish rules and routines for their children's behavior outside of school has been tied to students' school success. Rules most clearly tied to literacy learning and school performance include rules about media use and bedtime. Family routines conducive to establishing a reading habit or being prepared for school each day are also important.

Television (TV) viewing has been much discussed as an influence on children's reading. The relationship between TV viewing and student's academic achievement is complex and depends in part on the amount and the quality of TV they watch. In general, it can be concluded that heavy viewing of entertainment TV tends to be detrimental to children's reading skills (Ennemoser & Schneider, 2007; Koolstra & Van der Voort, 1996). Notably, though, those researchers defined heavy viewing in a way that includes most U.S. children. On average, children (8–18 years old) in the United States spend four hours and twenty-nine minutes each day watching TV and only thirty-eight minutes reading print with Black and Hispanic children in the U.S. watching more TV than White children (Kaiser Family Foundation, 2010). Children from affluent homes seem to be more negatively influenced by TV watching than children from low-income families possibly because more stimulating literacy resources and activities than TV are available as alternative to TV in affluent homes and communities (Comstock & Paik, 1991).

Not surprisingly, children watch less TV when parents limit their TV viewing (Barradas, Fulton, Blanck, & Huhman, 2007). Only 47 percent of elementary-school students, 27 percent of middle-school students, and 16 percent of high-school students reported having rules about how much TV they could watch (Kaiser Family Foundation, 2010); slightly more have rules about the content they can watch. Parents seeking to enforce limits encounter three main challenges: (1) children resist rules resulting in family discord, (2) replacing TV time with more meaningful activities requires time, effort, and resources that families don't think they have, and (3) TV is seen as useful for entertaining, occupying, and teaching children (Evans, Jordan, & Horner, 2011).

Parents have an important role in helping their children establish a reading habit. A study of middle school students' daily activities substantiated the importance of family engagement in reading for students Mario's age; adolescents did most of their leisure reading at home and tended to be with family members when they read (Shumow, Schmidt, & Kackar, 2008). Modeling also is important—children with educated parents (who tend to read) read more often than children with less educated parents (Roberts, Foehr & Rideout, 2005).

WHERE DOES MARIO'S
FAMILY FIT IN BOOK READING?

It appears that reading *books* and writing documents are not part of Mario's typical family routine. Importantly, reading books is not modeled or expected from Mario or his siblings in either English or Spanish. His parents are functionally literate and work hard to support the family. They have jobs that do not require extensive reading or writing, but like Mario, they are able to function *within the socio-cultural practices* that are *meaningful* to them. The family owns a computer and Mario is skilled at finding information that interests him on the Internet. Previously, Mario mentioned that his parents, but not his peers, listen to him talk about the books he likes. He is not deprived of the parents' attention or involvement. Reading "big books" and deciphering "long words" is not part of his family's reality and that is precisely what Mario struggles with in school.

Several caveats are essential. First, although parent education and family income are generally associated with home literacy resources, book distribution (or lending) and shared reading programs have succeeded with families who have low income and educational levels (Kreider, Morin, Miller, & Bush, 2011), demonstrating that many parents will read with their children given access to books. A study of middle-school students found that most did some leisure reading each day but children of parents without any postsecondary education read less than children of parents with more education (Shumow, Schmidt, & Kackar, 2008) and it is the volume of reading that predicts how well children will read (Cunningham & Stanovich, 2001).

Second, some cultural groups have rich oral literacy practices that do not mesh with traditional school literacy practices. Heath (1983, 1989) documented the way that instructional patterns predominate in elementary schools (I, initiation = teacher question, R, response = child answer, E = teacher evaluation) matched parent child verbal interactions in middle class families (e.g., What color is that? Blue. Yes! Or, How old are you? Five. That's right!). IRE interaction patterns almost never occurred in Black families with low-income living in the same geographical area; their family verbal interaction patterns were more sophisticated, open-ended, and creative than those in the middle class White families. Nevertheless, most of the Black children struggled with learning to read and write at school; they had difficulty participating in school literacy activities because they were unfamiliar with the IRE pattern and fell further and further behind. Others (Kreider et al., 2011; Cazden, John, & Hymes, 1972) also note rich oral traditions inconsistent with school practices among some Native American Indian tribes.

Third, English (or any multiple) literacy attainment is complicated in a bi or multilingual home, but it is important to understand that being bilingual has cognitive advantages (Bialystok, 2002; Kaushanskaya & Marian, 2009; Olusola, Adesope, Lavin, Thompson, & Ungerleider, 2010), promotes psychological well-being in immigrant families (Zentella, 2002), and opens many opportunities in a global economy. Unfortunately, home language and literacy practices are perceived as a problem in some pre-K–12 classrooms. Shin and Krashen (1996) found that many teachers understood that bilingualism was an advantage, yet only about half actually welcomed the use of the first language in any form in their classrooms. In a more recent study, 70 percent of the teachers did not want English language learners in their classroom, believing these students had deficits (Walker, Shafer, & Liams, 2004). As bilingual children entered school, educators often told parents that native language use at home threatened their children's academic success in English, which prompted several families to switch completely or partially to the English language at home (Lyutykh, 2011). Some of these parents were multilingual and had high income, occupational status, and educational level, which are characteristics that enable immigrant families to foster academic success in their children (Fan & Chen, 2001; Strickland & Shumow, 2008). Importantly, teachers' implicit attitudes are known to impact parents' school engagement (Green, Walker, Hoover-Dempsey, & Sandler, 2007).

Informal educational activities and resources. Parents who provide, facilitate, and talk with their children about leisure reading and other literacy experiences tend to have children who are more successful in school based literacy. Studies of young children illustrate that point; children learned more vocabulary and had higher reading comprehension and achievement when their parents conversed with them about the text of storybooks in a relaxed positive climate and made connections to their own experiences (Baker, Mackler, Sonnenschein, & Serpell, 2001). Throughout the elementary years, exposure to reading material and to reading and discussing books together with parents at home fosters reading achievement (Walberg, 2011). Studies of older adolescent students, like Mario's brother, reported strong links between the amount and variety of reading material in the home and amount of leisure reading (Kirsch et al., 2002).

Children's participation in culturally rich out-of-school activities also has been associated with higher literacy learning. In one study high achieving students spent twenty hours each week outside of school in constructive learning activities, such as music practice, reading, writing, visiting museums, and participation in youth groups, with the support of parents or other adults (Redding, 2000). Among adolescents, communication with parents, such as discussing books, films, television programs, and political/social issues, as well as cultural activities, such as attending museums, concerts, and live theater, had positive effects on literacy performance across nations (Moore, Guzman, Hair, Lippman, & Garrett, 2004).

Direct teaching at-home. There are a considerable number of studies about parents directly teaching skills to their young children. Parents who teach their children directly about reading and writing words at home aid the development of their children's early literacy skills, which, in turn, predicts reading at the end of grades one and three (Senechal & LeFevre, 2002). Few studies of older children distinguish teaching of reading and writing skills at home from homework help. One study found that mothers who helped children construct autobiographical narratives matched the level of their assistance to their children's developmental level (Habermas, Negele, & Brenneisen Mayer, 2010).

Mario's family is bilingual. They often switch from Spanish to English at home probably because they had been led to believe that speaking English at home would help Mario's education. However, in many cases, immigrant parents' limited English proficiency does not afford them an opportunity to directly teach valuable literacy skills in English at a level that meets school expectations. Literacy-rich family practices in a native language facilitate the learning of reading and writing in English, because many literacy skills transfer from one language to another (Cummins, 1979, 2000). Thus, Mario's family could play a valuable supportive role by supporting vocabulary development, reading, and writing in Spanish.

Researchers have demonstrated that difficulties with the acquisition of oral English are typically short term (Bialystok, 2002; 2009). Basic spoken language is acquired within six months to a year. However, at least five to seven years of uninterrupted instruction is required for second-language students to develop cognitive academic language proficiency (CALP) in English such as advanced vocabulary knowledge and reading comprehension (e.g. Cummins, 2000; Hakuta, Butler, & Witt, 2000). Children who are continuously supported with instruction in the home language and English literacy perform as well as or better than monolingual children on literacy tasks (Francis, Lesaux, & August 2006; Hernández, 2001; Thomas & Collier, 2002). Lack of literacy in the native language often translates to poor literacy in English. It is therefore important to encourage immigrant parents to read and write with their children in the native language as well as in English. Good quality reading material in the native language fosters literacy development (Tse, 2001, Jones, 2004).

Homework. Teachers use homework to give students additional opportunities to practice skills (Markow, Kim, & Liebman, 2007) and to foster development of achievement motivation and self-regulation in students (Bempechat, 2004). Productive family involvement in well-designed, standards-based homework can promote academic achievement and generate positive emotional benefits for both students and parents (Van Voorhis, 2003, 2011). Researchers who combined and analyzed fourteen different studies about programs that educated parents to be more involved in their children's homework concluded that students' achievement in language arts subsequently increased (Patall, Cooper, & Robinson, 2008). That study also suggested that, among elementary students, parental help with homework led to more homework completion and reduced problems with homework.

Parents' background knowledge, educational experience, and social capital contribute to them being effective helpers. For example, parents who have knowledge about both their own child's literacy level and the typical pathways through which children learn are able to provide especially effective guidance when helping their children with homework (Shumow, 2010). According to a large national survey conducted by the federal government, parents and school leaders disagree to some extent about whether parents are provided with information to help them help their children do homework, with fewer parents than administrators reporting that this information is provided (Herrold & O'Donnell, 2008). That discrepancy suggests either that the information is not reaching parents or that they do not understand it.

Jeynes (2007) reported that the positive relationships between parental help with homework and students' academic performance appears to be diminished in homes where parents belong to marginalized groups who have had restricted educational opportunity. Yet, when researchers (Epstein & VanVoorhis, 2001) designed language arts writing assignments for children from a high poverty school that involved parents in listening and reacting to their middle school students' writing, the children's grades improved in language arts and writing. Their parents said the homework program helped them understand what their children were learning.

INFLUENCES OF AT-SCHOOL
PARENT ENGAGEMENT ON LITERACY

Children whose parents are actively involved at school tend to do better in school than children whose parents are not. This association might be because parents learn about academic requirements and therefore know what to expect and encourage their children to do. Parent involvement at school includes going to conferences, attending events, volunteering at the school, and attending parent education programs.

Conferences. Many schools schedule routine parent teacher conferences once or twice per year; conferences are also sometimes scheduled for addressing specific problems or issues. The routine conference offers parents and teachers the opportunity to build partnership and share information, but, in one study at the elementary school level, parents reported that the communication was one-way from teacher to parent and that they often did not share the teacher's perspective and did not have their questions addressed (Murphy, 2009). Communication across cultures adds a

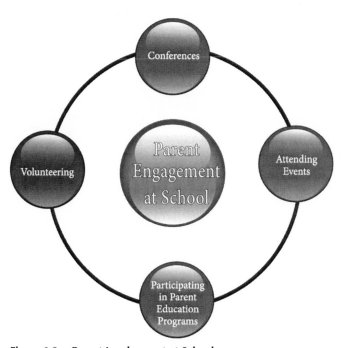

Figure 6.2.   Parent Involvement at School.

level of complexity that has exacerbated misperceptions between parents and teachers during conferences (Eberly, Joshi, & Konzal, 2007). Student-led conferences, for which the teacher prepares the student to assume the role and responsibility of primary communicator in sharing work, progress, and goals, have many advantages including excellent attendance, satisfaction, and outcomes (Hiatt-Michael, 2010). The advent of high stakes testing has made sharing and explaining assessment results with parents, and students, critically important. Weiss and Lopez (2011) describe three essential elements to consider in sharing data with families: 1) families need timely access to results; 2) they need to understand the results; and 3) they need to know what action they can take. Much more needs to be learned about how parents interpret and respond to assessment results.

Literacy events at school. Different types of literacy events for families can be held at school. Parents are most likely to come to school to be an audience for their children, so events that showcase student performance of their writing, songs (lyrics which have been read), or plays can be very successful in terms of creating a partnership around literacy. Many schools also hold book fairs which serve the dual purpose of promoting reading and fund raising.

Volunteering. Many schools offer opportunities for parents to volunteer at school. Volunteering that involves working with individual students or with small groups of students on instructional tasks (i.e., tutoring) tends to be most popular in elementary schools. Tutors need some instruction, clear directions, and prepared materials. That investment tends to pay off because students who work with a tutor make significant gains in literacy skills compared to those who do not (Ritter, Barnett, Denny, & Albin, 2009). Parents who cannot work in the classroom can be recruited as volunteers to use their skills outside the classroom (Church & Dollins, 2011). Literacy-related voluntary contributions might include parent work on classroom or school newsletters, websites, or on publicity for school events as well as on organizing and preparing compilations of student writing into books, literary magazines, or displays.

Luis Moll and his colleagues (1992) powerfully demonstrated that teachers who base school learning activities, like writing, on family and community culture and practices build successful relationships with families around school. Parents who were asked to come to school as experts on a topic were especially willing to come; adolescents, in particular, endorse this as a good reason for parents to participate at school (Hill & Tyson, 2009).

Parent education and family literacy programs. Many schools offer various forms of parent education to families. These might include one-time lectures or presentations, structured classes, or workshops. In general, parents will be more engaged if they perceive the education as pertinent to their needs, trust the sources of information, and can participate with their children. Although parents identify teachers as a preferred source of information, they do not tend to choose literacy topics among their most important needs but they do want information on how to engage their children in learning (Mullis & Mullis, 2009). Family literacy programs do usually involve parent-child interactions; evidence shows that family literacy programs positively impact children's literacy skills (Steensel, McElvany, Kurvers, & Herppich, 2011). Family literacy programs that taught parents how to teach their children specific reading skills and programs that taught parents to listen to their children read were both successful at enhancing reading achievement in primary grade children in comparison to control groups (see Senechal and Young, 2008 for a review). Parents of struggling readers who establish a literacy-supportive home environment help increase reading achievement by motivating their children to do more voluntary reading (Baker, 2003). Programs that have parents and children work together on writing projects that are culturally meaningful motivate children to read (Kreider, et al., 2011).

IMPLICATIONS: HOW CAN EDUCATORS HELP MARIO & HIS FAMILY?

In this era of accountability for student performance educators can build partnerships with parents to maximize students' literacy learning and development. Despite widely recognized benefits of home-school partnerships, teachers often find it challenging to engage parents. Most teachers receive little preparation for working effectively with parents during either pre-service or in-service teacher education (Katz & Bauch, 2001) and school policies tend to be limited in both breadth and specificity. As a result, teachers are left with little information about how to establish and maintain partnerships. This is unfortunate because a well-functioning partnership between the home and the school will maximize students' literacy development.

GUIDING PRINCIPLES

Several useful guiding principles for working with parents can be derived from the work of scholars and practitioners who have concentrated on family school partnerships (Shumow, 2011). These principles apply across grade levels and communities. They are:

1. Two-way communication is essential: listening and responding to parents help promote trust and true partnership grounded in understanding.
2. Parents and teachers have different and complementary expertise which they can share with one another to enrich literacy learning: parents are experts on their particular child with deep knowledge about the child's interests, history, personality, and emotions. Teachers are experts on curriculum, pedagogy, and students in general.
3. In almost every case parents and teachers hold a central shared goal that needs to be acknowledged and made explicit: both want the student to succeed academically (Hill, Tyson, & Bromell, 2009). To the extent that teachers communicate that shared goal clearly and sincerely to parents and students, they will very likely find staunch allies.

4. Understand and accept that teachers and parents have different roles. As professionals, educators have a responsibility to take the lead in promoting partnership with parents and for acting in the best interest of all students. Parents have a deep enduring emotional tie to their own child; parental advocacy for a child is often rooted in that emotional tie. It can be deeply painful for a parent to see a child struggle (Rogoff, 1990).

5. Optimism combined with a plan to realize goals builds a strong foundation for a partnership. Initial interactions and communications between teachers and parents should be positive and hopeful. Approaches to problems that arise should be solution focused and incorporate aspects of the previous four principles. For example, parents are unlikely to know how to solve a reading problem but can share insights into the child that will help craft a solution and can support solution paths.

STRATEGIES FOR INVOLVEMENT

In order to build relationships with parents the teachers can:

- Invite the parents to get involved
- Be good observers and listeners
- Follow through on commitments
- Be flexible and relevant to the needs and interests of the family
- Provide resources

Invitations. At the most basic level, a teacher's and/or a child's invitations to a parent often successfully initiate parental engagement (Green, Hoover-Dempsey, Ice, & Whitaker, 2007; Walker, Wilkins, Dalaire, Sandler, & Hoover-Dempsey, 2005). Teachers are often surprised to learn that parents, especially those from low-income, immigrant, and/or disenfranchised groups fear them (Finders & Lewis, 1994; Lareau, 2000). The first invitation needs to reach out to parents and welcome them into a partnership. An early invitation needs to ask parents to share important information about their child with the teacher; the wealth of information gained from parents is invaluable to a teacher. Klassen-Endrizzi (2008) describes how teachers can continue to extend invitations to family members via surveys, ceremonies, and celebrations. Teachers can have students create and write invitations for their parents, which promotes the development and use of literacy skills for a meaningful task.

Observations. Teachers can work most effectively with parents and students if they understand children's families and communities. Demographic, economic, and cultural diversification has made it less likely that teachers and the families of their students share a common background. It is important for teachers to put aside their preconceived notions about particular groups because there is a great deal of variation within groups. Home visits have been a highly successful method for promoting teacher-parent relationships. Studies have shown that the visits lead to improved: (a) communication with parents, (b) understanding of the child, and (c) understanding of the impact of the child's home environment as it relates to school performance (Carger, 1997; Lin & Bates, 2010; Meyer & Mann, 2006). However, home visits are logistically difficult. Photo narrations at school (Cappello, 2005; Clark-Ibanez, 2004) are a culturally responsive way to engage in "virtual home visits" which bridge home and school (Strickland, Keat, & Marinak, 2010). Children's photos and voices provide an opportunity for teachers to become aware of their assumptions or storylines they bring into their interactions with children from backgrounds different from their own (Keat, Strickland, & Marinak, 2009).

Listening. Active listening is another strategy for teachers to learn about families and their students, establish a positive relationship, and honor parents for their expertise about their child. Strickland, Keat, and Marinak (2010) found that without exception, all teachers in one diverse preschool reported a desire to know about the immigrant children in their classroom. However, they felt unable to connect with immigrant families because of their limited English language and, as a result, the teachers resorted to "guessing as to the origin of the children and their parents" and, therefore, remained unfamiliar with the child's context outside of school.

Children can serve as a source of linguistic, cultural, and family knowledge (McNaughton, 2001; Souto-Manning, 2007). Children's literature and the extensive intercultural information about characters and context within books can be used to transform implicit cultural understandings into explicit concepts that could be discussed by child and teacher (Akrofi, et al., 2008). Baghban (2007) also recommended using children's books and subsequent discussions to help children connect family life to academic literacy.

Follow through. Hands (2009) identified follow through as an essential component in establishing trust. Simply put, teachers should always strive to do what they have said or promised to do. Follow through on the initial invitation to partner with parents, in deeds as well as words, is critical. For example, Pushor (2009) advocates changing the conventional beginning of the year "Meet the Teacher" open houses to "Meet the Parents" night during which families work together to create representations of their families that they leave in the classroom. She argues convincingly that such a small but fundamental shift in thinking and practice could profoundly improve home–school trust and relationships. Teachers of older students have had parents of students write and leave letters for their children.

Design literacy activities that link the student & family. There are many ways to involve the students and families in meaningful assignments and project. For example, students can be assigned to interview family members and write about those interviews. Alternatively, students can create and write materials that communicate to their parents about what is going on at school; some schools are surprised to see how much traffic school websites get when students post write up about experiences like their outdoor education overnight replete with photographs!

Build in flexibility. Many parents face time and logistical conflicts which restrict their engagement. They may work multiple jobs or have limited child care, for example. Technology-enabled tools afford more flexibility and help overcome language barriers in ongoing communication with parents, enhancing traditional venues of communication such as telephone calls, notes home, and face-to-face conferences (Ramirez, 2001; Swaim, 2006). Computer conferencing, email, and discussion boards, blogs, and chats remove time-constraints associated with coming to school. Many of these tools also allow users to purposefully compose, edit, and organize their ideas in a low-pressure, non-threatening environment, increasing the parents' willingness to participate in school-home interaction and dialogue (Rogers and Wright, 2008). Teachers find many of these tools useful because communication can take place asynchronously.

Provide information that fits family needs and interests. Teachers can use the knowledge and understanding they gain from learning about families to understand what information the parents need and want. Students, especially those who are struggling, do not always accurately report information to parents. Rogers & Wright (2008) suggested that school websites are an asset in keeping parents informed of homework and important due dates. Bauch (1998) reported that an implementation of the Transparent School Model program, which included a voice messaging system, increased school to home exchange of information by about 500 percent. Teachers reported that improved communication positively affected both homework completion and accuracy. Parents used the offered communications technologies and reported feeling better informed about assignments believing this information could positively affect student progress. Posting assignments and other helpful tips for parents in guiding children to complete their homework will be useful for many families (Abdal-Haqq, 2002).

Most parents purchase gifts for their children at some time during the school year, whether it is for a birthday or cultural holiday. Mario is happy to receive a book as a gift. Teachers can provide lists or links to lists of books by category/interest for parents to consult when they are choosing gifts or helping their child select books at the public library.

Utilize available resources. Teachers have resources available to help engage families. For example, some schools are located in areas with community libraries. The youth and reference librarians can assist teachers in setting aside or identifying books and materials for students and parents. Some will even establish parent-child book clubs. Many schools have a PTA/PTO. That organization can assist with resources for parent engagement around literacy; perhaps they would sponsor a storyteller or a film based on an excellent children's book. They might also be willing to help in communicating messages about things like the importance of reading and limiting entertainment television. When such requests come from other parents, they can be especially influential. Many communities also have literacy related events like author visits, spoken word poetry "slams," and plays put on at local high schools. Notices about these low-cost fun family events that enrich children's literacy experiences can be posted. Table 6.1 displays on-line resources available to assist teachers in engaging parents.

Table 6.1. Resources that Educators can Use in Engaging Parents

Resource	Description
American Library Association www.ala.org	Provides numerous booklists and other resources for parents about reading. Search site for parent resources.
Collaborative for Early Adolescence www.niu.edu/cea	Links to array of resources for involving parents of middle school students in literacy. (Resources for educators, and parents).
Harvard Family Research Project www.hfrp.org/family-involvement	Synthesizes, summarizes, and distributes research on family involvement in education, including literacy.
International Reading Association http://reading.org	Provides numerous resources for engaging parents in reading for all age levels (search site for parents).
National Center for Family Literacy www.ncfl.org	Provides a wide array of resources that teachers can share with families and use in planning initiative (most are free).
National Parent Teacher Association (PTA) www.pta.org	Parent Guides to Student Success explain Common Core standards for parents in English and Spanish.
Read, Write, Think. www.readwritethink.org	Joint project of International Reading Association and National English Teachers Association. Provides links to numerous resources for parents from home page.

WORK WITH PARENTS TO MEET COMMON CORE STANDARDS

Teachers can use the strategies outlined in Table 6.2 to engage parents in a partnership aimed at meeting the standards. Students will be more likely to succeed if parents and teachers work together in helping students achieve these standards.

Table 6.2. Parent Involvement Strategies to Support Common Core Learning Standards

Strategy	Common Core Learning Standards-ELA
Informal Educational Activities	
Ask parents to discuss their children's leisure reading with them. Consider providing conversation starters or suggestions for parents.	SL.1: Engage effectively in a range of collaborative discussions on *grade-level topics* and texts, building on others' ideas and expressing their own clearly.
Alert parents about activities for families in the community such as library programs, bookstore events, live theater, concerts, and exhibits or programs at local museums, nature centers, or universities.	RI.9: Integrate information from several texts/resources on the same topic in order to write or speak knowledgeably about the subject. RL.7: Analyze how visual and multimedia elements contribute to meaning.

(continued)

Table 6.2. *(Continued)*

Strategy	Common Core Learning Standards-ELA
Encourage parents to discuss themes and character development in books, films, and television shows with their children.	RL.2: Discuss a theme and characters' responses to challenges; RL.3: Compare and contrast characters.

Direct Teaching at Home	
Ask parents to review skills at home and to listen to their children read.	RF.3: Know and apply grade-level phonics and word analysis in reading; RF.4: Read with sufficient fluency to support comprehension.
Ask parents to provide a dictionary in their heritage language and in English. Ask them to use specialized words in their heritage language to expand vocabulary.	L.4: Clarify meanings of unknown words; RL.6: Acquire use of grade-appropriate general academic and domain-specific words and phrases.
Encourage parents to read and write with their children in any language.	L.3: Use knowledge of language and its conventions when reading and writing.

Homework	
Assign homework that requires students to get information from a family member.	W.2: Write informative texts to examine a topic and convey ideas.

At-school Parent Engagement	
Parents can be invited to attend and participate in student led conferences. If their work schedules do not allow them to come to school, technology can be used to facilitate "attendance" either by attending remotely or by trading audio or video files of discussion at school and at home.	SL1a: Come to discussions prepared, having read or studied required material; explicitly draw on that preparation and other information known about the topic to explore ideas under discussion; SL.1b: Follow agreed-upon rules for discussions and carry out assigned roles.
Parents can be invited to attend literacy events that showcase student performance of their writing, songs (lyrics which have been read), or plays.	RF.4b: Read grade-level prose and poetry orally with accuracy, appropriate rate, and expression on successive readings. SL.4: Present a topic, sequencing ideas and speaking clearly; SL.5: Include visual displays to enhance development of ideas.

Strategy	Common Core Learning Standards-ELA
Ask for volunteers to help organize and create newsletters, websites, publicity for school events, compilations of student writing, literary magazines, or displays. Work can be done at home or at school.	W.4: Produce coherent writing developed and organized for purposeful sharing; W.6: With guidance and support from adults, use technology to produce or publish ideas or products.

Strategy	Common Core Learning Standards-ELA
Parent Education and Family Literacy Programs	
Offer programs for parents and students to work together to write about topics or events meaningful to their family.	W.3: Use writing to develop real experiences.

QUESTIONS FOR THOUGHT

1. How does Mario's family life and background influence his literacy practices, learning, and success? Think of a child you know well and answer the same question. Compare and contrast Mario with that child.
2. How can teachers use Mario's emerging competencies in two languages and understanding of two cultures to engage his parents and to connect literacy activities at school with Mario's family?
3. What would you recommend Mario's parents do at home to help him develop strong literacy skills and become more successful at school?
4. What are common challenges that immigrant parents face when communicating with teachers? Think of an immigrant parent who you know is not often a visitor at school. Do you know what prevents him or her from coming more often? Brainstorm strategies to make your classroom more inviting for this parent.

REFERENCES

Abdal-Haqq, I. (2002). *Connecting schools and communities through technology.* Washington: National School Boards Association.

Akrofi, A., Swafford, J., Janisch, C., Liu, X., & Durrington, V. (2008). Supporting immigrant students' understanding of U.S. culture through children's literature. *Childhood Education, 84,* 209–29.

Baghban, M. (2007). Immigration in childhood: Using picture books to cope. *Social Studies (Maynooth), 98,* 71–77.

Baker, L. (2003). The role of parents in motivating struggling readers. *Reading & Writing Quarterly, 19*(1), 87–106.

Baker, L., Mackler, K., Sonnenschein, S., & Serpell, R. (2001). Parents' interactions with their first-grade children during storybook reading and relations with subsequent home reading activity and reading achievement. *Journal of School Psychology, 39*(5), 415–38.

Barradas, D., Fulton, J., Blanck, H., & Huhman, M. (2007). Parental influences on youth television viewing, *The Journal of Pediatrics, 151(4),* 369–73.

Barton, P. E. & Coley, R. J. (2007). *The Family: America's Smallest School.* Princeton, NJ: Educational Testing Service.

Bauch, J. P. (1998). Applications of technology to linking schools, families, and students. Retrieved from http://ceep.crc.illinois.edu/eecearchive/books/fte/links/bauch.pdf.

Bempechat, J. (2004). The motivational benefits of homework: A social-cognitive perspective. *Theory Into Practice, 43*(3), 189–96.

Bialystok, E. (2002). Acquisition of literacy in bilingual children: A framework for research. *Language Learning, 52*(1), 159–99.

Bialystok, E. (2009). Bilingualism: The good, the bad, and the indifferent. *Bilingualism: Language and Cognition, 12,* 3–11.

Bronfenbrenner, Y. (1993). Ecological models of human development. In M. Gauvain & M. Cole (Eds.), *Readings on the development of children,* 2nd ed. (pp. 37–43). NY: Freeman.

Bronfenbrenner, U. (1979). The ecology of human development. Cambridge, MA: Harvard University Press.

Bronfenbrenner, U. (2005). Ecological Systems Theory In U. Bronfenbrenner (Ed.) *Making Human Beings Human: Bioecological Perspectives on Human Development* (pp 106–73). Thousand Oaks CA: Sage.

Carger, C. L. (1997). Attending to new voices. *Educational Leadership, 54*(7), 39–43.

Cappello, M. (2005). Photo interviews: Eliciting data through conversations with children. *Field Methods, 17,* 170–82. doi: 10.1177/1525822X05274553.

Caspe, M., Lopez, M. E., & Wolos, C. (2006/2007, Winter). Family involvement in elementary school children's education. *Family Involvement Makes a Difference,* Retrieved from http://www.hfrp.org/publications-resources/browse-our-publications/family-involvement-in-elementary-school-children-s-education.

Cazden, C., John, V., Hymes, J. (1972). *Functions of language in classroom.* New York: Teachers College Press.

Church, K. & Dollins, C. (2010). Parent engagement at school. In D. Hiatt-Michael (Ed.) *Promising practices to support family involvement in schools* (pp.75–95). Charlotte, NC: Information Age Publishing.

Clark-Ibanez, M. (2004). Framing the social world with photo elicitation interviews. *American Behavioral Scientist, 47*(12), 1507–27.

Comstock, G. & Paik, H. (1991) *Television and the American Child.* Orlando: Academic Press.

Cummins, J. (1979). Linguistic interdependence and the educational development of bilingual children. *Review of Educational Research, 49,* 222–51.

Cummins, J. (2000). *Language, power and pedagogy: Bilingual children in crossfire.* Clevedon: Multilingual Matters.

Cunningham, A. C., & Stanovich, K. E. (2001). What reading does for the mind. *Journal of Direct Instruction, 1*(2), 137–49.

Eberly, J. L., Joshi, A., & Konzal, J. (2007). Communicating with families across cultures: An investigation of teacher perceptions and practices. *The School Community Journal, 17*(2), 7–26.

Eccles, J., & Harold, R. (1996). Family involvement in children's and adolescents' schooling. In A. Bloom & J. Dunn (Eds.), Family-school links: How do they affect educational outcomes (pp. 3–34). Mahwah, NJ: Erlbaum.

Ennemoser, M. & Schneider, W. (2007). Relations of television viewing and reading: Findings from a 4-year longitudinal study," *Journal of Educational Psychology, 99,* 349–68.

Epstein, J. & VanVoorhis, F. (2001). More than minutes: Teachers' roles in designing homework, *Educational Psychologist, 36*(3), 181–93

Evans, C, Jordan, A., & Horner, J. (2011). Only Two Hours? A Qualitative Study of the Challenges Parents Perceive in Restricting Child Television Time. *Journal of Family Issues, 32*(9), 1223–44.

Fan, X., & Chen, M. (2001). Parental involvement and students' academic achievement: A meta-analysis. *Educational Psychology Review, 13*(1), 1–22.

Finders, M. & Lewis, C. (1994). Why some parents don't come to school, *Educational Leadership, 51(8)*, 50–54.

Francis, D., Lesaux, N. K., & August, D. (2006). Language of instruction. In D. L. August & T. Shanahan (Eds.), *Developing literacy in a second language: Report of the National Literacy Panel* (pp. 365–410). Mahwah, NJ: Erlbaum.

García Coll, C. T. & Pachter, L. (2002). Ethnic and Minority Parenting. In M. H. Bornstein, (Ed.), *Handbook of Parenting, Volume 4: Social Conditions and Applied Parenting*, (2nd ed.). Mahwah, NJ: Lawrence Erlbaum Publishers.

Goldenberg, C., Gallimore, R., Reese, L., and Garnier, H. (2001). Cause of effect? A longitudinal study of immigrant Latino parents' aspirations and expectations, and their children's school performance. *American Educational Research Journal, 38*(3), 547–82.

Green, C., Walker, J., Hoover-Dempsey, K., Sandler, H. (2007). Parents' motivations for involvement in children's education: An empirical test of a theoretical model of parent involvement, *Journal of Educational Psychology, 99(3)*, 532–44.

Habermas, T., Negele, A., & Brenneisen Mayer, F. (2010). "Honey, you're jumping about"— Mothers' scaffolding of their children's and adolescents' life narration. *Cognitive Development, 25*, 339–51. doi:10.1016/j.cogdev.2010.08.004

Hakuta, K., Goto Butler, Y., & Witt, D. (2000). How Long Does It Take English Learners to Attain Proficiency? University of California Linguistic Minority Research Institute Policy Report 2000-1.

Hands, C. (2009). The evolution of trust relationships in school-community partnerships. In L. Shumow (Ed.), Promising Practices for Family and Community Involvement during High School (pp. 53–72). Charlotte, NC: Information Age Publishing.

Heath, S. B. (1983). *Ways with Words*. NY: Cambridge University Press.

Heath, S. B. (1989). Oral and literate traditions among black Americans living in poverty. *American Psychologist, 44*, 367–73.

Hernández, A. (2001). The expected and unexpected literacy outcomes of bilingual students. *Bilingual Research Journal, 25*(3), 301–26.

Herrold, K., & O'Donnell, K. (2008). *Parent and family involvement in education, 2006–07 school year, from the National Household Education Surveys Program of 2007 (NCES 2008-050)*. Washington, D.C.: National Center for Education Statistics, Institute of Education Sciences, U.S. Department of Education. Retrieved from http://nces.ed.gov/pubs2008/2008050.pdf.

Hiatt-Michael, D. (2010). Communication practices that bridge home with school. In D. Hiatt-Michael (Ed.), *Promising practices to support family involvement in schools* (pp.25–55). Charlotte, NC: Information Age Publishing.

Hill, N. & Craft, S. (2003). Parent-school involvement and school performance: Mediated pathways among socioeconomically comparable African American and Euro-American families. *Journal of Educational Psychology, 95(1)*, 74–83.

Hill, N. E., & Taylor, L. C. (2004). Parental school involvement and children's academic achievement: Pragmatics and Issues. *Current Directions Is Psychological Science, 13*(4), 161–64.

Hill, N., & Tyson, D. (2009). Parental involvement in middle school: A meta-analytic assessment of the strategies that promote achievement. *Developmental Psychology, 45*(3), 740–63.

Hill, N., Tyson, D., & Bromell, L. (2009). Developmentally appropriate strategies across ethnicity and socioeconomic status: Parental involvement during middle school. In N. Hill & R. Chao (Eds.) *Families, schools, and the adolescent: Connecting research, policy, and practice* (pp53–72). New York, NY: Teachers College Press.

Hoover-Dempsey, K., Ice, C. & Whitaker, M. (2009). "We're way past reading together:" Why and how parental involvement in adolescence makes sense. In Hill & Chao (Eds.). *Families, schools, and the adolescent: Connecting research and practice* (pp. 19–36). New York: Teachers College Press.

Huss-Keeler, Rebecca L. (1997). Teacher perception of ethnic and linguistic minority parental involvement and its relationships to children's language and literacy learning: A case study. *Teaching and Teacher Education, 13*(2), 171–82.

Jeynes, W. (2007). The relationship between parental involvement and secondary school student academic achievement: A meta-analysis. *Urban Education, 42*, 82–112.

Jones, S. (2004). Shaping identities: the reading of young bilinguals. *Literacy, 38*(1), 40–45.

Kaiser Family Foundation (2010). *Generation M2: Media in the lives of 8–18 year olds.* Retrieved from http://www.kff.org/entmedia/.

Kaushanskaya, M. & Marian, V. (2009). The bilingual advantage in novel word learning. *Psychonomic Bulletin & Review, 16*(4), 705–10.

Katz, L., & Bauch, J. (2001). The Peabody family involvement initiative. In S. Redding & L. G. Thomas (Eds.), *The community of the school* (pp. 185–204). Lincoln, IL: Academic Development Institute.

Keat, J., Strickland, M., & Marinak, B. (2009). Child Voice: How Immigrant Children Enlightened Their Teachers with a Camera. *Early Childhood Education Journal, 37*, 13–21.

Kirsch, I., de Jong, J., Lafontaine, D., McQueen, J., Mendelovits, J., & Monseur, C. (2002). *Reading for change: Performance and engagement across countries: Results from PISA 2000.* OECD. Retrieved from http://www.oecd.org/dataoecd/43/54/33690904.pdf.

Klassen-Endrizzi, C. (2008). *Becoming Teammates: Teachers and Families as Literacy Partners.* Urbana, IL: National Council of Teachers of English.

Koolstra, C. & Van der Voort, T. (1996). Longitudinal effects of television on children's leisure time reading: A test of three explanatory models," *Human Communication Research, 23*, 4–35.

Kreider, H., Morin, G., Miller, G. E., & Bush, A. (2011). Promoting language and literacy outcomes from share reading at home. In D. B. Hiatt-Michael & H. Westmoreland (Eds.). *Promising Practices for Family Engagement in Out-of-School Time* (pp. 97–107). Greenwich, CT: Information Age Publishing.

Lareau, A. (2000). Home Advantage. Second Edition. Lanham, MD: Rowan & Littlefield.

Lee, J. & Bowen, N. (2006). Parent involvement, cultural capital, and the achievement gap among elementary school children. *American Educational Research Journal, 43*(2), 193–218.

Lee, C. D., & Smagorinsky, P. (Eds) (2000). *Vygotskian perspectives on literacy research: Constructing meaning through collaborative inquiry.* New York: Cambridge University Press.

Lin, M. & Bates, A. B. (2010). Home visits: How do they affect teachers' beliefs about teaching and diversity? *Early Childhood Education Journal, 38*, 179–85.

Lyutykh, E. (2011). *Russian language schools: Exploring heritage language literacy beliefs in families, instruction, and communities.* (Doctoral dissertation).

Markow, D., Kim, A., & Liebman, M. (2007). *The MetLife survey of the American teacher: The homework experience.* New York, NY: Metropolitan Life Insurance Company.

McNaughton, G. (2001). Silences and subtexts of immigrant and nonimmigrant children. *Childhood Education, 78*, 30–37.

Meyer, J. A., & Mann, M. B. (2006). Teachers' perceptions of the benefits of home visits for early elementary children. *Early Childhood Education Journal, 34*, 93–97.

Moll, L., Amanti, C., Neff, D. (1992). Funds of knowledge for teaching: Using a qualitative approach to connect homes and classroom. *Theory into Practice.*

Moore, K., Guzman, L., Hair, E., Lippman, L., & Garrett, S. (2004). *Parent-teen relationships and interactions: Far more positive than not.* Child Trends Research Brief 2004-25. Retrieved from http://www.childtrends.org/Files/Parent_TeenRB.pdf.

Mullis, A. & Mullis, R. (2009). Parent education: Perceived needs and sources of information. North Dakota State University. http://library.ndsu.edu/repository/bitstream/handle/10365/4730/farm_40_04_04.pdf?sequence=1.

Murphy, J. (2009). Survey study of the relationship between parents' and teachers' perception of what constitutes effective school-to-home communications. (Doctoral Dissertation). Available from Proquest (ATT 3344457).

Neuman, S., Koh, S. & Dwyer, J. (2008). CHELLO: The child/home environmental, language and literacy observation. *The Early Childhood Research Quarterly, 23,* 159–72.

Olusola, O., Adesope, O., Lavin, T., Thompson, T., & Ungerleider, C. (2010). A Systematic Review and Meta-Analysis of the Cognitive Correlates of Bilingualism. *Review of Educational Research, 80,* 207–45.

Patall, E., Cooper, H., & Robinson, J. (2008). Parent involvement in homework: A research synthesis. *Review of Educational Research,78*(4), 1039–1101.

Pushor, D. (2009) Are schools doing enough to learn about families? In T. Marsh & T. Turner Vorbeck (Eds.) *(Mis)Understanding Families: Learning from Real Families in Our Schools* (pp. 4--16). NYC: Teachers College Press.

Ramirez, F. (2001). Technology and parental involvement. *Clearing House, 75*(1), 30–31.

Redding, S. (2000). *Parents and learning.* Education practices series—2. Brussels, Belgium: International Academy of Education; Geneva, Switzerland: The International Bureau of Education. Retrieved from www.families-schools.org. [See Resources for Schools and Parents.]

Ritter, G., Barnett, J., Denny, G., & Albin, G. (2009). The effectiveness of volunteer tutoring programs for elementary and middle school students: A meta-analysis. *Review of Educational Research, 79,* 3–38.

Roberts, D., Foehr, U., & Rideout, V. (2005). *Generation M: Media in the lives of 8–18 year olds* (Kaiser Family Foundation Report). Retrieved from http://www.kff.org/entmedia/upload/Generation-M-Media-in-the-Lives-of-8-18-Year-olds-Report.pdf.

Rogers, R., & Wright, V. (2008) You've got mail: Using technology to communicate with parents. *Electronic Journal for the Integration of Technology in Education, 7,* 36–58.

Rogoff, B. (1990). *Apprenticeship in thinking: cognitive development in social context.* New York: Oxford University Press.

Saint-Laurent, L. & Giasson, J. (2005). Effects of a family literacy program adapting parental intervention to first graders' evolution of reading and writing abilities *Journal of Early Childhood Literacy, 5,* 253–78.

Senechal, M., and LeFevre, J-A. (2002). Parental involvement in the development of children's reading skills: A five-year longitudinal study. *Child Development,73*(2),445–60.

Senechal, M., & Young, L. (2008). The effect of family literacy interventions on children's acquisition of reading from kindergarten to grade 3: A meta-analytic review. *Review of Educational Research, 78*(4), 880–907.

Shin, F., & Krashen, S. (1996). Teacher attitudes toward the principles of bilingual education and toward students' participation in bilingual programs: Same or different? *Bilingual Research Journal, 20*(1), 45–53.

Shumow, L. (2003). The task matters: Parental assistance to children doing different homework assignments. *The School Community Journal, 13*(2), 7–23.

Shumow, L. (2010). Parent involvement at home. In D. Hiatt-Michael & C. Hands (Eds.) *Promising Practices to Support Family Involvement in Schools* (pp. 57–74). Charlotte, NC: Information Age Publishing.

Shumow, L. (2011). Homework. In S. Redding, M. Murphy, & P. Sheley (Eds), *Handbook on Family and Community Engagement* (pp. 77–80). Lincoln IL: Academic Development Institute. http://www.families-schools.org/downloads/FACEHndbkFamEngRegSpec.pdf.

Shumow, L., Lyutykh, E., & Schmidt, J. A. (2011). Predictors and outcomes of parental involvement with high school students in science. *The School Community Journal, 21*(2), 81–98.

Shumow, L., Schmidt, J., & Kackar, H. (2008). Reading in class and out: An Experience Sampling Method Study. *Middle Grades Research Journal, 3*(3), 97–120.

Shumow, L., & Miller, J. (2001). Father's and mother's school involvement during early adolescence. *The Journal of Early Adolescence, 21,* 69–92.

Sonnenschein, S., Munsterman, K. (2002). The influence of home-based reading interactions on 5-year-olds' reading motivations and early literacy development. *Early Childhood Research Quarterly, 17(3),* 318–37.

Souto-Manning, M. (2007). Immigrant families and children (re)develop identities in a new context. *Early Childhood Education Journal, 34,* 399–404.

Spera, C. (2005). Review of the relationship among parenting practices, parenting styles, and adolescent school achievement. *Educational Psychology Review, 17(2),* 125–46.

Steinkuehler, C. (2011). *The mismeasure of boys: Reading and online videogames* (WCER Working Paper No. 2011-3). University of Wisconsin–Madison, Wisconsin Center for Education Research website: http://www.wcer.wisc.edu/publications/workingPapers/papers.php.

Steensel, R., McElvany, N., Kurvers, J., Herppich, S. (2011). How effective are family literacy programs? Results of a meta-analysis, *Review of Educational Research, 81,* 69–96.

Strickland, M., Keat, J., & Marinak, B. (2010). Connecting worlds: Using photo narrations to connect immigrant children, preschool teachers, and immigrant families. *The School Community Journal, 20*(1), 81–102.

Strickland, M., & Shumow, L. (2008). Family matters: Exploring the complexities of families of immigrant adolescents and achievement in four G8 countries. *The Open Family Studies Journal, 1,* 39–48.

Strommen, L., & Mates, B. (2004). Learning to love reading: Interviews with older children and teens. *Journal of Adolescent and Adult Literacy, 48,* 188–200.

Swaim, S. (2006). Make the home-school connection. *Middle Ground, 9*(3), 5.

Taylor, L. Clayton, J., & Rowley, S. (2004). Academic socialization: Understanding parental influences on children's school-related development in the early years. *Review of General Psychology, 8(3),* 163–78.

Thomas, W. P., & Collier, V. (2002). *A national study of school effectiveness for language minority students' long-term academic achievement* (Final Report). Berkeley, CA: University of California, Center for Research on Education, Diversity & Excellence. Available online at http://crede.berkeley.edu/research/crede/research/llaa/1.1_es.html.

Tse, L. (2001). Heritage language literacy: A study of U.S. biliterates. *Language, Culture, and Curriculum, 14*(3), 256–68.

Turney, K., and Kao, G. (2009). Barriers to school involvement: Are immigrant parents disadvantaged? *The Journal of Educational Research, 102*(4), 257–71.

Valdes, G. (1996). *Con respeto: Bridging the distance between culturally diverse families and schools.* New York, NY: Teachers College Press.

Van Voorhis, F. L. (2003). Interactive homework in middle school: Effects on family involvement and science achievement. *Journal of Educational Research, 96*(6), 323–38.

Van Voorhis, F. L. (2011). Costs and benefits of family involvement in homework. *Journal of Advanced Academics, 22*(2), 220–49.

Vygotsky, L.S. (1986). *Thought and Language* (A. Kozulin, Ed.). Cambridge, MA: MIT Press.

Vygotsky, L. S. (1978). *Mind in society: The development of higher psychological processes.* Cambridge, MA: Harvard University Press.

Walberg, H. (2011). Curriculum of the Home. In S. Redding, M. Murphy, & P. Sheley (Eds.), *Handbook on Family and Community Engagement* (p. 69). Lincoln IL: Academic Development Institute.

Walker, J., Wilkins, A., Dalaire, J., Sandler, H. & Hoover-Dempsey, K. (2005). Parent involvement: Model revision through scale development. *The Elementary School Journal, 106(2),* 85–104.

Walker, A., Shafer, J., & Liams, M. (2004). "Not in my classroom": Teacher attitudes towards English language learners in the mainstream classroom. *NABE Journal of Research and Practice, 2*(1), 130–60.

Weiss, H. & Lopez, E. (2011). Making data matter in family engagement. In S. Redding, M. Murphy, & P. Sheley (Eds.), *Handbook on Family and Community Engagement.* Lincoln, IL: Academic Development Institute.

Zentella, A. C. (2002). Latin, Languages and Identities. In M. Suárez-Orozco & M. Páez (Eds), *Latinos: Remaking America* (pp. 321–28). Berkeley: University of California Press.

7

Mathematics Talk

Literacy Development in a Mathematics Context

Brian R. Evans

Literacy has increasingly become an integral component of mathematics instruction (Bosse & Faulconer, 2008; Pierce & Fontaine, 2009), particularly considering the interest in teaching mathematics from a problem solving perspective (Posamentier & Krulik, 2008; Posamentier, Smith, & Stepelman, 2008; Schoenfeld, 1985). While students may accept the need to read their mathematics textbooks, some students will object when required to write in a mathematics class. A student may say, "This is mathematics class, we write in English class, but not here." It is important that we help students understand that literacy transcends any one particular subject area and carries across all subject areas. This chapter addresses literacy development in the mathematics classroom.

In mathematics problem solving is one of the five National Council of Teachers of Mathematics (NCTM) process standards (NCTM, 2000), and is critically important in how students best learn mathematics (Posamentier et al., 2008). NCTM (2000) said, "Problem solving is not only a goal of learning mathematics but also a major means of doing so" (p. 52). Problem solving is considered the principal reason for studying mathematics by the National Council of Supervisors of Mathematics (NCSM) (NCSM, 1978), and it is the foundation for constructivist and reform- and inquiry-based teaching in mathematics (Clark, 1997). Another issue involves the issues of teaching mathematics in multicultural contexts, specifically honoring the information and approaches to learning that second language learners or international learners bring to diverse classrooms (Whiteford, 2009). Some researchers believe that we need to develop mathematical knowledge using more inclusive strategies (Crafter, 2012) with culturally aware teaching through cooperative learning and multiple representations (Jao, 2012). This chapter addresses mathematical literacy development in mathematics classrooms.

Charles and Lester (1982) defined a mathematical problem as a task in which (a) the person confronting it wants or needs to find a solution; (b) the person has no readily available procedure for finding the solution; and (c) the person must make an attempt to find a solution. Authentic mathematical problems are more than a collection of word problems. More specifically, problems need to be unfamiliar to the student. Authentic problem solving is defined as a process in which an individual uses previously acquired knowledge, skills, and understanding to satisfy the demands of an unfamiliar situation (Krulik & Rudnick, 1989). When teachers demonstrate solving a word problem using direct instruction by providing several examples for students, and then give students an identical type of problem with some slight changes, such as changing several of the quantities involved, they are not engaging students in authentic problem solving.

In order for students to be effective problem solvers, they need to possess strong literacy skills in order to extract the necessary information from the problem and understand what is being asked of them. Polya (1945) put forth a general problem solving strategy in his classic work, *How to Solve It*: (a) understanding the problem; (b) making a plan; (c) carrying out the plan; and (d) looking back. Reading comprehension is a necessary skill in order to engage in the problem solving process given that most problems will be presented in textual form. In the past teachers often encouraged students to look for key words throughout the word problem. Today we realize that it is much more important to truly understand what information is given and what we need to do in order to satisfy the demands of the problem. In real world problem solving the problems will not be neatly presented to us with mathematical key words readily available and easy to find. Reading comprehension becomes a critical skill in the mathematics classroom.

Although the human brain may have been capable of thinking before the development of language, literate people think primarily in language. Language helps us better formulate, refine, and express our ideas more efficiently. Mathematical and scientific inquiry is a systemic and concentrated means of thinking. Mathematics is a way of thinking about the world (Countryman, 1992). Student gain literacy skills first by listening and speaking, and then move on to reading and writing (Carter, 2009). However, writing expresses our thinking to others, and it also allows us to organize our own thinking. Writing in mathematics class allows students to communicate their mathematical and scientific thinking for others and gives them the opportunities to evaluate and reflect upon their own mathematical thinking.

CONNECTION TO THE
COMMON CORE STATE STANDARDS

In addition to NCTM Standards and the influence on the mathematics curriculum, the Common Core Standards have become very influential in nearly all U.S. states in the last several years. The Common Core State Standards were developed by the

National Governors Association Center for Best Practices and the Council of Chief State School Officers in 2009 in order to have the same standards and goals for all students throughout the United States. States participating in the initiative were permitted to include up to 15 percent of their own standards, which means 85 percent would be common between the states. Three of the Standards for Mathematical Practice are directly related to the literacy and mathematics connection: (1) make sense of problems and persevere in solving them; (2) construct viable arguments and critique the reasoning of others; and (3) use appropriate tools and strategies. Both of these practice standards require strong literacy skills in order to read mathematical problems and the reasoning of others, as well as in writing mathematical arguments.

CONNECTION TO MARIO'S CASE STUDY

The same issues that the struggling reader and writer encounter in English class may be encountered in mathematics. Fortunately, mathematics and English teachers can use the strategies in this chapter, among others, to improve student reading and writing skills. In chapter 4 we encountered a self-described poor reader, Mario. He stated that in order to perform effectively in mathematics, reading was not necessary. He claimed that one only needs to be able to simply read a mathematics problem, but implied that this does not require additional reading skills. However, in order to fully comprehend mathematics problems, students need to have strong reading comprehension skills, in addition to mathematical proficiency. In the teacher questioning, the teacher speaking with Mario implied that mathematics, along with social studies and science, could be among the most difficult subject areas for reading. Reading within other subject contexts, particularly in a technical subject like mathematics, can indeed provide students with challenges beyond reading comprehension alone.

In Mario's case study in chapter 4, he indicates that he does not come from a family of readers, in addition to describing himself as a poor reader. By connecting reading and writing to mathematics, teachers are giving Mario yet another opportunity to practice literacy skills and encourage reading and writing to be intertwined with other aspects of Mario's life. Mario had indicated that he did not think reading was very important, but by connecting to another content area, such as mathematics, Mario receives an opportunity to see the importance of literacy.

An additional problem with literacy skills exists for English Language Learners (ELL). Mario's parents came from a Spanish speaking country, but Mario seems to have learned English from a very young age and indicated that he does not speak Spanish. However, other children who arrive in the United States and learn English as a second language may have anxiety about their English classes in which they are required to read and write in English exclusively. They may enjoy mathematics class in which they are familiar with the nearly universal Hindu-Arabic numerals and operational symbols. Requiring these students to read and write in mathematics may further increase mathematics anxiety. This issue will be addressed later in the chapter.

Outside of reading and writing, Mario may benefit from work with his numeracy skills. Numeracy is reasoning with and understanding the basic numerical concepts, and it is analogous to literacy for the mathematics classroom. A strong numeracy foundation could give poor readers and ELL students the confidence they need in their abilities before the English language skills are fully developed without the added stress of literacy. While connections between reading and writing with mathematics are important, focusing first on basic mathematical concepts could develop student self-efficacy that could serve the students moving forward with their language skills.

It is recommended that teachers use the information in this chapter to connect reading and writing to the mathematics class for students such as Mario. It is the lack of connection for many years of mathematics instruction that promoted Mario to think mathematics was unrelated to these essential skills. This chapter will focus on practical ways in which teachers can make this connection.

THEORETICAL FRAMEWORK

The ideas of this chapter are grounded in sociocultural theory (Vygotsky, 1987), which proposes that individual learning is framed by social learning experiences with others. In the classroom context this interaction occurs between instructor and student and among the students. While traditionally reading could be considered a solitary activity, reading for the objective of engaging in the problem solving process is a social activity as students negotiate the meaning and context of the problem with their peers to collectively develop a solution to the problem. This chapter is grounded in teaching mathematics from a problem solving perspective (NCSM, 1978; NCTM, 2000; Schoenfeld, 1985). Teaching mathematics from a problem solving perspective necessitates that students are solving unfamiliar problems using previously acquired knowledge, skills, and understanding to satisfy the demands of unfamiliar situations (Krulik & Rudnick, 1989). In mathematics this is akin to developing the critical thinking process.

Bosse and Faulconer (2008) said that students learn mathematics best through reading in mathematics, and writing in mathematics increases understanding and content knowledge. Further, Bosse and Faulconer (2008) cited numerous studies that reported increased mathematical learning through the use of writing in mathematics (Brandau, 1990; Doherty, 1996; Drake & Amspaugh, 1994; Gopen & Smith, 1990; Grossman, Smith, & Miller, 1993; Miller, 1992; Nahrgang & Peterson, 1986; Porter & Masingila, 2000; Pugalee, 1997; Rose, 1989; Stehney, 1990). Particularly, several researchers have said that writing in mathematics can improve conceptual understanding (Gopen & Smith, 1990; Nahrgang & Peterson, 1986; Porter & Masingila, 2000; Pugalee, 1997). Porter and Masingila (2000) said that while writing can improve conceptual understanding, other methods and activities that promote conceptual understanding may have comparable value to writing in mathematics class. The benefits of writing across the curriculum for mathematics provide grounding for this chapter.

LITERACY IN MATHEMATICS

In addition to problem solving as one of the five NCTM process standards, communication is another process standard. NCTM (2000) said, "Students who have opportunities, encouragement, and support for speaking, writing, reading, and listening in mathematics classes reap dual benefits: they communicate to learn mathematics, and they learn to communicate mathematically" (p. 60). Wilcox and Monroe (2011) acknowledged that many teachers struggle with integrating writing in mathematics class, while maintaining the integrity of both subjects. However, Carter (2009) said that students who have strong writing skills should be able to apply these skills in other contexts, such as mathematics. Moreover, reading and writing in mathematics can help facilitate better mathematics learning (Bosse & Faulconer, 2008; Winsor, 2008). Bosse and Faulconer (2008) said that students "learn mathematics more effectively and more deeply when reading and writing is directed at learning mathematics" (p. 8). Winsor (2008) listed three conditions for more effective mathematics learning: (a) students write to communicate the mathematics they are learning; (b) students learn collaboratively in groups; and (c) student learning is situated in context (i.e., real world learning).

The literature is replete with strategies for both the integration of literacy with mathematics and the use of literacy in improving mathematics education. The following sections will briefly summarize some of the common reading and writing strategies teachers can use in the mathematics classroom.

READING STRATEGIES IN MATHEMATICS

Learning mathematics is similar to learning another language. Students must know the basics of mathematics vocabulary, must be able to put the vocabulary into sentences and context, and must work within the mathematical language. Posamentier et al. (2008) said, "To be mathematically literate in today's classroom, a student must be comfortable with the rich and diverse language that is mathematics" (p. 97). Posamentier et al. (2008) continued, "Just as teachers in a language course, mathematics teachers guide their students toward developing a sound vocabulary" (p. 97). While Burns (2007) warned that mathematics vocabulary is not the goal of mathematics instruction, nor the primary indicator of mathematical success, the purpose of learning mathematics vocabulary is "for communicating about mathematical ideas, and first it's necessary to acquire knowledge about those mathematical ideas" (p. 43). In other words, while mathematics vocabulary is needed for effective communication, students must first develop conceptual understanding before learning the appropriate mathematics terminology. For example, it is more important for students to understand the concepts behind fractions before knowing the "top number" is the numerator and the "bottom number" is the denominator. However, eventually students should use the proper terminology once they have a solid grasp on conceptual understanding. Once students understand the concepts (Burns, 2007), it is important for students to put vocabulary definitions in their own words (Pierce & Fontaine, 2009).

Guided Reading and Strategies from English Class

Just as English teachers can help guide student reading for those who struggle, mathematics teachers can provide the same support for students. Teachers should supply just enough support to appropriately scaffold students who need extra help. Scaffolding, a concept developed by Vygotsky, is "the specific strategies or structures that help people move along in their development" (Nakkula & Toshalis, 2006, p. 10). Nakkula and Toshalis (2006) argued that teachers should provide an optimal level of scaffolding, or supports, to have students operate at the top of their potential. Not enough scaffolding leads to frustration, and too much scaffolding leads to boredom. There are specific strategies mathematics teachers can employ to help improve reading comprehension in mathematics. Teachers can read along with students who struggle and assist students with difficult words. Teachers can ask the appropriate questions such as, "What is the problem asking of us?" and "What information does it provide?" Careful questioning can lead students in the correct direction while allowing them the independence to arrive at their own conclusions. Guided reading could be effective in helping students read their mathematics textbooks, an exercise that many students find challenging.

Many of the other strategies that English teachers employ to help their students could be used by mathematics teachers as well. These techniques apply both to vocabulary building and problem solving reading comprehension. See Tables 7.1 and 7.2 at the end of the chapter in Appendix B for a summary of the strategies.

Think-Alouds: Think-Alouds help the students to experience the thinking process that teachers go through while they read through a mathematics problem. Teachers "talk through" the problem in their own words, and students can model teacher thinking (Unrau, 2008).

Vocabulary Self-Collection Strategy (VSS): VSS requires students to select mathematics vocabulary words that they do not know but wish to know. Students take responsibility and control for their learning by finding out for themselves the meaning of unknown words (Haggard, 1982; Unrau, 2008).

Word Knowledge Check (WKC): WKC allows teachers to know how strong the students' mathematics vocabulary skills are. For a given word the students can check one of the following categories: "I never saw it before," "I heard it but don't know what it means," "I recognize it in context as related to something I know," "I know it well," and "I can use it in a sentence" (Unrau, 2008; p. 168).

Know—Want to Know—Learned Strategy (KWL): KWL has students communicate to the teacher and themselves what they know, what they want to know, and what they have learned. This strategy could be used for mathematics vocabulary building in a similar manner to VSS and WKC. KWL can also be used for the problem solving process by which students categorize aspects of the problem they understood, would like to understand, and have learned (Ogle, 1986; Unrau, 2008).

Directed Inquiry Activity (DIA): DIA requires students to answer the who, what, where, when, why, and how questions of a word problem. Students skim the text to get an overview while considering these questions (Thomas, 1986; Unrau, 2008).

Survey, Question, Read, Recite, and Review (SQ3R): SQ3R can be a systematic way for reading through a mathematics problem as students survey what it says by skimming the text, employ self-questioning, read for detail, recite in their own words what it says, and go back over the text for clarification. This approach is similar to DIA (Robinson, 1946; Unrau, 2008).

Word Wall: A Word Wall can be used as a place in the classroom for students to write unfamiliar mathematics vocabulary words. Students can find the definitions and place them in their personal glossaries in their notebooks. Many students may find that they share similar vocabulary words with other students in the class (Posamentier et al., 2008).

Verbal and Visual Word Association

A useful strategy for helping students learn mathematics vocabulary is the Verbal and Visual Word Association (VVWA) strategy (Barton & Heidema, 2002; Posamentier et al., 2008), also called a Word Square (Quinn & Molloy, 1992). The VVWA strategy has a two-by-two matrix that gives the student four different perspectives on the vocabulary word in an area divided into four quadrants. For example, Posamentier et al. (2008) presented a matrix presented by Barton and Heidema (2008) for the concept of mathematical slope. In the top left corner students would see the concept: slope of a line. In the top right corner students would see a graphic: the slope of the line using the Cartesian coordinate plane. In the lower left corner students would see the formula for the slope of the line: $m = \dfrac{y_2 - y_1}{x_2 - x_1}$.

In the lower right corner students are given a real world picture of the concept along with an explanation in more understandable terms: a picture of a person climbing a mountain with a caption, "Think steepness of a hill. The higher the absolute value of the slope, the steeper the incline of the line" (p. 97).

Comparison of Mathematics Words to English Words

Posamentier et al. (2008) recommended that mathematics vocabulary be compared and contrasted with the English word meaning outside of mathematics. For example, Posamentier et al. (2008) presented the English language regarding the type of angle. An acute angle is an angle less than ninety degrees. In English "acute" means "sharp," which indicates the sharp point of a small acute angle. An obtuse angle is an angle more than ninety degrees. In English "obtuse" means "dull," which indicates the blunt nature of a large obtuse angle. A right angle is an angle that measures ninety degrees. The label "right" comes from the Latin "rectus" meaning "upright," since a right angle is perpendicular and stands upright. However, when students first encounter the right angle, many may think of the colloquial meaning of the word "right," which could be that something is correct or moral, or perhaps opposite to the left direction. It would be helpful for students to know the etymology of mathematical terminology when available. One can speculate how many children wonder exactly what is wrong with "odd" and "irrational" numbers and "improper" fractions.

Mathematics Literature

There are generally two types of mathematics literature books. The first type is books designed to be used in a mathematics class containing a mathematics theme. Children's books of this type generally introduce and reinforce mathematics ideas throughout the book while providing an enjoyable context for children. The second type is books that are not necessarily intended for mathematics class, but teachers and students can find use for mathematics in specific sections or throughout the book. An example of this would be when an English teacher selects a book for students to read and in conjunction with the mathematics teacher students create mathematics problems from the text. Usually the mathematics will derive from real world quantitative applications alluded to in the book. For example, a book read in English class may have a character travel a specified distance or purchase items from a store.

There are numerous benefits to reading literature for mathematics class. First, reading literature connects mathematics to other subject areas, particularly, but not limited to, English. Reading a social studies paper involving statistics and graphs that require interpretation may be appropriate for high school students. Second, connecting mathematics to literature can lead to student engagement and interest in the subject. Literature contextualizes mathematics and connects it to the real world. Price (2009) said, "The variety in literature provides countless opportunities for students to become engaged in a mathematics concept being taught, thereby creating a meaningful context for the student" (p. 1). Third, for students who enjoy reading books in mathematics could help develop their confidence and reduce mathematics anxiety if mathematics is taught in a more comfortable setting. Reading in mathematics class could develop healthy attitudes and dispositions toward mathematics (Price, 2009; Whitin & Whitin, 2004). Burns (2007) said,

> Connecting math to literature can boost confidence for children who love books but are wary of math. While the goal after reading a book aloud is to launch a math lesson, it's important first to provide time for students to enjoy the book, savor the text, and examine the illustrations. (p. 45)

Integrating reading into mathematics benefits both low and high achieving students. Price (2009) said, "Students who struggle with concepts can benefit from an approach that is often less intimidating and more entertaining. Students who excel can add to their understanding of mathematical concepts by more fully understanding the real-world applications of those contexts" (pp. 4–5). It is important that teachers select books that represent diversity and include people and contexts from a variety of cultures (Price, 2009; Whitin & Whitin, 2004). For a list of children's literature to use in mathematics class, see the list developed from Ojose (2008), Beaudoin (2011), and Hopkin (1993) in Appendix A.

Newspaper, Magazines, and Online Articles

Students can be encouraged to read newspaper, magazine, and online articles in order to search for mathematics in the real world. Younger children could be asked to identify decimals or percentages in newspapers, magazines, and online articles, and present their findings to the class (Burns, 2007). Older children could interpret graphs and connect social studies to mathematics (Posamentier et al., 2008).

WRITING STRATEGIES IN MATHEMATICS

Most educators would agree that reflection upon, and then revision of, one's own thinking and work is an important component in the educational process. By requiring students to express their own mathematical thinking in writing we not only help them improve and refine their writing skills, but we also help them refine their mathematical thinking. Countryman (1992) said, "writing can provide opportunities for students to construct their own knowledge of mathematics" (p. vi). Wilcox and Monroe (2011) recommended students engage in writing activities that both allow for students to express themselves without worrying about revising their writing, and recommended writing activities that require students to revise their papers in order to reflect upon and improve their writing and mathematics skills. See Table 7.3 at the end of the chapter in Appendix B for a summary of the strategies.

Freewriting

Countryman (1992) recommended having students engage in freewriting, which is an exercise that permits students to write whatever they would like. Countryman (1992) began her classes with five minutes of freewriting to give students the opportunity to express their thoughts on paper without restriction. Students were surprised by how easy this exercise is to begin. It is important to give students the opportunity to write without concern about spelling and grammar in freewriting activities. Students need to be able to quickly place their thoughts on paper in a manner similar to brainstorming. A possible option for the teacher is to have students switch papers and then explain to each other what was not clear in their writing. This combination of writing and clarification through language moves thinking from unorganized fragments to coherent organization.

Mathematics Logs

A common strategy for integrating writing in mathematics is to employ the use of mathematics logs. A mathematics log allows students to record their mathematics learning on paper. Countryman (1992) defined a mathematics log as a "personal record of what is transpiring in the course" (p. 15), and recommend that students be given some time at the end of the week to assess their understanding. The mathematics log is a place where students record what they have learned and ask questions about information they have not fully understood. Mathematics logs can be concise and allow students to quickly keep record of their learning progress.

Mathematics Journal

A mathematics journal is generally longer and more detailed than a log, and it is more reflective than the factual information that may appear in a log. Mathematics journal writing is one of the most common forms of writing in the mathematics classroom (Borasi & Rose, 1989; Bosse & Faulconer, 2008). Students should be permitted to engage in freewriting in mathematics journals, but journal writing is different than freewriting in that it is conducted more consistently every day or once every several days. The mathematics journal is an outlet for students to reflect freely and deeply on their learning without judgment, but it can be used as a means of communicating with the teacher.

Students will need guidance on how to reflect upon their mathematics learning and writing in their journals. Burns (2007) suggested giving students prompts to get them started on their writing. Alternatively, teachers can provide guiding questions for students such as the following:

1. What did I learn in mathematics class today?
2. What new mathematical insights do I now possess?
3. What was an aspect of today's class in which I had trouble?
4. What strategies could I employ to overcome my misunderstandings?
5. Was I able to solve problems in class because I followed what the teacher did, or was I able to solve problems in class because I actually understood the concepts behind the mathematics? What can I do to increase understanding?
6. What kind of support do I need to solve the problems from class today?
7. What kind of support do I need to better understand the mathematics in class today?
8. How do I best learn mathematics? Do I best work alone, with classmates, or with the teacher?
9. Do I best learn mathematics when I experiment with problems alone or have someone show me what to do? Do I need concrete hands-on materials?
10. Do I best learn mathematics when I see someone solving a problem, hear someone talking about how a problem is solved, or solve problems by myself or with the help of mathematics manipulatives/technology?

Mathematics Autobiography

A mathematics autobiography is a student's expression of mathematical successes and challenges throughout schooling, which could serve as a diagnostic evaluation of not only student ability and past performance, but also give teachers insight on student mathematics anxiety, confidence, self-perceptions of efficacy, and attitudes toward the subject, which could help inform instructional decisions including differentiated instruction and remediation. If it could be determined that some students have severe anxiety about studying mathematics, teachers could include strategies in the curriculum to alleviate the anxieties. According to Countryman (1992), a mathematics autobiography at the beginning of the school year,

> Gives them permission to talk about what they know best: themselves, what they care about, and what they know. It also helps students focus on their own learning styles and think about what works and does not work for them. In addition, writing enables students to take more responsibility for what goes on in the class, for as they write about doing mathematics they come to see themselves as central to the process of learning. (p. 22)

A mathematics autobiography may prove therapeutic for student as it allows them to express themselves on paper and have direct communication with their teachers, who could provide constructive feedback for student successes, challenges, and anxieties in the mathematics classroom. The mathematics autobiography could be used as the first of many journal entries so that teachers could track growth and development over the course of the school year. A mathematics autobiography gives students the opportunity to not only reflect upon previous performance, but also set goals for the current school year. It allows the students to set expectations for themselves and communicate to their teachers what expectations they have for them. Sample guiding questions for writing a mathematics autobiography are as follows:

1. How would you describe your mathematical experiences throughout your schooling?
2. What successes have you had in your mathematics classes?
3. What challenges have you encountered in your mathematics classes?
4. What areas of mathematics have you found enjoyable?
5. What areas of mathematics have you not found enjoyable?
6. What studying techniques have worked well for you in mathematics?
7. What studying techniques have not worked well for you in mathematics?
8. Have you found that you have learned mathematics better working with others or by yourself? Why do you think you feel the way you do?
9. What are your goals and personal expectations for yourself in mathematics for this school year? How will you know if you have achieved those goals and have met your expectations?
10. What are your expectations from your mathematics teacher? How will you know if he or she has met your expectations?

Mathematics History

Mathematics history is full of interesting stories that bring mathematics to life for the students and show that mathematicians were real people who had their own struggles and triumphs throughout life just like everyone else. Requiring students to write a journal entry or mathematical essay about the life of a particular mathematician, the historical development of a particular concept, or the discoveries from a particular time period or culture allow students to connect writing to mathematics. Not only does having students write about diverse cultural contributions to mathematical development, but it allows students to gain perspective about the global developments of mathematics. A careful historical analysis of mathematics reveals that mathematics is not the exclusive domain of European males, but rather very significant developments were made in North and Sub-Sahara Africa, the Middle East, South and East Asia, and the Pre-Columbian Americas. Sample journal or essay questions follow.

1. How did Babylonian mathematics influence today's mathematics?
2. How would you explain the development and transmission of the Hindu-Arabic numeral system?
3. Which people and cultures contributed to the development of calculus? Justify your response.
4. During the Early Middle Ages, how did Islamic culture contribute to mathematical development?
5. How did the discovery of irrational number pi develop?
6. What is the origin of the discovery of the irrationality of the square root of two?
7. How did mathematics in India affect mathematics in Europe?
8. How would you describe the mathematics of the Maya and Inca civilizations?
9. Which historical period would you argue had the greatest mathematical contributions? Provide evidence to support your claim.
10. Who is your favorite mathematician and why? Provide two contributions that this mathematician made.

Composing Word Problems

Creating word problems is another good way to have students write in mathematics. Students can create their own problems for other students in the class to solve. By creating their own word problems students must have a strong grasp of the mathematical content. In order to create word problems that reflect the appropriate conditions given by the teacher, the students authoring the problems must understand the underlying mathematics concepts in order to create solvable problems with the information given, and solvable using the techniques in the unit being studied. Teachers can guide students in the word problem authoring process by giving students the conditions needed for writing. For example, if students are studying motion problems, which are problems that have the relationship that distance is equal to the rate of an object multiplied by its time, teachers may require students to supply two out of the three variables (e.g., a student may supply the rate and distance at which a person runs), use reasonable numbers in a real world context (e.g., a problem that has a person running at forty-five miles per hour would be unreasonable), and use consistent units of measurement (e.g., a person running at six miles per hour and traveling fifteen kilometers may be academically inappropriate until conversions between the two systems of measurement have been discussed). Teachers can require creativity and promote literacy skills by requiring students to base their problems on real world settings that require more than two or three calculations embedded in a story using between 150 and 200 words. This would eliminate the possibility that a student creates a word problem that simply states a person ran at six miles per hour for two hours, and inquire how far the runner had run. Not only is this problem too simple and involves only one calculation, but it is also quite boring. The result of the student word problem authoring, along with teacher guidance, may be as follows.

Martina, a sixth grade student at Cobble Hill Elementary School, has never enjoyed sports. She felt that she was clumsy and uncoordinated, and she always tried to stay out of sight in gym class. One day while walking home from school she was startled by a very large angry dog. While the dog was safely locked behind a fence, the loud barking gave her such a start that she bolted down the street and ran for five blocks. She could not believe how quickly she had run the remaining blocks of her walk home. Inspired by her speed she decided to time herself and run for 15 minutes to determine how many blocks she could cover. She knew that 20 blocks was equal to 1 mile. She set her timer and ran as fast as she could. After she completed her 15 minutes she realized that she had run 25 blocks as she was catching her breath. Martina sat down and began working to figure out how fast she ran. She was pleasantly surprised that her speed was so high. What was Martina's speed in miles per hour?

The student needs to find out how far Martina had run. Since she ran for 25 blocks the student can figure that Martina ran 25/20 miles, which is 1.25 miles. Since the problem wants us to give Martina's speed in miles per hour, it would be best to convert her time into hours. The student can calculate that 15 minutes is 15/60 hours, which is 0.25 hours. Since the student knows that distance equals rate multiplied by time, the student now has 1.25 miles = r(0.25 hours). Solving for r the student gets r = 1.25 miles/0.25 hours, which is 5 miles per hour.

Notice that the numbers used in this problem are reasonable, and running five miles per hour for a sixth grade student who feels that she is not athletic is quite an accomplishment. Additionally, notice that the problem requires the student to calculate three separate times in order to arrive at the correct answer. A problem like this one is relatable to the students' lives, requires creativity, encourages healthy behavior (i.e., physical activity over a sedentary lifestyle), may encourage students to explore new options such as athletics, and makes motion problems more engaging for students. The experiment that Martina undertook is one in which the students themselves could and should conduct. While it is very unlikely that a sixth grade student could write a word problem of this type on the first draft, consider that in English class students often write essays, submit to the teacher, receive feedback, and then are required to re-write or edit their work. The same process can be used in mathematics class to create a refined finished product. Students who engage in this activity reinforce their writing skills while learning mathematics. While it may inhibit some creativity, it may be beneficial for teachers to direct the story themes around healthy positive behavior. For example, while acceptable for students to compose motion problems around motor vehicles, it is better if they instead composed problems around walking, running, bicycling, or swimming, modes of transport that lead to better physical health. If a student wrote a story around a child riding in a car to a fast food restaurant, it might be better to guide the student toward a story about a child walking with his or her parents to a farmer's market to purchase fresh organic produce. While it may appear that the teacher is promoting an agenda, albeit a positive one, all mathematics problems are political by the content that is either included or excluded (e.g., contextualized in unhealthy behavior such as unhealthy eating, sedentary lifestyle, low-wage employment, environmental degradation, etc.). Gutstein and Peterson (2005) said, "Simply put, teaching math in a neutral manner is not possible. No math teaching—is actually 'neutral,' although some teachers may be unaware of this" (p. 6). Gutstein and Peterson further elaborated that if teachers ignore politics in mathematics programs then teacher choices teach students three things:

1. They suggest that politics are not relevant to everyday situations.
2. They cast mathematics as having no role in understanding social injustice and power imbalances.
3. They provide students with no experience using math to make sense of, and to change, unjust situations. (Gutstein & Peterson, 2005, p. 6)

Reflecting Upon Solving Word Problems

Not only should teachers have students create their own word problems, but they should allow their students to reflect upon their own problem solving process while solving word problems for themselves. Using Polya's (1945) steps for problem solving, teachers could have students reflect on the process as follows.

1. Understand the problem: What information does the problem give me? What is the problem asking of me? Can I restate what the problem is asking in my own words?
2. Make a plan: How could I use the information I have to solve this problem? Do I have enough information or too much information? What else do I need outside of this problem in terms of background knowledge?
3. Carry out the plan: What will be my best approach in carrying out my plan? Am I correctly carrying out my plan or am I making mistakes? Is my approach satisfying the demands of the problem?
4. Look back: Does my solution to this problem check out? Is there another way to solve this problem? Could I generalize or extend this problem to a larger situation?

ADDRESSING OBJECTIONS TO
READING AND WRITING IN MATHEMATICS

Although this chapter has focused upon reading and writing in mathematics and its benefits, the negative aspects of reading and writing in the mathematics classroom should be addressed. Some students are weak in literacy skills, but strong in quantitative thinking. Further, some students cannot read or write at all, but are able to manipulate mathematical symbols to some extent. As mentioned earlier, English Language Learners (ELL) may dread going to English class in which they're required to read and write in English, but enjoy mathematics class in which they are familiar with the nearly universal Hindu-Arabic numerals and operational symbols. Requiring these students to read and write in mathematics may further increase mathematics anxiety. While these are legitimate concerns, a focus on a purely computational mathematics curriculum is an irresponsible decision because students learn mathematics best when situated in a contextual problem solving focused curriculum (NCSM, 1978; NCTM, 2000; Posamentier & Krulik, 2008; Posamentier, Smith, & Stepelman, 2008; Schoenfeld, 1985). The contextual problem solving focus in mathematics requires students to develop their reading and writing skills. While this may prove challenging for some students, particularly for students who struggle with reading and writing, the cross curriculum support of their reading and writing skills may improve their skills more quickly than leaving the development to the English teacher alone.

Winsor (2008) specifically addresses language, reading, and writing development for ELL students. Winsor (2008) labels ELL students in the mathematics classroom as Mathematics as a Second Language (MSL) students. Winsor's (2008) strategy is to combine vocabulary learning, group work, and student journal writing to help improve the mathematics vocabulary and communication skills of his MSL students.

A technique Winsor (2008) uses to reinforce mathematics vocabulary is an adaptation of VVWA, or Word Square, for ELL students. Winsor (2008) divided the Word Square into four quadrants and gave an example using even numbers in mathematics. In the top left corner students would write the concept in their native language, in this case Spanish: numeros pares. In the top right corner students would write the concept in English: even numbers. In the lower left corner students would write the concept in their own words: Son los multiples de dos. In the lower right corner students would write the concept as a representation: 2, 4, 6, 8, 10, etc. Winsor (2008) found that the Word Square required that students understand the vocabulary rather than only use memorization, which would be less beneficial for them.

Winsor (2008) recommended heterogeneous grouping of students based upon English literacy proficiency so that students could translate for each other when less advanced ELL developed difficulties. Students who are proficient in English also benefit from this exercise because they are required to understand the material in order to explain it to group members. Additionally, Winsor (2008) recommended using student journal writing and allowing them to write in the language in which they were most comfortable. However, students are required to write the mathematics vocabulary in English for reinforcement of the vocabulary.

CONCLUSION

It is clear that there are multiple ways of integrating literacy into the mathematics classroom. While mathematics teachers may at first be resistant to the idea of adding more to the material they must cover, many will find that students gain literacy skills, increase mathematics understanding, and more quickly learn mathematics vocabulary. Literacy activities equip mathematics teachers with more tools to communicate with their students and help them understand their students' learning. It is important that while students may resist literacy activities in the mathematics class, teacher must reinforce that interdisciplinary nature of the curriculum and that both literacy and mathematics skills are a necessary condition for good career, thinking, and life skills.

REFERENCES

Barton, M. L., & Heidema, C. (2002). *Teaching reading in mathematics* (2nd ed.). Aurora, CO: Mid-Continental Research for Education and Learning.

Beaudoin, C. (2011). *Teaching mathematics with children's literature.* Retrieved from http://fcit.usf.edu/math/resource/bib.html.

Borasi, R., & Rose, B. (1989). Journal writing and mathematics instruction. *Educational Studies in Mathematics, 20,* 347–65.

Bosse, M. J., & Faulconer, J. (2008). Learning and assessing mathematics through reading and writing. *School Science and Mathematics, 108*(1), 8–19.

Brandau, L. (1990). Rewriting our stories of mathematics. In A. Sterrett (Ed.), *Using writing to teach mathematics* (pp. 73–77), Washington, D.C.: Mathematical Association of America.

Burns, M. (2007). *About teaching mathematics: A K–8 resource* (3rd ed.). Sausalito, CA: Math Solutions Publications.

Carter, S. (2009). Connecting mathematics and writing workshop: It's kinda like ice skating. *Reading Teacher, 62*(7), 606–10.

Charles, R. I., & Lester, F. K., Jr. (1982). *Teaching problem solving: What, why, & how.* Palo Alto, CA: Seymour.

Clark, D. M. (1997). The changing role of the mathematics teacher. *Journal for Research in Mathematics Education, 28*(3), 278–308.

Countryman, J. (1992). *Writing to learn mathematics: Strategies that work.* Portsmouth, NH: Heinemann.

Crafter, S. (2012). Parental cultural models and resources for understanding mathematical achievement in culturally diverse school settings. *Educational Studies in Mathematics, 81*(1), 31–46.

Doherty, B. J. (1996). The write way: A look at journal writing in first-year algebra. *Mathematics Teacher, 89*(7), 556–60.

Drake, B. M., & Amspaugh, L. B. (1994). What writing reveals in mathematics. *Focus on Learning Problems in Mathematics, 16*(3), 43–50.

Gopen, G. D., & Smith, D. A. (1990). What's an assignment like you doing in a course like this?: Writing to learn mathematics. *The College Mathematics Journal, 21*(1), 2–19.

Grossman, F. J., Smith, B., & Miller, C. (1993). Did you say "write" in mathematics class? *Journal of Developmental Education, 22*(4), 2–6.

Gutstein, E., & Peterson, B. (2005). *Rethinking mathematics: Teaching social justice by the numbers.* Milwaukee, WI: Rethinking Schools.

Haggard, M. R. (1982). The Vocabulary Self-Collection Strategy: An active approach to word learning. *Journal of Reading, 27,* 203–207.

Hopkins, M. H. (1993). Ideas: Mathematics and children's literature. *The Arithmetic Teacher, 40*(9), 512–19.

Jao, L. (2012). The multicultural mathematics classroom: Culturally aware teaching through cooperative learning and multiple representations. *Multicultural Education, 19*(3), 2–10.

Krulik, S., & Rudnick, J. A. (1989). *Problem solving.* Boston, MA: Allyn and Bacon.

Miller, L. D. (1992). Teacher benefits from using impromptu writing prompts in algebra classes. *Journal for Research in Mathematics Education, 23,* 329–40.

Nahrgang, C. L., & Peterson, B. T. (1986). Using writing to learn mathematics. *Mathematics Teacher, 79,* 461–65.

Nakkula, M. J., & Toshalis, E. (2006). *Understanding youth: Adolescent development for educators.* Cambridge, MA: Harvard Education Press.

National Council of Supervisors of Mathematics. (1978). Position paper on basic mathematical skills. *Mathematics Teacher, 71*(2), 147-152.

National Council of Teachers of Mathematics. (2000). *Principles and standards for school mathematics.* Reston, VA: National Council of Teachers of Mathematics.

Ogle, J. (1986). K-W-L: A teaching model that develops active reading of expository text. *The Reading Teacher, 39,* 564–70.

Ojose, B. (2008). Applying Piaget's theory of cognitive development to mathematics instruction. *The Mathematics Educator, 18*(1), 26–30.

Pierce, M. E., & Fontaine, L. M. (2009). Designing vocabulary instruction in mathematics. *The Reading Teacher, 63*(3), 239–43.

Polya, G. (1945). *How to solve it.* Princeton, NJ: Princeton University Press.

Porter, M. K., & Masingila, J. O. (2000). Examining the effects of writing on conceptual and procedural knowledge in calculus. *Educational Studies in Mathematics, 42*(2), 165–77.

Posamentier, A. S., & Krulik, S. (2008). *Problem-solving strategies for efficient and elegant solutions grades 6–12.* Thousand Oakes, CA: Corwin Press.

Posamentier, A. S., Smith, B. S., & Stepelman, J. (2008) *Teaching secondary mathematics: Teaching and enrichment units* (8th ed.). Boston, MA: Allyn & Bacon.

Price, R. R. (2009). *Using children's literature to teach mathematics.* Retrieved from http://www.quantiles.com/resources/LiteratureMathematics.pdf.

Pugalee, D. (1997). Connecting writing to the mathematics curriculum. *Mathematics Teacher, 90*(4), 308–10.

Quinn, M. E., & Molloy, M. (1992). I learned to talk mathematics: Using cooperative groups with college minority students. In C. Kessler (Ed.), *Cooperative language learning: A teacher's resource book.* Englewood Cliffs, NJ: Prentice Hall.

Robinson, F. P. (1946). *Effective study* (2nd ed.). New York, NY: Harper & Row.

Rose, B. (1989). Writing and mathematics: Theory and practice. In P. Connolly & T. Vilardi (Eds.), *Writing to learn mathematics and science* (pp. 15–30). New York, NY: Teachers College Press.

Schoenfeld, A. (1985). *Mathematical problem solving.* New York, NY: Academic Press.

Stehney, A. K. (1990). A writing program and its lessons for mathematicians. In A. Sterret (Ed.), *Using writing to teach mathematics* (pp. 26–29). Washington, D.C.: Mathematical Association of America.

Thomas, K. J. (1986). The Directed Inquiry Activity: An instruction procedure for content reading. In E. K. Dishner, T. W. Bean, J. E. Readence, & D. W. Moore (Eds.), *Reading in the content area* (2nd ed., pp. 278–91). Dubuque, IA: Kendall Hunt.

Unrau, N. (2008). *Content area reading and writing: Fostering literacies in middle and high school cultures.* Upper Saddle River, NJ: Merrill Prentice Hall.

Vygotsky, L. S. (1987). Thinking and speech. In R. W. Rieber & A. S. Carton (Eds.), *The collected works of Vygotsky, L. S. (vol. 1): Problems of general psychology,* 39–285. New York, NY: Plenum.

Whiteford, T. (2009). Is mathematics a universal language? *Teaching Children Mathematics, 16*(5), 276–83.

Whiten, D. J., & Whiten, P. (2004). *New visions for linking literature and mathematics.* Urbana, IL: National Council of Teachers of English.

Wilcox, B., & Monroe, E. E. (2011). Integrating writing and mathematics. *Reading Teacher, 64*(7), 521–29.

Winsor, M. S. (2008). Bridging the language barrier in mathematics. *Mathematics Teacher, 101*(5), 372–78.

APPENDIX A: LIST OF CHILDREN'S LITERATURE TO USE IN MATHEMATICS CLASS (DEVELOPED FROM OJOSE (2008), BEAUDOIN (2011), AND HOPKINS' (1993) LIST)

Adler, D. A. (1996). *Fraction fun.* New York, NY: Holiday House.

Allen, P. (1982). *Who sank the boat?* New York, NY: Coward-McCann.

Anno, M. (1982). *Anno's counting house.* New York, NY: Philomel Books.

Anno, M. (1994). *Anno's magic seeds.* New York, NY: Philomel Books.

Anno, M., & Anno, M. (1983). *Anno's mysterious multiplying jar.* New York, NY: Philomel Books.

Ash, R. (1996). *Incredible comparisons.* New York, NY: Dorling Kindersley.

Axelrod, A. (1996). *Pigs on a blanket.* New York, NY: Simon & Schuster.

Axelrod, A. (1997). *Pigs go to market: Halloween fun with math and shopping.* New York, NY: Simon & Schuster.

Axelrod, A. (1997). *Pigs will be pigs.* New York, NY: Simon & Schuster.

Barry, D. (1994). *The Rajah's rice: A mathematical folklore from India.* New York, NY: W. H. Freeman.

Birch, D. (1988). *The king's chessboard.* New York, NY: Puffin Pied Piper Books.

Burns, M. (1994). *The greedy triangle.* New York, NY: Scholastic Press.

Carle, E. (1969). *The very hungry caterpillar.* New York, NY: Putnam.

Carle, E. (1977) *The grouchy ladybug.* New York, NY: Harper Collins.

Chalmers, M. (1986). *Six dogs, twenty-three cats, forty-five mice, and one hundred sixty spiders.* New York, NY: Harper Collins.

Christaldi, K. (1996). *Even Steven and odd Todd.* New York, NY: Scholastic Press.

Clement, R. (1991). *Counting on Frank.* Milwaukee, WI: Gareth Stevens Children's Book.

Cushman, R. (1991). *Do you wanna bet? Your chance to find out about probability.* New York, NY: Clarion Books.

Dee, R. (1988). *Two ways to count to ten.* New York, NY: Holt.

Demi. (1997). *One grain of rice: A mathematical folktale.* New York, NY: Scholastic Press.

Edens, C. (1994). *How many bears?* New York, NY: Atheneum.

Falwell, C. (1993). *Feast for 10.* New York, NY: Clarion Books.

Friedman, A. (1994). *The king's commissioners.* New York, NY: Scholastic Press.

Gag, W. (1928). *Millions of cats.* New York, NY: Coward-McCann.

Giganti, P. (1988). *How many snails? A counting book.* New York, NY: Greenwillow.

Giganti, P. (1992). *Each orange had 8 slices.* New York, NY: Greenwillow.

Greenfield, E. (1989). *Aaron and Gayla's counting book.* Boston, MA: Houghton Mifflin.

Hajdusieicz, B. B. (1991). *Shape up, curvy snake.* Austin, TX: Steck-Vaughn Company.

Haskins, J. (2006). *Count your way through. . . .* Minneapolis, MN: Carolrhoda Books.

Hightower, S. (1997). *Twelve snails to one lizard: A tale of mischief and measurement.* New York, NY: Simon & Schuster.

Hoban, T. (1981). *More than one.* New York, NY: Greenwillow.

Hoban, T. (1985). *Is it larger? Is it smaller?* New York, NY: Mulberry Paperbacks.

Hoban, T. (1999). *Let's count.* New York, NY: Greenwillow.

Hong, L. T. (1993). *Two of everything.* Morton Grove, IL: Whitman.

Hopkinson, D. (1993). *Sweet Clara and the freedom quilt.* New York, NY: Random House.

Hulme, J. N. (1991). *Sea squares.* New York, NY: Hyperion Books.

Hulme, J. N. (1995). *Counting by kangaroos: A multiplication concept book.* New York, NY: W. H. Freeman.

Hulme, J. N. (1991). *Sea sums.* New York, NY: Hyperion Books.

Hutchins, P. (1986). *The doorbell rang.* New York, NY: Greenwillow.

Jaspersohn, W. (1993). *Cookies.* Old Tappan, NJ: Macmillan.

Jenkins, S. (1995). *Biggest, strongest, fastest.* New York, NY: Ticknor & Fields Books.

Juster, N. (1961). *The phantom tollbooth.* New York, NY: Random House.

Kellogg, S. (1976). *Much bigger than Martin.* New York, NY: Dial Books.

Linden, A. M. (1994). *One sailing grandma: A Caribbean counting book.* New York, NY: Heinemann.

Lionni, L. (1960). *Inch by inch.* New York, NY: Mulberry Books.

Lobal, A. (1970). *Frog and toad are friends.* New York, NY: Harper-Collins.

Losi, C. A. (1997). *The 512 ants on Sullivan Street.* New York, NY: Scholastic Press.

Maccarone, G. (1997). *Three pigs, one wolf, and seven magic shapes.* New York, NY: Scholastic Press.

Matthews, L. (1979). *Gator pie.* New York, NY: Dodd, Mead and Company.

McMillan, B. (1991). *Eating fractions.* New York, NY: Scholastic Press.

Medearis, A. S. (1990). *Picking peas for a penny.* New York, NY: Scholastic Press.

Merriam, E. (1993). *12 ways to get to 11.* New York, NY: Simon & Schuster.

Most, B. (1994). *How big were the dinosaurs?* San Diego, CA: Voyager Books.

Munsch, R. (1987). *Moira's birthday.* Toronto, ON: Annick Press.

Murphy, S. J. (1996). *Give me half!* New York, NY: HarperCollins Publishers.

Murphy, S. J. (1997). *Divide and ride.* New York, NY: HarperCollins Publishers.

Myller, R. (1990). *How big is a foot?* New York, NY: Dell.

Neuschwander, C. (1997). *Sir cumference and the dragon of pi.* Watertown, MA: Charlesbridge.

Neuschwander, C. (1997). *Sir cumference and the first round table.* Watertown, MA: Charlesbridge.

Nolan, H. (1995). *How much, how many, how far, how heavy, how long, how tall is 1000?* Toronto, ON: Kids Can Press.

Norton, M. (1953). *The borrowers.* New York, NY: Harcourt Brace.

Parker, T. (1984). *In one day.* Boston, MA: Houghton Mifflin.

Pinczes, E. J. (1993). *One hundred angry ants.* Boston, MA: Houghton Mifflin.

Pinczes, E. J. (1993). *A remainder of one.* Boston, MA: Houghton Mifflin.

Pittman, H. C. (1986). *A grain of rice.* New York, NY: Bantam Skylark Book.

Pluckrose, H. (1988). *Pattern.* New York, NY: Franklin Watts.

San Souci, R. (1989). *The boy and the ghost.* New York, NY: Simon-Schuster Books.

St. John, G. (1975). *How to count like a Martian.* New York, NY: Walck.

Schwartz, D. (1985). *How much is a million?* New York, NY: Lothrop, Lee, & Shepard.

Schwartz, D. (1989). *If you made a million.* New York, NY: Lothrop, Lee, & Shepard.

Scieszka, J., & Smith, L. (1995). *Math curse.* New York, NY: Viking.

Sharmat, M. W. (1979). *The 329th friend.* New York, NY: Four Winds Press.

Tahan, M. (1993). *The man who counted. A collection of mathematical adventures.* New York, NY: Norton.

Tang, G. (2001). *The grapes of math.* New York, NY: Scholastic Press.

Tompert, A. (1990). *Grandfather's tang story: A tale told with tangrams.* New York, NY: Crown Publishers.

Tompert, A. (1993). *Just a little bit.* Boston, MA: Houghton Mifflin.

Viorst, J. (1978). *Alexander, who used to be rich last Sunday.* New York, NY: Aladdin.

Walpole, B. (1995). *Measure up with science: distance.* Milwaukee, WI: Gareth Stevens Publishing.

Wells, R. E. (1993). *Is the blue whale the biggest thing there is?* Morton Grove, IL: Whitman.

Wells, R. E. (1997). *What's faster than a speeding cheetah?* Morton Grove, IL: Whitman.

Wolkstein, D. (1972). *8,000 stones.* New York, NY: Doubleday.

APPENDIX B: SUMMARY OF STRATEGIES

Table 7.1.   Summary of Reading Strategies

Strategy	Summary	Common Core Connection
Think-Alouds	This can be used to "talk through" the problem.	Use appropriate tools and strategies.
Vocabulary Self-Collection Strategy	Select vocabulary words students do not know.	Use appropriate tools and strategies.
Word Knowledge Check	Students check category in regard to their sense of familiarity.	Use appropriate tools and strategies.
Know-Want to Know-Learned Strategy	This is what students know, want to know, and have learned.	Use appropriate tools and strategies.
Directed Inquiry Activity	Who, what, where, when, why, and how questions are used.	Make sense of problems and persevere in solving them.
Survey, Question, Read, Recite, and Review	Skim text, self-question, read for detail, recite in own words, go back to text.	Make sense of problems and persevere in solving them.
Word Wall	Identify and record unfamiliar words.	Use appropriate tools and strategies.

Table 7.2.   Summary of Mathematics Reading Strategies

Strategy	Summary	Common Core Connection
Guided Reading and Strategies from English Class	Mathematics teachers can provide the support employed by English teachers as summarized in Table 1.	Use appropriate tools and strategies.
Verbal and Visual Word Association	Two-by-two matrix to give students different perspectives.	Use appropriate tools and strategies.
Comparison of Mathematics Words to English Words	Mathematics vocabulary can be compared and contrasted with the English word meaning outside of mathematics.	Use appropriate tools and strategies.
Mathematics Literature	Connects mathematics and literature	Use appropriate tools and strategies.
Newspapers, Magazines, and Online Articles	Search for mathematics in the real world.	Use appropriate tools and strategies.

Table 7.3. Summary of Writing Strategies in Mathematics

Strategy	Summary	Common Core Connection
Freewriting	This is an exercise that permits students to write whatever they would like.	Use appropriate tools and strategies.
Mathematics Logs	A mathematics log allows students to record their mathematics learning on paper.	Use appropriate tools and strategies.
Mathematics Journal	A mathematics journal is generally longer and more detailed than a log, and it is more reflective than the factual information that may appear in a log.	Use appropriate tools and strategies.
Mathematics Autobiography	A mathematics autobiography is a student's expression of mathematical successes and challenges throughout schooling.	Use appropriate tools and strategies.
Mathematics History	Students can write about a mathematics historical figure, the historical development of a particular concept, or the discoveries from a particular time period or culture.	Use appropriate tools and strategies.
Composing Word Problems	Creating word problems is another good way to have students write in mathematics.	Construct viable arguments and critique the reasoning of others.
Reflecting Upon Solving Word Problems	Students should reflect upon their own problem solving process while solving word problems for themselves.	Make sense of problems and persevere in solving them.

8

Literacy and the Arts

How Artistic Perspectives Enhance Literacy Learning

Merryl Goldberg and Laurie Stowell

Learning *about* the arts is every student's right (not privilege); but it is just one aspect of the range of arts possibilities within classrooms. The power of the arts as a pedagogy, i.e. process for working with concepts, opens classroom teachers to many possibilities from motivating students to want to learn and ask questions, to assessing their understanding of subject matter. Arts are both *products*, such as finished paintings, poems, dances, plays, songs, as well as a *process* through which individuals communicate and express information, ideas, and emotions. The process of engaging with arts involves discipline, practice, reflection, imagination, persistence, and often . . . passion. The integration of the process of the arts combined with the process of learning to engage students in becoming better readers can be a powerful combination.

The arts can also serve to provide access for all learners. English language learners who might not be confident in reading, writing, or describing concepts in English, might very well be mistaken for not understanding concepts. However, when a child is given the opportunity to draw or act out a concept, a teacher might realize her student's capability was only limited by an ability to express via words. Students who may be identified as the "low" students according to standardized testing may completely surprise teachers with hidden abilities that show they are not "low" at all.

ARTS INFUSED PEDAGOGY

Arts infused pedagogy focuses on learning *with* and *through* the arts, and brings multiple and unique benefits to the overall process of learning, including functioning as mirrors, windows, and bridges. Bella Lewitsky (1989), dancer, wrote that, "The arts are a mirror for society—critic, teacher and forecaster—and teach the value of individual differences." As windows, the arts have the potential to open up teachers and students to wonder, take risks, be curious, creative, imaginative, question, reflect and revise, feel confident, explore deeply, and find voice. The arts also serve as bridges insomuch as they enable students to connect to ideas, peoples, cultures, and more. "[The arts] can nurture a sense of belonging, of community; or, they can foster a sense of being apart, of being an individual. The arts provide a vehicle for individuals, communities and cultures to explore their own world and journey to new ones, thus enriching their understanding of the varied peoples and cultures that exist on our planet" (Goldberg and Phillips, 1992, p. v).

Art infused pedagogy melds the process of creating art with specific classroom content. It encompasses "habits of mind" including envisioning, exploring, and engaging and persisting (Hetland, et al., 2010). Karen Gallas, in her seminal article, "Arts as Epistemology: Enabling Children to know What They Know," (1991), was among the first educators to dig deeply into the power of the artistic process as a teaching methodology. "For both children and teacher," she wrote, "the arts offer opportunities for reflection upon content and the process of learning, and they foster a deeper level of communication about what knowledge is and who is truly in control of the learning process" (p. 50). She described the artistic process adapted to children's learning as "Arts as Epistemology."

Since Gallas, several terms have been used to express the arts as a vehicle for working with subject matter including arts integration, arts-infused curriculum, interdisciplinary studies, and multidisciplinary studies. Gail Burnaford (2007) in cooperation with the Arts Education Partnership published a thorough review of arts integration literature that also highlights its uses. The uses include learning in, with, and through the arts, the arts as a curriculum "connections process," and the arts as "collaborative engagement." While many of the phrases, from "arts as epistemology" through to arts integration capture a sense of the arts possibilities beyond being taught in and of themselves as disciplines, we believe to further the potential of the arts in this arena of learning, the phrase "arts infused pedagogy" more fully describes the role of arts as a pedagogical tool for teaching and learning.

DREAM: DEVELOPING READING EDUCATION WITH ARTS METHODS

To illustrate the potential of arts infused with literacy, we will focus on an ongoing professional development program for teachers we have developed and researched, called DREAM. The program provides professional development through an institute and optional workshops to elementary grade teachers in high poverty settings (with high English Language Learner populations) to use visual arts and theater to improve students' reading and language arts skills. DREAM grew out of another long-term and well documented project, SUAVE (Socios unidos para Artes Via Educacion—United Community for Arts in Education) (Goldberg, 2004), which for over twenty years has provided teachers with methods to integrate the arts throughout the curriculum.

Students are keenly adept at understanding their world through visual means. In DREAM's arts infused pedagogy, teachers learn specifically about visual literacy as it relates to utilizing illustrations in the reading text as supplementary, complementary, and contrasting information (Goldberg, 2012, pp.187–89). In viewing the illustrations, teachers guide students with questions such as: Why did the artist make the choices he or she did? This can be posed broadly or more specifically to artistic elements such as medium, color, line, shape, perspective, etc. What additional information do the illustrations add to the text? Are there details left out of the illustrations that are in the text? Or vice versa? From whose perspective is the illustration and what does that say about the characters and why? The questions are limitless!

The illustrations in the reading texts as well as chapter books can be used directly for grammar lessons as well. For example, several DREAM teachers have assessed students' understanding of nouns, verbs, adjectives, and adverbs by asking them to describe the illustration in detail using only one group of words, such as adjectives or nouns. Of course this technique is not limited to illustrations; it can be used more broadly with works of art such as paintings and sculptures. In addition, this technique translates easily to other content areas as well, such as math, science, and social studies.

In addition to utilizing the illustrations in the reading texts, teachers learn how to guide their students to create their own illustrations of stories, characters, plot, and settings. They can also learn how to create puppets and other props that enable students to bring stories to life. Teachers delve into creating alternative visual book reports in creative forms such as accordion books that they then introduce to their students.

Theater is an effective forum for learning to read and involves acting out scenes or paragraphs from the reading texts to develop an understanding of characters, plot, and setting; or improvising as the characters in a story. A popular activity DREAM teachers learned was "tableau," or "frozen scenes." Teachers learned to act out or mime a piece of a story from the reading text and then freeze at an important moment. Many teachers engaged their students in the tableau activity and that served to motivate the students in uncovering the essence of the storyline. Some teachers built on this by having their students start in a tableau and then move into a scene depicting what came next in the story.

The concept of *inference* is a challenge for many readers. We have found that developing reading skills through theater methods offers a unique opportunity for students to dig deeper into the texts and engage with them such that inference becomes secondhand. By engaging theater techniques to understand what they are reading, children can become characters in a story (or nonfiction) through acting, and they are absolutely in the position of having to "read between the lines" and interpret how the character will enter the scene, facial expressions, gestures, vocalize, and so on. By "becoming the character" and gaining insight into the character's thoughts, actions, and motivations, students are able to enter into a deeper understanding of the text. It is truly what Rosenblatt (1938) called a transactional experience between the reader and the text in which both are transformed. This active engagement with the story sets the stage for students to dig into the reading, use their imaginations, and think reflectively as well as critically.

As teachers broaden their methodologies to include the arts, they begin to see their students in a new and sometimes surprising light. As happened in one classroom, a student who had a tendency to be the class bully became a story book character in such a personal and kind manner, that his teacher never looked at him in the same way again. Through the arts teachers will discover hidden (and not so hidden) talents of their students that would have been left unacknowledged without the art activities.

DREAM Research

In the realm of research relating to reading and the arts, there are a limited number of studies that look at student learning in particular, such as Ann Podlozny's research (2000). Podlozny's research was among the first to show a relationship between drama and the strengthening of verbal skills. Ellen Winner and Lois Hetland's meta-analysis reviewing research relating to arts and academic achievement (Winner &Hetland, 2000), highlighted the finding of causal relationships between classroom drama and verbal achievement, music listening and spatial reasoning, and music learning and spatial reasoning. The DREAM program and research built upon and expanded these studies.

DREAM narrowed the arts disciplines to visual arts and theater. We knew from our previous work in SUAVE that visual arts provided a "safe zone" for teachers in that it was comfortable, an easy entry point and perhaps above all, a quiet activity. Furthermore, the potential in visual literacy opened many venues for working with teachers and students. We also knew that in SUAVE research and in the literature, theater provided a rich arena for potential with regard to its integration in language arts.

In contemplating how to design a research project in light of an arts infused pedagogical professional development framework, the DREAM partners focused in on creating a study that would primarily examine the effectiveness, benefits, and challenges of training teachers in this pedagogy. To further complicate the design, however, we were also compelled to track student test scores as was required by our funder, the U.S. Department of Education Office of Innovation and Improvement (OII), Arts Education Model Development and Dissemination program (AEMDD). The test scores weren't a huge concern because in most of our previous studies, test scores always went up. Therefore, we looked at this requirement as merely a requirement. In the end, however, as the study unfolded, the test scores came into play much more than could have been anticipated.

The context for the DREAM research is rooted in several conversations, i.e., best practices in arts infused strategies, particularly in drama (Mages, 2008); arts integration as a methodology for improving student learning (Gallas, 1994; Goldberg, 2012; Saraniero &Goldberg, 2008); and research models of professional development and coaching (Batt, 2010; Desimone, 2009; Rudd, Lambert, Satterwhite, & Smith, 2009; Goldschmidt & Phelps, 2009; Garet, Cronen, Eaton, Kurki, Ludwig, Jones, et al., 2008). In reading education, literature concerning motivation and the importance of engaging students in wanting to read (Gambrell, 2011) has guided the development and implementation of arts activities.

Research Methodology

DREAM is implemented through a collaboration between California State University San Marcos and the San Diego County Office of Education called NCPDF (North County Professional Development Federation). NCPDF is a consortium of school districts that work collaboratively on professional development for the teachers in their districts. Teachers from ten school districts within NCPDF representing rural, suburban, and urban communities participated in this study that included one year of planning and three years of implementation. Over the four years of the study, 141 teachers and approximately 3,000 students participated in the research.

There were three research groups in DREAM—two treatment groups and one comparison group. All treatment teachers attended the weeklong DREAM summer institute. Following the institute, half of the treatment teachers worked independently to integrate theater and visual art into their reading curriculum. The other half of the teachers received in-class personal training with a professional artist for an additional 20–25 hours throughout the school year.

For all years, a lottery was conducted of eligible third and fourth grade teachers, all of whom volunteered to be a part of the research and program. To be eligible, teachers had to work in a participating district at a school with a population of students, at least 35 percent of whom qualified for free or reduced school lunch. However, the average overall percentage of students qualifying for free or reduced lunch was much higher. In accordance with our research protocol, DREAM teachers were compensated for attending the summer institute and participating in other research-related activities throughout the year.

Over the course of the study, the teachers in all three research groups were found to be similar. There were few differences between study groups on key demographic information, such as teachers' educational attainment, teaching experience, and previous professional development in the arts. The study teachers were an experienced group with an average tenure in the classroom of 15–16 years across the three groups. The average number of years spent teaching their current grade level was between six and seven years.

The vast majority of teachers had no formal professional development focused on arts in the year prior to the DREAM institute, and we also compared a variable concerning previous SUAVE training since many of our participating school districts implemented SUAVE. Not surprisingly, most of the teachers were women, but each year there were a handful of men in the mix. Finally, as a whole, before DREAM, teachers reported that they used visual arts more than theater in their classrooms, when they implemented an art activity.

Data Analysis Tools

A variety of quantitative and qualitative data analyses were used throughout the evaluation. Focus group transcripts of the teachers and art coaches were coded and analyzed for themes. The teachers' lesson plans were scored with the project rubric and the rubric results were quantified with descriptive statistics, as were the coaches' weekly logs. Teachers' pretest and posttest surveys were analyzed with descriptive statistics, ANOVA, t-tests, and linear regression. Finally, the teachers' responses to open-ended survey questions were coded and analyzed for themes. Students' standardized test scores were analyzed using linear regression and t-tests.

DREAM Institute and Coaching

The institute was carefully designed to combine a mix of activities, reflection, and provide numerous resources for the teachers. Specific learning outcomes addressing what teachers would come to know about the use of arts integrated pedagogy, specific skills they would acquire, and what they would come to appreciate and understand were developed and later shared with the teachers.

The weeklong institute was designed primarily as a hands-on experience. A grid was created that demonstrated the relationships among the California state standards (prior to the adoption of the Common Core Standards) in reading, visual arts, and theater (an excerpt is provided below) that helped guide workshop leaders in creating specific institute activities. This resource later became a powerful tool for teachers as they recognized how concretely the arts and reading standards matched and complimented each other. It also served to ease teachers' anxiety about "taking time away" from reading instruction. They learned that they were actually enhancing reading instruction and providing richer educational experiences for their students. A small portion of the grid excerpted here:

Table 8.1. Alignment of California State Reading Standards with Arts Standards

Theater Standard	Reading Standard	Visual Art Standard
1.1 Use the vocabulary of the theater, such as character, setting, conflict, audience, motivation, props, stage areas, and blocking to describe theatrical experiences.	1.7 **Vocabulary and Concept Development:** use a dictionary to learn the meaning and other features of unknown words	1.5 Identify and describe elements of art in work of art, emphasizing line, color, shape/form, texture, space, and value.
1.1 Use the vocabulary of the theater, such as character, setting, conflict, audience, motivation, props, stage areas, and blocking to describe theatrical experiences.	1.8 **Vocabulary and Concept Development:** use knowledge of prefixes (e.g., un-, re-, pre-, bi-, mis-, dis-) and suffixes (e.g., -er, -est, -ful) to determine the meaning of words	1.5 Identify and describe elements of art in work of art, emphasizing line, color, shape/form, texture, space and value.
	Reading Comprehension	
1.2 Identify who, what, where, when, and why (the five Ws) in a theatrical experience.	2.4 **Comprehension and Analysis of Grade-Level-Appropriate Text:** recall major points in the text and make and modify predictions about forthcoming information	1.4 Compare & contrast two works of art made by the use of different art tools and media (e.g. watercolor, tempera, computer). 5.3 Look at images in figurative works of art and predict what might happen next, telling what clues in the work support their ideas.

During the week of the summer institute the teachers were guided through numerous activities including theater games, illustration activities, puppet-making, tableau, acting, and directing. In addition, time was dedicated to discussion, evaluation, assessment, planning, and online reflective blogging.

Teachers consistently described in written reflections, blogs, and video-taped "MIMs" (Magical Institute Moments) their experience as "engaging, hopeful, inspiring, challenging, validating, motivating, refreshing, emboldened, and full of life and laughter." One teacher remarked, "This institute is an amazing opportunity for teachers to step out of the classroom and experience something different, something fun, something exciting and get the excitement back into teaching." Another echoed the feeling of excitement, "I feel energized. I'm excited to start our new year in August and I'm overwhelmed with excitement." While I was always heartened by the institute experience and by the teachers' joy, the question lingered; would it make a difference in the classroom?

Per our research protocol, following the institute, half of the teachers would implement the arts integrated pedagogy on their own, and half would continue to receive professional development in the DREAM pedagogy by having art coaches visit them in their classrooms over the year. Research from one of our previous studies that focused on the SUAVE program (Goldberg, 2004) came into play with regard to the coaching aspect of our research. The findings underscored the benefits of what we found to be a "professional-professional" relationship, whereby teachers gained from the artists and artists gained from the teachers.

A unique aspect of the SUAVE program that we implemented into the DREAM protocol, was systematic support and training for the art coaches. The coaches (who were primarily artists or art instructors, not reading teachers) met together for several hours every other week in what became affectionately known as the "coaches meeting." These meetings provided an opportunity for the artists to brainstorm new ideas and lessons, and discuss how to engage reluctant or overly exuberant teachers. Several times a year during our DREAM research, our university specialist on reading education joined the coaches meetings to provide feedback on how the classroom arts activities measure up with regard to good reading instruction.

The coaches meetings provided the opportunity to delve into interesting questions directly related to finding ways to best reach teachers. For instance, the vast majority of DREAM teachers reported on their pre-program survey, that they were more comfortable implementing visual arts activities than theater activities. In the coaches meeting we examined aspects of the visual arts that might make that so, things like visual art activities are familiar and safe physically and emotionally. Teachers did not have to have extensive knowledge to conduct a visual art activity or "put themselves out there" with regard to exposing themselves emotionally. Students are quieter and contained during the activities. If the principal walks in the door, the class looks attentive. We then brainstormed ways in which theater activities could provide that same "safe" ground for teachers. We also decided to hand out a checklist previously developed by the County Office of Education for administrators on what to expect when walking in to an arts infused classroom.

An example of one of our more animated and important conversations during a coaching meeting connected the act of theater directing, to the teaching of inference. Theater coaches and our reading specialist drew a direct line between directing and inference insomuch as the job of the theater director is essentially to read between the lines and interpret how scenes will be enacted. Thus, in having directing as an outcome for DREAM teachers, we realized in the coaches' meeting that the teachers themselves were also learning techniques directly linked to deeper aspects of reading comprehension. By teaching students how to interpret a scene to act out or mime, they were also teaching them to make inferences.

The coaching meetings proved important because the actual in-class personal training for the participating teachers is not prescribed; nor are there any coaching "recipes." Art coaches worked individually with teachers to support their learning and implementation of the DREAM methods and lesson plans within the teacher's particular context. The implementation and personal training varied widely; sometimes teams decided to co-teach, other times teachers asked their coach to demonstrate, or a teacher decided to try a lesson on her own and asked for the coaches' critique. Each teacher/coach pairing proved unique, and was enacted based on both the learning styles of the individual teachers, as well as what the teacher chose as their reading focus for the lesson(s).

PRINCIPAL FINDINGS AND DISCUSSION: TEACHERS' PROFESSIONAL DEVELOPMENT

The coaching professional development model and arts infused pedagogy both proved successful. Some of the outcomes included:

- Professional Development in arts-infused pedagogy: Teachers newly learned strategies were successfully implemented in classrooms and had a positive effect on student learning in the areas of vocabulary, reading comprehension, understanding plot, and inference.
- Theater proved to be an especially effective tool for literacy learning.
- Teachers noted particular success with ELL students, taking ownership of their learning, more motivated, empowered, and taking risks.
- Teachers felt joy, reinvigorated, and reconnected to teaching.

Both versions of the professional development, the a) institute only group and the b) institute plus coaching group experienced significant positive results in terms of the teachers' learning and implementation in their classroom practice. Not surprisingly, however, we found that the coaching intervention was especially impactful. Coached teachers integrated arts more frequently (particularly theater) and into more areas of the reading curriculum than institute-only or comparison teachers. The coached teachers reported being more confident in integrating the arts compared to the institute-only and comparison teachers, and were better able to demonstrate their learning as evaluated through their work samples. In addition, the coached teachers' work samples showed greater improvement over the course of treatment years than those of the institute-only teachers. It should be noted that the institute only teachers also made significant improvements in their practice, however, not as much as the coached teachers and not continuous improvement as did the teachers with the coaches. In other words, the institute had a definite positive impact, which is also reflected in the student test scores, but fell short of the gains made by the coached teachers. The majority of the teachers perceived the coaching intervention contributed significantly to improvements in reading instruction and student learning. This perception strengthened over the course of the school year. This finding is consistent with the literature in professional development, especially in literacy in that "drive by" (guest speaker at a staff meeting) or "one time" workshops do not generally have long term affects. Teachers need support and feedback as they implement new strategies for those strategies to become part of their practice.

Nearly all the coached teachers agreed that the coaching contributed to student learning *in the arts* as well as learning to read through the arts. This is an important finding in so much as one of our goals for the program was to connect teachers directly to the visual and performing arts standards for their grade. We made the standards evident by introducing them intentionally at the institute as well as placing them on the grid alongside the reading standards (example provided). Since there were virtually no arts specialists in our schools, finding that the students were also learning about the arts as a result of learning through the arts was a key positive.

The coaches reported that the majority of the coached teachers understood the fundamentals of arts infused pedagogy; and were able to successfully demonstrate the use of the arts as pedagogy in the reading curriculum. The coaches reported that a majority of the teachers were able to independently integrate the arts throughout the year, and expected they would be able to continue successful use of the arts after the coaching year.

Treatment teachers (coached and institute-only) overwhelmingly described the DREAM arts infused pedagogy as having a positive impact on student learning, both in learning about the arts as well as reading through the arts. As a result of their new strategies, teachers reported greater student engagement and enthusiasm for learning, deeper learning in and retention of reading curriculum, and improved participation and greater focus in class. According to one teacher, "The students were more motivated and involved in their learning. Teaching with art gives the students a sense of ownership and empowerment."

Many teachers described how the pedagogy motivated students. One teacher told a compelling story concerning how she came upon one of her reading groups, and realized they had moved ahead in their text onto the next story and were thoroughly immersed in reading it. She told them they were on the wrong story; that they were supposed to be on the previous story. The kids enthusiastically said they were reading ahead because they couldn't wait to see what art activities they would get to do with the story! The teacher was incredibly heartened; it was one of those "Aha! I get why this works!" moments.

"The integration of the arts," one institute only teacher reported, "has helped me connect to reading comprehension in ways that testing can simply not measure. The students are engaged and interested in reading because they know that I will ask them to create something and not just do something like a test when we complete a story. I try to always connect the art to the comprehension strategy or skill . . . I believe in my classroom, art is helping students unlock their own love for reading." Another institute only teacher put it this way, "It helped to draw the students into the stories and characters in a deeper way. They were better able to identify with the characters and the plot as well as use the vocabulary." Many teachers from both treatment groups noticed that the reading touched their students in ways it hadn't previously, for example, this teacher described how her students were able to connect more readily to the characters in their texts. "I saw my students become adept at connecting with characters we read about on an emotional level."

In the realm of relating teaching to student ownership of learning, this institute only teacher put it this way, "It has helped me to be more creative especially when a student doesn't comprehend what he/she is reading. I begin to think outside the box and try to have them make connections on how the character feels, the setting, the time and so on. They now own the information, not just rent it."

While both groups made improvements and reported glowingly about the changes in their teaching, coached teachers were better able to demonstrate their learning. Teachers in both treatment groups improved in the quality of their lesson plan over the course of the intervention year. However, coached teachers made greater improvement than did institute-only teachers, as measured on the DREAM lesson plan rubric.

In terms of aspects of reading such as vocabulary comprehension, understanding plot, and inference, teachers noted great gains in their students' abilities, which as the reader will see later in the discussion is also borne out in the test scores. Inference is an exceptionally interesting area and probably the least concrete of all the areas measured, i.e. in comparison to word comprehension, plot, or character analysis. In the institute we were intentional with regard to teaching visual literacy; however we were not intentional about connecting it to inference. In fact, it took nearly a year of discussing the use of the illustrations in practice and brainstorming activities for the DREAM team to make the connection ourselves. We realized that explicit instruction about the choices illustrators make regarding perspective, line, color shape, design, etc. enable young readers to read more into and gain more information about characters, setting, plot, or even details that an illustrator would like the reader to notice in the text or absent from it. Connecting visual literacy to inference also led us (inspired us!) to examine the connection between theater activities such as directing and its direct relationship to inference. The nature of the theater activities such as learning to act, create tableaus, improvise, or create puppet shows, provided an opportunity to search for what is "between the lines." In so doing, students consider the gestures, actions, and vocalizations of particular characters and must make those "between the lines" decisions as to how the characters come off the page and into real life.

Teachers recognized that the pedagogy was an especially effective tool for motivating and engaging their students in creative expression (a VAPA standard emphasized at the institute), especially in reaching their English Language learners:

> My students were more willing to take a risk in their second language (English), while performing, creating. They were not afraid to take chances using academic English, especially in their writing when in other years it has been difficult to build their self-esteem in the second language. They felt very motivated and extremely enthusiastic about learning core subjects. It created a bigger impact on learning.

In additional to motivating this teacher's students, the arts infused strategies increased their desire to learn: "My entire class were non-readers at the start of the year. The arts helped students improve comprehension, as well as increase their desire to learn to read."

A benefit we hadn't expected at the start of the study was the extent to which DREAM would reinvigorate teachers and bring them back to a state of being able to enjoy, even love teaching. DREAM strategies served to engage not only students in reading, but teachers in enthusiastic teaching. "[DREAM] invigorated my teaching and reminded me that even though test scores remain supreme, students love and deserve arts in their education." "I enjoy my job more. It's made me a better, happier teacher." DREAM also served to rekindle teachers' priorities even under pressure from district mandates.

A common concern that arose centered on having enough time, "How do I integrate the arts when every minute is filled with activities in the pacing guide?" One answer to this question was that the arts integrated so seamlessly into the teaching of reading, that it was not "taking time away" but rather serving as a means to teach reading skills in the curriculum. However, and despite the district mandates, teachers began to feel comfortable questioning the mandates: "DREAM reminds me that I need to make time for the arts because our kids need it. It helps me find the courage to do less 'test prep' and isolated skill work when I am under significant pressure to do prescripted lessons that kill the joy and creativity our kids can bring to learning when we allow them."

Teachers provided a wide range of responses on the open ended questions as to how the DREAM project had an effect on their teaching practice including that the project provided tangible lessons and practices, and an acknowledgment that the arts are important to a child's development/education. Institute teachers recognized that they still had more to learn. For example, one teacher wrote, "I could have been more confident if I had a coach."

Principal Findings and Discussion

Three themes emerged from our findings:

- **Arts integration pedagogy is a powerful strategy for teaching literacy in the 3rd grade:** arts integration supports reading comprehension and language arts.
- **Student reading test scores in DREAM improved by 87 points:** During DREAM's first two years of implementation, 3rd grade students in DREAM classrooms have consistently excelled on year-end test scores. In year 2, the 3rd grade students in classrooms with art coaches did exceptionally well. They began the school year as the lowest performing of all the study groups (both treatment and comparison) on the California state language arts test. However, they ended the year as the highest performing group, improving on their prior year test scores by 87 points on average.
- **Theater is an effective instructional tool in reading education:** Teachers who integrated theater into their language arts curriculum to teach reading comprehension, inference, and detail had students score higher on the state language arts test. Analysis identified that the more frequently teachers integrated theater, the more effective they perceived it as a tool for reading instruction.

As per requirements of the Arts in Education Model Development and Dissemination (AEMDD) grant, DREAM was required to develop project goals to report to the U.S. Department of Education relating to student test scores. In the first year of implementation, we found a modest impact in test scores. However, between year one and year two we adapted the institute and refocused the instructional activities and the coaching to directly relate to the reading texts and the test score exploded. Year two data, which is the focus of this next section, is where we found notable and significant results.

The overall mean 2010 and 2011 California State Test (CST) English Language Arts (ELA) scores for third and fourth grade students in each treatment group along with the comparison group are shown in Table 8.2.

Table 8.2. Student CST ELA Scores

Group	2010 Mean ELA Scores (SDs)	2011 Mean ELA Scores (SDs)	Improvement	Paired t-test
3rd Grade				
Coached (N = 361)	278.80	366	87.20	7.028, p <.001
Institute-only (N = 259)	299.15	339.86	40.71	5.331, p <.001
Comparison (N = 275)	295.58	320.87	25.29	3.246, p <.01
4th Grade				
Coached (N = 251)	325.21	354.52	29.31	6.496, p <.001
Institute-only (N = 238)	281.22	334.23	53.01	7.572, p <.001
Comparison (N = 303)	318.73	317.83	−.90	Not significant

As is evident, the treatment groups significantly outpaced the comparison groups in both grades. Third grade students in coached classrooms made the biggest improvement between 2010 and 2011 with a stunning gain of over eighty-seven points, and third grade students in the institute-only classrooms made the second largest gains of the three groups. The fourth grade students in the institute-only classrooms made the biggest improvement between 2010 and 2011 with a fifty-three point gain in test scores. Both treatment groups made statistically significant improvement between their 2010 and 2011 scale scores. The comparison group, however, did not. When we dug deeper into the subscales of the language arts test, reading comprehension, word analysis, and literary analysis sections indicated the most improvement was seen by students in treatment groups, which matched very closely to the teachers' self-reporting.

Admittedly, we were thrilled by the test scores, and at the same time we found them oddly puzzling, perhaps even a little troubling. Since our main focus for the DREAM project was teacher professional development, we weren't entirely prepared for the dramatic result.

At first glance, the findings make sense for the third grade insomuch as the students with coached teachers fared considerably better, than the other two groups. In California, students are placed on the point scale and rated according to the standards of "far below basic," "below basic," "basic," "proficient," and "advanced." The state goal is to have all students reach or exceed the proficient category in language arts and math every year. On average the majority of our treatment students began the year in the ELA at below basic. With the coaching intervention, students in the third grade DREAM classrooms on average went from below basic through basic and all the way to end the year as proficient. This is significant as California's goal is for all students to be proficient. Generally, moving students from one rating to the next in a year's time is considered successful growth.

It seems incongruent, however, that the fourth grade students in classrooms with institute-only teachers would make more gains on the standardized test than the coached teacher group. However, in both third and fourth grades, the students who made the most gains were the students who started out on average with the lowest test scores. In third grade that was the coached group, and in the fourth grade, that was the institute-only group. Furthermore, both the third and fourth graders in the treatment groups made significantly greater improvements than did the comparison group students.

As with the third grade students, fourth grade students whose teachers had the benefit of the arts coaches also ended the year having made gains on the test scores. While the fourth grade students did not make the same gains with their test scores as the institute only group (who started out much lower), they still ended with the highest average score for the fourth grade. These findings are consistent with our previous research in SUAVE. In that study we also found that third grade students outscored fourth graders on the standardized tests.

There are a few noteworthy common denominators found in the test scores. First, children in both grades who started the year with the lowest test scores, ended the year with the most gains in the test scores. Second, in both grades, students in the classrooms with the coached teachers ended the year with the highest test scores. A possible explanation for the first could be that the professional development, even on the reduced level of the institute-only training, is especially effective in helping teachers reach the students who, according to test scores, need the most help. Secondly, it could be possible that in fourth grade, there is limit on how much the arts integration professional development will impact test scores, and we have reached that limit.

Several differences distinguish third from fourth grade. Class size often increases in fourth grade. There is also a significant shift from grade three to grade four in the reading curriculum itself. In third grade, students are immersed in reading literature whereas in fourth grade there is a distinct shift to reading as an expository function. Additionally, third grade reading is more supported while fourth grade students are expected to become more independent readers. Reading test scores generally drop from third to fourth grade due to increased reading demands. The DREAM intervention is focused on literary reading, thus, it probably matches better with the third grade curriculum and expectations.

Setting the Stage for Success

To set the stage for more effective teaching in addition to enthusiasm for teaching, DREAM teachers demonstrated that they learned specific strategies within the institute and successfully applied them to their classrooms. While coached teachers were able to more effectively implement the strategies, institute-only teachers still made gains as was shown in their lessons as well as in the gains their students made on the standardized tests. After the second year of implementation in fact, we had a moral dilemma of whether or not to continue the institute-only portion of our study having seen the gains made by the coached teachers, and especially their students as exemplified through the eighty-seven point gain on the standardized test. We persevered however to more fully compare and identify the benefits and challenges of the respective models.

A challenge we faced after year one was redesigning the institute to more closely include the reading texts that the teachers used in their classrooms, so that they could see the immediate connection to their practice. Teachers don't need more to do, they need to be able to teach their curriculum more effectively and engagingly. In so doing, we built planning time into the institute so that teachers could work at grade level with each other to develop lessons. We also shaped the hands-on activities during the institute such that the teachers utilized their grade level texts and stories. The goal was not specific to a particular story within the reading textbook so much as it was to show how each story could be taught employing the arts infused pedagogy. In this way, we provided the tools for the teachers, and had them apply them directly to their curriculum, which they proved they could do.

An important question we've asked ourselves is, is DREAM replicable outside of our study and context? And, if so, how would it need to be adapted? To answer this we've considered the pros and cons of several aspects of the program, including grade level. In our opinion, and experience beyond the research study, DREAM works extremely well in lower grades, and we would like to research its effectiveness in K–2. We also believe the strategies are applicable to expository reading as well as to writing. In terms of bringing DREAM strategies to other districts and states, and for that matter toward other subjects such as math and science, the possibilities are clear. Since the emphasis on the program is pedagogy versus curriculum, the potential to adapt the strategies and implement across settings and subject matter is rich.

The Common Core Standards presents another tangible opportunity for literacy and the arts. To indicate some examples of best practice for integrating literacy and the arts, we have also adapted the chart earlier in the chapter to include the direct connections to Common Core Anchor Standards from which all grade level standards flow, as well as examples for third and fourth grade Common Core Standards. The appendix of this chapter includes the chart connecting Common Core to the arts.

MARIO AND THE ARTS

Mario, like many boys, finds reading to be a "boring activity" and doesn't think he is a good reader. He would rather be engaged in video games or doing something active with friends. Mario also says he "always talks about my ideas." Talking out loud seems to help Mario process what he reads or what he is learning. Reading infused with theater activities would be a wonderful match for Mario. Theater utilizes speaking and listening and can be very active. Mario could speak about a character, setting or plot through a puppet or by acting it out. Theater activities could engage Mario's interest in reading. Theater as a social activity is highly motivating and provides middle school students like Mario the opportunity to work in a group with their peers to create a theatrical experience together. Mario's answers to the questions also indicate that he reads at a literal level. Theater activities would be a good support to enable him to develop comprehension skills beyond the literal level to move into interpretation, application, and even analysis. We have found theater activities enabled students to read between the lines and read beyond the lines on the page.

Mario also talks about comics and how the pictures help him understand. Graphic novels have become mainstream for many ages and are popular in middle school. They could engage Mario and would be a good support to Mario's reading comprehension. Picture books can be very effective for teaching visual literacy in a middle school classroom. Adolescents see aspects of familiar picture books they did not see as young children. They can also begin to appreciate the art of illustration and how illustrations also provide details and tell stories. Understanding visual literacy and how the pictures support the story or tell the story would strengthen Mario's comprehension and engage him in reading. By reading more, he could expand his vocabulary and that in turn increases comprehension. Reading graphic novels could encourage him to write his own version of a graphic story. Becoming an author and understanding the choices authors and illustrators make provides valuable insight into the creation of a text. This understanding of the reciprocal nature of reading and writing is essential for developing and deepening the skills of both.

In DREAM, one of the delightful observations was seeing teachers reawakened to their own potential to make a difference in children's lives and learning. No doubt the spirit of joyfulness, passion, and wonder that teachers described as a result of their DREAM experiences mattered to them and their students. The arts-enabled teachers were re-engaged in teaching and learning. This is a far cry from the drudgery of following pacing guides and other imposed district curriculum that only prepare students through a narrowly focused test-prep lens. Given the opportunity to feel reinvigorated about teaching inspired and reinvested teachers to become more engaged and effective teachers and thus set the stage to become more effective in their teaching.

Sadly, over the last decade, students in high poverty schools have had less and less access to arts education overall, and low performing school sites as measured by test scores are the first to lose their arts programs. Teachers have been systematically forced into narrowing the curriculum by district mandates focusing on reading and math to the detriment of other non-tested subjects such as history and sciences. The erosion and elimination of the arts is well documented in a longitudinal study released by National Center for Education Statistics (U.S. Department of Education, 2012).

Our DREAM research, however, indicates that the stripping down of the arts, especially arts-infused pedagogy is counterproductive to the goal of raising students' academic achievement and test scores. The standardized test scores of the students in the DREAM program indicate that rather than eliminate the arts, schools should focus on infusing the arts as pedagogy in order to raise test scores. The DREAM results also serve as a poignant reminder of the limitations of traditional teaching in getting at the core of children's capabilities. We can't help but think about all the children in the control group whose teachers did not have access to the professional development. Had these children been in DREAM classrooms, their test scores would almost surely be higher as well.

Art, noted the poet Adrienne Rich (1993, p. 162), is "a vital way of perceiving and knowing." As subjects in and of themselves, the arts engage the imagination, open the spaces to be creative and innovative, and teach lessons of complexity. The teachers in the DREAM program have learned how to embrace and harness the power in the arts as a way to engage, inspire, motivate, and assess their students. Arts infused pedagogy provides significant opportunities to literacy teachers to re-engage with the art of teaching, provide effective strategies to teach reading, and set the stage for students who desire to learn, be more fully engaged and confident in learning, and feel an ownership of their learning. As we look toward a vision for arts education in the years to come, it is crystal clear, that "the arts ain't fluff." And, ensuring a place for arts in education pays big dividends. Our children deserve all of it.

REFERENCES

Batt, E. (2010). Cognitive Coaching: A Critical Phase in Professional Development to Implement Sheltered Instruction. *Teaching and Teacher Education: An International Journal of Research and Studies, 26*(4), 997–1005.

Burnaford, G. (2007). Arts Integration: Frameworks, Research and Practice, A Literature Review. Arts I.

Carson, R. (1965/1998). *The sense of wonder.* NY: HarperCollins Publishers.

Chomsky, C. (1971). Invented spelling in the open classroom. *Word,* 27, pp. 499–518.

Csikszentmihalyi, M. (2008). *Flow.* NY: Harper Perennial Modern Classics.

Desimone, L. (2009). Improving impact studies of teachers' professional development: Toward better conceptualizations and measures. *Educational Researcher, 38* (3), 181–99

Duckworth, Eleanor (2006). The having of wonderful ideas and other essays on teaching and learning (2 ed.). NY: Teachers College Press.

Gallas, K. (1991). Arts as epistemology: Enabling children to know what they know. *Harvard Educational Review, 61*(1)

Gallas, K. (1994). *The languages of learning: How children talk, write, dance, draw and sing their understanding of the world.* New York: Teachers College Press.

Gambrell, L. (2011). Seven rules of engagement: What's most important to know about motivation to read. *The Reading Teacher.* Vol. 65. Issue 3 pp. 172–78.

Gardner, H. (2006). *Multiple Intelligence*: New Horizons, NY: Basic Books.

Gardner, H. (1993). *Frames of mind: The theory of multiple intelligences* (10th anniversary ed.). New York: Basic Books.

Garet, M., Cronen, S., Eaton, M., Kurki, A., Ludwig, M., Jones, W., et al. (2008). The Impact of Two Professional Development Interventions on Early Reading Instruction and Achievement. NCEE 2008-4030. *National Center for Education Evaluation and Regional Assistance.*

Goldberg, M. & Phillips, A. (Eds.) (1992). *Arts as education.* Cambridge, MA: Harvard Educational Review Reprints Series #24.

Goldberg, M. (Ed.) (2004). *Teaching English language learners through the arts: A SUAVE experience.* NY: Pearson Education, Inc.

Goldberg, M. (2012). *Arts Integration: teaching subject matter through the arts in multicultural settings* (4 Ed.). New York: Pearson Publishing.

Goldschmidt, P. & Phelps, G. (2009). Does teacher professional development affect content and pedagogical knowledge: How much and for how long? *Economics of Education Review, 29,* 432–39.

Heath, S. B. (1999). Imaginative actuality: Learning in the arts during nonschool hours. In *Champions of change: The impact of learning on the arts.* The President's committee on Arts and Humanities.

Hetland, L., Winner, E., Veenema, S., Sheridan, K. (2007). *Studio thinking: the real benefits of visual arts education.* NY: Teachers College press.

Lewitsky, Bella (1989). Why art? University of California, San Diego regent's lecture, May 31, 1989.

Mages, W. K. (2008). Does creative drama promote language development in early childhood? A review of methods and measures employed in the empirical literature. *Review of Educational Research, 78* (1), pp. 124–52.

National Center for Education Statistics (U.S. Department of Education, 2012): http://nces. ed.gov/pubsearch/pubsinfo.asp?pubid=2012014.

Pennypacker, S. (2007). *The talented Clementine.* NY: Hyperion Books.

Podlozny, A. (2000). Strengthening verbal skills through the use of classroom drama: A clear link. *Journal of Aesthetic Education*, Vol. 34, No. 3/4, Special issue: The Arts and Academic Achievement: What the Evidence Shows (Autumn-Winter 2000).

Rich, A. (1993). *What is found there: Notebooks on poetry and politics.* NY: W.W. Norton.

Rosenblatt, L. (1994) The reader, the text and the poem: The Transactional Theory of the literary work. Southern Illinois University Press.

Rudd, L., Lambert, M., Satterwhite, M., & Smith, C. (2009). Professional Development + Coaching = Enhanced Teaching: Increasing Usage of Math Mediated Language in Preschool Classrooms. *Early Childhood Education Journal, 37*(1), 63–69.

Saraniero, P. & Goldberg, M. (2008). The Impact of Arts Integration on English Language Learners, Paper presented at the Annual meeting of the American Educational Research Association.

Winner, E. & Hetland, L. (2000). The arts and academic achievement: What the evidence shows. Double issue of *Journal of Aesthetic Education*, 34 (3–4). Fall-Winter 2000.

Table 8.3. Alignment of Title 1, Arts, and Common Core Standards

Arts activities that can be funded under Title 1	Examples of appropriate activities (illustrative)	How to determine what is allowed with Title 1 funds	Examples of activities that do not fall under Title 1
Arts integration in English Language Arts: Reading	Established programs such as: DREAM (Developing Reading Education with Arts Methods) Visual Literacy Activities connecting illustration to text and inference to support conclusions drawn from the text Theater activities to explore and understand character, setting, plot, inference Use of theater scripts, or music lyrics as reading texts	Funds may not be used to supplant direct arts instruction or be used to hire music, visual art, theater, or dance teachers. Funds may be used, however, for arts integration activities that support English language arts.	Sequential arts education in discipline-specific instruction do not fall under Title 1: Music classes Visual Arts classes Theater classes Dance classes
Arts integration in English Language Arts: Writing	Creative writing exercises to develop real or imagined events through vehicles including one-act plays, music lyrics, poetry Lessons may focus on writing about the arts, art history, or events in history that centered on arts-based movements such as the role of music in the civil rights movement. Write reviews of arts events	Funds may not be used to fund arts teachers, however, they may be used to fund activities which incorporate the arts into the writing curriculum	
Arts integration in English Language Arts: Speaking and Listening	Theatrical presentations that involve collaborations with diverse partners and that build on other's ideas and expressing their own ideas persuasively Presentation with visual media and visual displays (graphic design, video, poster boards, 3d printing)	Funds may not be used to fund arts teachers, however, they may be used to fund activities which incorporate the arts into activities that support speaking and listening standards	

(continued)

Table 8.3. (Continued)

Arts activities that can be funded under Title 1	Examples of appropriate activities (illustrative)	How to determine what is allowed with Title 1 funds	Examples of activities that do not fall under Title 1
Arts integration in English Language Arts: language (conventions, knowledge, and vocabulary acquisition)	Act out words and meanings Picto-spells (drawing the meanings of spelling words) Create dances to depict word meaning or punctuation	Funds may not be used to fund arts teachers, however, they may be used to fund activities which incorporate the arts into the curriculum for such purposes as vocabulary acquisition, grammar, etc.	
Arts Integration in mathematics	Identify works of art by artists who have incorporated symmetry as a part of their work and then create a work of art, using bilateral or radial symmetry. Create single digit addition problems by using sounds and/or movement	Funds may not be used to fund arts teachers, however, they may be used to fund activities which incorporate the arts into the math curriculum	
Arts and ELL	ELL student benefit from all of these activities as it expands their ability to communicate, express ideas, and work collaboratively with success.	Funds may not be used to fund arts teachers; however, they may be used to fund activities which incorporate the arts into supporting the learning of ELL students.	

Table 8.4. Common Core Standards alongside VAPA Standards (California) Using Grade 4 as Illustration

Common Core College and Career Readiness Anchor Standards	Arts Connections	CA Theater Standards	CA Visual Art Standard
Reading: Key ideas and details **Anchor:** Read closely to determine what the text says explicitly and to make logical inferences from it; cite specific textual evidence when writing or speaking to support conclusions drawn from the text.	**Art is Text/Art as Text** Theater scripts provide wonderful reading material perfect for close reading and for inference.	Identify universal themes in stories and plays [from different periods and places].	Look at images in figurative works of art and predict what might happen next, telling what clues in the work support their ideas.
Refer to details and examples in a text when explaining what the text says explicitly and when drawing inferences from the text.	Art pieces, i.e. paintings, sculptures, murals, as well as pieces of music are texts. Many important details can be found in illustrations. Teaching students to distinguish important details from less important details is a valuable skill that can be learned from viewing illustrations and applyingto printed text. The reverse is also true in that students can create illustrations that demonstrate their understanding of important details.		
Anchor: Determine central ideas or themes of a text and analyze their development; summarize the key supporting details and ideas.	The work of a director, or an actor developing a character depends on understanding and analyzing the script with a special attention to inference.	Identify who, what, why, where, and when in a theatrical experience.	Read biographies and stories about artists and summarize the readings in short reports, telling how the artists mirrored or affected their time period or culture.

(continued)

Table 8.4. *(Continued)*

Common Core College and Career Readiness Anchor Standards	Arts Connections	CA Theater Standards	CA Visual Art Standard
Anchor: Analyze how and why individuals, events, or ideas develop and interact over the course of a text.	Analysis is essential to both understanding and producing theater, or discussing works of art.	Use the vocabulary of the theater such as character, setting, conflict, audience, motivation, props, stage areas, and blocking to describe theatrical experiences. Identify character's objectives and motivations to explain that character's behavior. Demonstrate the emotional traits of a character through gesture and action.	Look at images in figurative works of art and predict what might happen next, telling what clues in the work support their ideas.
Describe in depth a character, setting, or event in a story or drama, drawing on specific details in the text (e.g., a character's thoughts, words, or actions).		Identifying and describing characters' traits, motivations, and feelings would most effectively be done in a theatrical performance: Readers Theater, Tableaux, or writing and acting out scripts from a story.	Predicting is an important strategy for readers. The prediction must be based on textual evidence. "Telling what clues in the work support their ideas" is using textual evidence. Illustrations in a story or picture book are works of art and students can learn to read the art. Illustrations of characters or settings provide great "text" for students to identify specific details that demonstrate mood, thoughts of characters, and motivations.

Reading: Craft and Structure

Anchor: Interpret words and phrases as they are used in a text, including determining technical, connotative, and figurative meanings, and analyze how specific word choices shape meaning or tone.

Anchor: Analyze the structure of texts, including how specific sentences, paragraphs, and larger portions of the text (e.g., a section, chapter, scene, or stanza) relate to each other and the whole.

Explain major differences between poems, drama, and prose, and refer to the structural elements of poems (e.g., verse, rhythm, meter) and drama (e.g., casts of characters, settings, descriptions, dialogue, stage directions) when writing or speaking about a text. (There are very similar standards for informational text in the standards asking students to utilize text features to locate information.)

Creative Expression and Artistic Perception (VPA standards) focus on craft and technique. Creative expression involves interpretation in addition to technical ability. Artistic perception is an ability to understand an analyze works of art.

The Language Arts standards specifically name drama and theater vocabulary in the grade standards (look left!). These standards beg for teachers to use theater in the reading classroom.

Demonstrate how voice (diction, pace, and volume) may be used to explore multiple possibilities for a live reading.

Reading aloud stories, dramas, and poems utilizing aspects of voice can help readers understand the differences between these types of texts.

Identify and describe elements of art in work of art, emphasizing line, color, shape/form, texture, space, and value.

Describe and analyze the elements of art (color/shape, line, texture, space, value), emphasizing form, as they are used in works of art and found in the environment.

(continued)

Table 8.4. *(Continued)*

Common Core College and Career Readiness Anchor Standards	Arts Connections	CA Theater Standards	CA Visual Art Standard
Anchor: Assess how point of view or purpose shapes the content and style of a text.	This fits into aesthetic valuing, a core standard in the arts—in all disciplines.		Describe and analyze the elements of art (color/shape, line, texture, space, value), emphasizing form, as they are used in works of art and found in the environment.
Compare and contrast the point of view from which different stories are narrated, including the difference between first- and third-person narrations. (Point of view also appears in the informational text standards.)	Understanding point of view is essential for comprehension and visual art or theater.	Theater can be used to explore various points of view in a story, drama, or poem. Students can act out the same story from different points of view.	Illustration (as well as other works of art) utilize point of view in very distinct ways. Readers can distinguish the point of view or perspective represented in an illustration: is it the readers? The main characters? A secondary character? The illustrators? Someone else?
Anchor: Integrate and evaluate content presented in diverse media and formats, including visually and quantitatively, as well as in words.	Arts absolutely fit beautifully into this category: *"diverse media and formats, including visually."*		
Make connections between the text of a story or drama and a visual or oral presentation of the text, identifying where each version reflects specific descriptions and directions in the text. (There are very similar standards for informational text in the standards.)		Students can demonstrate their understanding of a text through dramatizing it. They could also transform a story or text into a script with stage directions to be acted out.	Common Core Standards call for specific integration of visual arts in reading. Students can explain aspects of a text's illustration and create an illustration of text: text they read or texts they write themselves. Students can demonstrate their understanding of a text through illustrating it.

Anchor: Delineate and evaluate the argument and specific claims in a text, including the validity of the reasoning as well as the relevance and sufficiency of the evidence.

Anchor: Analyze how two or more texts address similar themes or topics in order to build knowledge or to compare the approaches the authors take.

Compare and contrast the treatment of similar themes and topics (e.g., opposition of good and evil) and patterns of events (e.g., the quest) in stories, myths, and traditional literature from different cultures.

Develop and apply appropriate criteria or rubrics for evaluating a theatrical experience.
Use problem solving and cooperative skills to dramatize a story or a current event.
Dramatize different versions of similar stories from around the world.
Identify universal themes in stories and plays from different periods and places.
Students can create puppets (in a variety of ways) of interesting characters and dramatize dialogue and scenes from stories. They can create settings on paper, shadow boxes, chart paper (and the like) and characters from stories from different cultures like fairy tales, myths, or other traditional literature.

Identify successful and less successful compositional and expressive qualities of works of art (including students' own), and describe what might be done to improve them.

Compare and describe various works of art that have a similar theme and were created at different periods.

Author *and* illustrator studies across books are an excellent means to recognize particular styles of writing and art. Studying artists who have distinctive styles such as David Weisner, Chris Van Allsburg, Marla Frazee, Lois Ehlert, Steve Jenkins, and Dav Pilkey enable students to recognize artistic styles. Additionally, authors and artists have created distinctive characters from series books like Clementine by Sarah Pennypacker, illustrated by Marla Frazee; Lilly (and her purple

(continued)

Table 8.4. *(Continued)*

Common Core College and Career Readiness Anchor Standards	Arts Connections	CA Theater Standards	CA Visual Art Standard
			plastic purse) by Kevin Henkes; Henry and Mudge by Cynthia Rylant, illustrated by Sucie Stevenson; Captain Underpants by Dav Pilkey; and Gooney Bird Greene by Lois Lowry, illustrated by Middy Thomas.
Reading: Range of Reading and Level of Text Complexity **Anchor:** Read and comprehend complex literary and informational texts independently and proficiently. By the end of the year, read and comprehend literature, including stories, dramas, and poetry, in the grades 4–5 text complexity band proficiently, with scaffolding as needed at the high end of the range.	Aesthetic valuing is a key component in teaching and understanding complexity. Poetry and drama provide a wonderful entre into understanding and digging into complexity. Reading poetry and drama aloud utilizing a variety of voice techniques and expression engage readers and listeners. Readers have to have a deep understanding of a text to demonstrate that understanding through their voice. Repeated readings to prepare a read aloud, teaches students to reread and engage in close reading strategies.	"Who has seen the wind?" is one of the suggested texts for 3rd grade. The poem lends itself well to a dramatic reading. "Casey at the bat" is one of the suggested texts for 4th grade. The narrative poem is rich with possibilities for dramatizing.	Distinguish and describe representational, abstract, and non-representational works of art.

(continued)

College and Career Readiness Anchor Standards for Speaking and Listening

Anchor: Prepare for and participate effectively in a range of conversations and collaborations with diverse partners, building on others' ideas and expressing their own clearly and persuasively.	Theater skills in particular can prepare students to be persuasive in their presentation of arguments.	Develop problem-solving and communication skills by participating collaboratively in theatrical experiences. Demonstrate the emotional traits of a character through gesture and action.
Anchor: Integrate and evaluate information presented in diverse media and formats including visually, quantitatively, and orally.	Information is routinely presented in videos, charts, and orally in arts.	Students apply what they learn in theater, film/video, and electronic media across subject areas. They develop competencies and creative skills in problem solving, communication, and time management that contribute to lifelong learning and career skills. They also learn about careers in and related to theater.
Anchor: Evaluate a speaker's point of view, reasoning, and use of evidence and rhetoric.	Aesthetic valuing in the arts teaches these skills.	Students critique and derive meaning from works of theater, film/video, electronic media, and theatrical artists on the basis of aesthetic qualities. Develop and apply appropriate criteria or rubrics for critiquing performances as to characterization, diction, pacing, gesture, and movement.

Table 8.4. *(Continued)*

Common Core College and Career Readiness Anchor Standards	Arts Connections	CA Theater Standards	CA Visual Art Standard
Anchor: Present information, findings, and supporting evidence such that listeners can follow the line of reasoning and the organization, development, and style that are appropriate to task, purpose, and audience.		Create for classmates simple scripts that demonstrate knowledge of basic blocking and stage areas.	Construct diagrams, maps, graphs, timelines, and illustrations to communicate ideas or tell a story about a historical event.
Anchor: Make strategic use of digital media and visual displays of data to express information and enhance understandings of presentations.	Art skills will come in handy in this category!	Students apply processes and skills in acting, directing, designing, and script writing to create formal and informal theater, film/videos, and electronic media productions and to perform in them.	
Anchor: Adapt speech to a variety of contexts and communicative tasks demonstrating command of formal English when indicated or appropriate.			

Note: To build a foundation for college and career readiness, students must have ample opportunities to take part in a variety of rich, structured conversations—as part of a whole class, in small groups, and with a partner. Being productive members of these conversations requires that students contribute accurate, relevant information; respond to and develop what others have said; make comparisons and contrasts; and analyze and synthesize a multitude of ideas in various domains.

Note: New technologies have broadened and expanded the role that speaking and listening play in acquiring and sharing knowledge and have tightened their link to other forms of communication. Digital texts confront students with the potential for continually updated content and dynamically changing combinations of words, graphics, images, hyperlinks, and embedded video and audio.

Look at images in figurative works of art and predict what might happen next, telling what clues in the work support their ideas. Identify successful and less successful compositional and expressive qualities of their own works of art and describe what might be done to improve them. Select an artist's work and, using appropriate vocabulary of art, explain its successful compositional and communicative qualities.

9

Promoting Agency, Access, and Acquisition Among Adolescent English Language Learners

Kathleen A. J. Mohr, Michelle Flory, and Lois Ann Knezek

It has been well documented that English Language Learners (ELLs) often need specialized support to achieve on par with their native-English-speaking peers in school. Although 65 percent of the ELLs in our schools were born in the United States (NCELA, 2007), approximately 75 percent of students classified as ELLs continue to score below the proficient level in reading on the National Assessment of Educational Progress assessments (NCES, 2009). The achievement gap between the ELL population and their native-speaking peers is marked. Interestingly, in both 4th and 8th grades, the gap between non-ELL and ELL Hispanic students was greater than those between White and non-ELL Hispanic students' scores. The achievement gap, therefore, is in some ways, a language proficiency gap. In part, this is because ELLs are assessed in content areas (i.e., math and science) before they have gained sufficient English language proficiency. Unfortunately, despite several years in U.S. schools, many ELLs remain behind their native-speaking peers. Moreover, approximately two-thirds of ELLs come from low-income families (NCELA, 2007), which correlates with reduced access to books, language interaction, and positive education experiences (Hart & Risley, 1995). The population of ELLs is projected to double by 2015 (NCELA, 2007,) which makes the need for improved educational opportunities for this population a national imperative.

The challenge to achieve is especially taxing for adolescent ELLs who are still developing English-language proficiency as they negotiate the emotional, social, and academic difficulties that characterize secondary school. Middle- and high-school students must adjust to different teachers and classes, manage school-related expectations outside of school, and negotiate peer-influenced social demands. For adolescent ELLs, doing well in school also involves developing both conversational and academic English and dealing with culturally bound social differences. These social and academic challenges demand much of adolescents who are quite vulnerable, even at-risk for disenfranchisement. Additionally, according to Wigfield, Eccles, and Pintrich, (1996) "Adolescents' success in making this developmental transition is complicated by a major increase in the difficulty of the academic work that is assigned in middle or junior high schools" (p. 46). With the challenge to succeed on school-based accountability measures and their social and economic exigencies, it is not surprising that the drop-out rate among ELLs, particularly Hispanic students, has been approximately 40 percent (NCELA, 2007).

Both higher-education and job opportunities in the United States expect proficiency in English (listening, speaking, reading, and writing,) as well as computer literacy skills. Politicians note that the U.S. economy needs a well-trained, capable workforce to participate in the global market. Essentially, a chance at the "American Dream" generally requires the ability to function and negotiate in English. Simply stated, to reach the expected levels of academic achievement, ELLs must learn in English while learning English. This is a challenging process. Essentially, ELLs must work doubly hard to achieve the same educational goals. They must acquire and learn the fundamentals of the English language system while learning academic content knowledge and are expected to make grade-level progress year after year. As recent state and federal funding efforts have evidenced, student achievement at the middle and high-school levels, especially among minority students is a national concern. Unfortunately, research in these areas is scant and professional development still insufficient (Ballantyne, Sanderman, & Levy, 2008; Dutro & Kinsella, 2010) at a time when the Common Core State Standards (CCSS) are stressing the need for more critical reading and rigorous language use among all students (National Governors Association Center for Best Practices, NGACBP & Council of Chief State School Officers, CCSSO, 2010).

Even if well intended, most teachers are not well prepared to teach English to nonnative speakers, especially those in middle and high school. Only four states require all prospective teachers to demonstrate competencies in teaching ELLs (Ballantyne et al., 2008) and many current teachers have had little formal training to support ELLs' language development and academic achievement. Much of what is currently offered as professional development regarding ESL concerns is superficial and difficult to put into action for long-term effects (Eun & Heining-Boynton, 2007). Content-area teachers tend to assume language proficiency, rather than take responsibility for fostering it among their ELL students, although recently there has been increased focus on the critical role of oral language as the foundation of subsequent learning across content areas (August & Shanahan, 2008; Dutro & Kinsella, 2010). Understanding how first language develops and is supported certainly relates to how second language can be developed. But, second-language development has its own peculiarities (Birch, 2002; Coleman & Goldenberg, 2010) that are not often addressed in teacher education programs (Ballantyne, et al., 2008).

Fortunately, although not adequately addressed in teacher education programs, much is known about how to support ELLs' acquisition of English. Stephen Krashen and others have been studying language acquisition processes for 30 plus years.

Many books have been published recently to equip teachers to attend to the needs of ELL students. Each month several articles in the field of education are devoted to the instructional support of ELLs. The available information about ELLs comes from several fields and philosophical perspectives, including linguistics, bilingual programs, heritage language pedagogy, socio-cultural literacy perspectives, and culturally relevant teaching premises. Consuming this, sometimes hodgepodge of, information can be somewhat overwhelming, especially for neophyte teachers or those who are assigned to work with older students who have a short time to achieve English proficiency. In addition to pedagogical issues, teachers of adolescents need to understand the psychological aspects of school achievement. The research of Wigfield and Eccles (2000) has shown that students' values for academics tend to decrease as they move through middle school.

Interestingly, although adolescents' ability-related beliefs and values become more negative about reading and math, there is an increase in the value of English. Explanations of these trends are speculative, but point to a need to understand students' views. Put simply, there remains a need for a more coherent framework about how to improve instruction and support achievement for ELLs, especially those who may be already lagging behind their peers in achievement. In a sense, there is a need for teachers to have hope and build hope in students who may lack an optimistic view of their futures. Such a framework must combine what is known from a variety of research fields and myriad theoretical perspectives. For example, what should middle school teachers know about ELLs' engagement and motivation to develop English as an academic language in an English language arts course, or how can a middle school science teacher support student achievement when ELL students are reading well below grade level? These are realistic problems that need a fresh perspective, a new frame of reference for practicing teachers.

A NEW FRAME OF REFERENCE FOR ENGLISH LANGUAGE LEARNERS IN MIDDLE SCHOOL CLASSROOMS

Despite renewed interest in bilingual programs, most ELLs spend the large majority of their time in regular classrooms. Classroom teachers have primary responsibility for all their students' academic success. Yet, many classroom teachers have limited knowledge of linguistics and second-language (L2) learning. Although trained in language pedagogy, many ESL teachers have limited experience in classroom teaching and have not experienced the second language process themselves. In addition, for various reasons, pull-out ESL programs have not proven particularly effective in serving the needs of most ELLs (De Jong & Harper, 2005; Ramirez, Yuen, & Ramey, 1991). Learning with and from native speakers has been shown to be better than being isolated from them in ancillary programs (Carhill, Suárez-Orozco, & Páez, 2008; Gersten, 1996; Short, 1999). It is the regular classroom where ELLs can and should thrive. August and Shanahan (2008) cite research that holds that instruction for ELLs should be "comprehensive and multidimensional" (p. 227); in other words, ELLs profit from enriched instruction rather than reductive approaches, especially from supportive and significant adults. It may seem counter-intuitive to propose that instead of basic instruction for those who are behind in their academic standing, teachers should consider how to enrich their teaching to help ELLs make accelerated progress (Mohr, 2004). However, remedial programs have never accelerated students nor covered the curriculum in a way that maximizes students' time in school. Thus, alternatives might afford a different approach to teaching ELLs that is both more effective and efficient.

To address the need for grade-level growth, classroom teachers need to use recommended practices to facilitate and accelerate the language and academic success of ELLs. Despite a plethora of scenarios, anecdotes, and examples of ELLs describing successes and failures, it can be difficult to come to a consensus about good ELL instruction. A key principle is that truly effective instruction targets the whole student within an understanding of their associated cultures and contexts. Especially at the middle-school level, teachers need to acknowledge the social, emotional, personal, and academic challenges that students face and consider a more holistic approach to meeting their needs.

As professionals, teachers should make carefully determined decisions to support their students. Teachers can influence students positively and negatively, largely in the quality of their teaching-learning interactions as they impact students' orientations toward learning tasks (Lehtinen, Vauras, Salonen, Olkinuora, & Kinnunen, 1995). As trivial as it may sound, teachers can make a difference. One way to approach their decision-making process regarding how to support ELLs is to consider recommended practices as a menu of instructional options. Rather than a checklist approach to improving instruction, using a menu of recommended practices enables teachers to make professional decisions about refining their instruction in a practical way. This chapter presents several domains of recommended practices that educators can use to evaluate their programs and to plan for more effective support of ELLs. Therefore, what follows will address the need to use research-based recommendations from several fields of study to provide ELLs with an environment that supports their personal agency so that they can access available resources in order to acquire the language and literacy that they need to achieve.

THEORETICAL FRAMEWORK

The perspective espoused in this chapter reflects some long-held tenets. For instance, Plato acknowledged the power of language and used higher-order questions to challenge his followers. Subsequently, advocates of associationism (Sternberg, 1996) emphasized making connections that for language learners can include noticing and utilizing the connections between their native tongue and the dominant language of their schools. From structuralism, an early school of psychology (Tracey & Morrow,

2006), came the notion that learning involves practiced skills and that rehearsal can promote accuracy and efficiency. The field of psycholinguistics advanced the study of discourse and contends that teachers can use language to promote more sophisticated cognition via elaboration. These perspectives offer some viable ways to broaden and improve teaching and learning processes. But, social cognitive theory as explained by Bandura (2006) and hope theory (Snyder, 2000), provide an enhanced perspective for helping adolescents maximize their time in school. If ELL youths are to make satisfactory progress in English-dominant classrooms, teachers must support their academic achievement, which, in part, is determined by their sense of self and views of their futures.

Perhaps one of the most useful theoretical perspectives for teachers of adolescent ELLs is social-cognitive theory and its fundamental tenet of self-efficacy. Self-efficacy, as defined by Zimmerman and Cleary (2000) is "the belief in one's effectiveness in performing specific tasks" (p. 45,) which "influences one's capability to originate and direct actions for given purposes" (p. 45). Zimmerman and Cleary go on to describe self-efficacy as "a forethought process within self-regulation models because of its proactive impact on performance and self-evaluative processes following performance" (p. 48).

In the vernacular, self-efficacy is "what we think about what we can do to get things done" and relates to personal agency. Adolescents need a strong sense of self— personal agency—to withstand peer-pressure and the "downward cycle of academic achievement that may involve aligning themselves with peers who possess unfavorable views about the value and importance of school" (Zimmerman & Cleary, 2000, p. 46). A key to personal agency is belief in one's ability to be self-regulating. From a social cognitive perspective, self-regulation has been defined as self-generated thoughts, feelings, and actions that are planned and cyclically adapted based on performance feedback to attain self-set goals (p. 56). Self-regulation can be thought of as a cycle that includes: forethought, performance control, and self-evaluation. Thus, self-regulated behavior begins with beliefs about what to do that is then put into action and the associated processes that are monitored. Self-regulated processes yield outcomes that can be evaluated for their effectiveness; this assessment process can, in turn, inform future processes.

Self-regulated behavior involves motivation, which has been defined by social cognitive researchers as a process in which goal-directed behavior is instigated and sustained (Pintrich & Schunk, 2002). "Motivation can manifest itself in various forms such as effort, persistence, and choice of activities—indexes that are hypothesized to be influenced by students' self-efficacy (Bandura, 1977, p. 51). Decisions to persist, exert effort, and select activities are cognitive judgments, not estimations of one's self-worth or equivalent to self-esteem (Zimmerman & Clearly, 2000). They contribute more to academic achievement than affective views.

Another field of psychology promotes hope theory (Snyder, 2000) and defines hope as "a positive motivational state that is based on an interactively derived sense of successful (a) agency (goal-directed energy) and (b) pathways (planning to meet goals)" (p. 8). Snyder and colleagues note that "goals provide the endpoints or anchors of mental action sequences; they are the anchors of hope theory" (p. 9). Having goals and recognizing possible pathways to reach them make hope a cognitive process, not an emotion. Extant research on hope recommends solution-focused, narrative, and cognitive retraining. According to hope theorists, building hope is a cognitive task, but both present-centered and future-oriented. Hopeful thinking uses the present to envision the future and focuses on setting goals and planning pathways to reach them. This process requires agency, that motivational component or "can do" attitude that keeps us moving along the pathway to a goal.

Fortunately, having hope, academic agency (Wigfield & Eccles, 2000) and the self-efficacy that reflects personal agency are related and can be developed. Therefore, ELL pedagogies should include an understanding of social cognitive aspects of achievement. This viewpoint counters the tendency to use more behavioristic, remedial, or socio-cultural pedagogies with ELLs. One over-riding issue related to success with ELLs is the need for communication that makes a difference in how they view themselves, their lives, their academic opportunities, and futures.

While social cognitive theorists provide extended discussion of students, there is much less mention of teachers and how they can use talk and tasks to persuade students and enhance their academic identities. Teachers can, in fact, help students who lack hope or agency by sharing them by proxy—teacher modeling of productive approaches. An important aspect of social cognitive theory is its assumption that an individual's social milieu is a primary determinant of his or her functioning, attitudes, and beliefs (Bandura, 1986). Classrooms can provide a context for teacher mentoring and modeling that promotes a more productive perspective for students who may need it the most.

> Adolescent students do not have to act or engage in an activity to learn or to feel confident in their abilities. Rather, their sense of efficacy can be either enhanced or lowered by the behaviors *and/or* feedback given by important individuals in their lives such as parents, teachers, counselors, and peers. Social agents promote positive perceptions of efficacy in adolescents by either using various forms of verbal persuasion (e.g., encouragement, progress feedback) or by modeling specific strategies, behaviors, or thoughts. (Zimmerman & Cleary, 2006, p. 63–64)

The premise for this chapter is that adolescent ELLs may need positive social agents in their lives to model and communicate productive perspectives about schooling. As part of positive educational experiences, teachers can serve as "learning coaches" in order to help ELLs deal with the emotional, social, linguistic, and academic challenges that they face in school. Similar to the concept of a life coach, a learning coach helps learners to understand their circumstances, set goals, and employ appropriate strategies to meet those goals. Additionally, life or learning coaches realize that they must equip their clients with how to deal with difficulties and how to persevere when they encounter setbacks. The goal is to develop the outlook, the skills, and tenacity to become independent of the coach.

Broadening the role of a content-area teacher to include that of learning coach may seem impractical. But, self-efficacy, hope, and agency are positively correlated to motivation, so teachers who coach their students toward success are promoting more motivated learning—a perennial challenge in educational settings. Increasing motivation benefits the teacher and students, individually and collectively. Motivation makes for more enlivened instruction and engaged students complete more assignments on time and are more successful on assignments, which makes grading them more gratifying and less arduous for teachers. Thus, the benefits of promoting students' self-efficacy as a part of the school program positively impact pupils and staff.

CONSIDERING MARIO RAMOS
FROM A SOCIAL-COGNITIVE PERSPECTIVE

Mario, the subject of the shared case study, affords an opportunity to apply a social cognitive framework to understand some missed opportunities to support his academic achievement in a middle school setting. A few key elements should be noted. Mario's English is considered fluent, but Spanish is often spoken at home, which likely indicates that his exposure to academic English happens primarily at school. His language and scholastic development seem sketchy. He is reportedly two to three years behind in his reading, which indicates a serious achievement gap. He is allowed to go to the Resource Room for forty minutes per day, which functions in some ways as a pull-out program. But as is common, it seems that this special support focuses on getting assignments done, not in catching him up with his peers in language skills or academic content. Nor does it likely contribute to building identity as a capable student.

Importantly, from the interview presented, Mario evidences low efficacy as a reader with limited value expressed for school reading. He does express an interest in fantasy as a genre, enjoys comics and computer-based gaming, which are also valued by his peers. But it appears from his comments that he doesn't recognize reading and writing as social activities, except for texting, which he classifies as a non-standard discourse. Otherwise, he doesn't acknowledge real-world applications of his reading and writing skills, including some twenty-first century literacy skills (NCTE, 2013,) such as choosing books at the appropriate level from the library, engaging in oral and written discourse socially and through technology, and using virtual outlets to engage in story narratives. He most likely is basing his "bad reader" status on his attempts to develop academic literacy skills. The running record confirms his insufficient decoding skills, but demonstrates stronger comprehension. He seems to have not developed the word analysis skills that would help him more accurately read grade-level texts. It would be interesting to know if he would perform as well or better on a comparable expository text or if his limited vocabulary might be even a more prominent factor with informational reading.

Mario reflects what many middle school ELLs who struggle in reading experience. Initially, Mario claims to not be a good reader, but with prompting from the interviewer, reveals many opportunities to interact with text and develop his language and reading skills. Mario is not necessarily a passive reader, nor is he resisting text (Brozo, 1991), which often happens to adolescents who struggle in reading. This knowledge provides the teacher with a jumping off point to help Mario see his own learning and literacy strengths.

Perhaps most salient in Mario's interview is his diminished sense of empowerment about his schooling. His words reveal a major disconnect between school, his personal life, and his future. He doesn't seem to see his bilingualism as a strength, which is unfortunate. He doesn't realize that he has a glimpse of some strategies that could stimulate his learning, when he ventures that he could improve by reading "harder books little by little." There are some highlights in his message, especially his mention of finding a preferred literary genre and a desire to write. Poetically, Mario acknowledges, "Each time I read a fantasy book, it's kind of like giving me thousands of ideas in my mind." (It would be interesting to learn if his teachers know his interest in reading or writing fantasy.) While the case study focuses on Mario as a strategic reader, it doesn't focus on determining if Mario could be a more strategic learner and problem-solver in general.

Mario's situation, as revealed in the interview, demonstrates that in typical school programs, many adolescent ELLs have developed a negative view of themselves as learners, which limits their participation and subsequent success in school. Can singular teachers offset such negative dispositions to meet the needs of such students? Although a challenge, classroom teachers must do what they can to reach and raise the hopes of their students, including those who may be most discouraged about their learning potentials. In fact, according to McDermott, Hasting, Callahan, & Gariglietti (1998, as cited in Snyder, 2000), Hispanic and Native American students score significantly lower than Caucasian and African American peers on hope scales.

From a social cognitive framework, Mario needs help in recognizing his strengths and how to use them to offset his weaknesses. Mario needs to realize that he has resources and by using available resources, he would have more opportunities, socially and scholastically. Mario would benefit from hearing a different message from his teachers and being able to talk about himself, his reading and writing development, from a more futuristic perspective. Could a teacher help Mario think differently about himself as a reader and writer and as a learner? What could a learning coach do for Mario and students like him?

SUPPORTING ADOLESCENT ELLS
WITH A SOCIAL COGNITIVE PERSPECTIVE

What follows are some practical ways for teachers to serve as learning coaches, especially for ELLs who are developing language while learning grade-level content. The numerous recommendations are clustered under three broad headings: agency, access, and accelerated acquisition. It is posited that disenfranchised students first need to see themselves as more capable learners who can, at least in part, orchestrate their futures by productive work in the present. Secondly, schools and classroom teachers must help students access the various resources available to them, especially their personal resources that often go unrecognized. Thirdly, the goal of accelerated progress must be communicated and facilitated in the classroom. The recommendations are intended as suggestions, not prescriptions, but teachers are encouraged to assess themselves and target which suggestions might be best to monitor or implement to improve their educational effectiveness.

AGENCY

According to Bandura (2005), "social cognitive theory analyzes developmental changes across the life span in terms of evolvement and exercise of human agency" (p. 1). Thus, from an agentic perspective (Bandura, 2005; Snyder, 2000), humans have the opportunity for continual self-renewal. Because people are potentially self-organizing, proactive, self-regulating, and self-reflective, "they are contributors to their life circumstances not just products of them" (Bandura, 2005, p. 3). Agency, thus, entails intentionality, forethought that includes making plans for the future, and self-regulation, which includes setting and abiding by personal standards. Self-regulation can be thought of as self-examination of thoughts and actions. That is, learners can intentionally plan for their success and monitor progress towards their goals. According to Bandura, "among the mechanisms of human agency, none is more central or pervasive than beliefs of personal efficacy. This core belief is the foundation of human motivation, well-being, and accomplishments" (p. 3). Personal efficacy—the belief that goals can be met via personal action—enables learners to take on challenges, to apply perseverant effort, view difficulties more positively, control their emotions, and make better choices.

To develop personal efficacy, the main ingredient to student agency, teachers should model personal efficacy, extend efficacy by proxy, and develop collective agency among their colleagues and students. Essentially, teachers can model, extend, and coach students to be more efficacious, to believe in themselves and their opportunities to succeed. To target the development of student efficacy and agency, teachers can consider the following refinements to their instructional approach.

Establish a Classroom Community That Welcomes and Challenges All Students

Although difficult to accomplish, classroom teachers should seek a balance between being warm and open (welcoming) and communicating high expectations for their students. Being friendly (and fun) does not necessarily challenge students to see learning as their "job." Teachers and students need to hold a vision for their futures that is connected to the work that they are doing in school. Some general ways to welcome and connect students to the classroom learning community include: knowing students and their families, personalizing learning with student examples, and honoring students' questions. More specifically, this approach can include standing at the door to welcome students into class, conversing positively with students as they enter, following up on personal incidents, noting individual achievements and qualities that will help students see themselves as capable. Essentially, welcoming classrooms are those where teachers strive to relate personally to and teach individual students, despite their being grouped as classes. Focusing on individuals rather than the class can make a powerful difference in the quality of student engagement.

A characteristic noted in research on effective teachers is the ability to share just enough humor and personal information to appear human, without becoming unprofessional (Mohr, 1998). The ability to be appropriately disclosive is often challenged by the current TMI-generation, but affords a valuable link between teacher and students.

Often it is the personal connection between teacher and student that helps disenfranchised students become motivated about learning and willing to be challenged at school. Such interactions can be facilitated by teachers appropriately using online communication networks that are established and monitored according to school safety policies.

In challenging classrooms, teachers establish clear learning expectations for their students and communicate them consistently. The instructional pace is swift and geared toward high-level, but obtainable, objectives. Lofty learning goals are reachable when the tasks are broken down into do-able components and clearly explained as parts of the whole. Put differently, teachers should foster a can-do spirit, modeling commensurate teacher-talk and coaching students to follow their example. For example, when a student queries, "Ah, do we have to do that?" can the teacher respond with, "Well, I don't see why we wouldn't want to do that?" Or, "we can do it together." In a study of effective reading teachers (Mohr 1998), it was found that they used a lot of collaborative discourse, such as "we" and "together" and "help one another" to communicate cooperation and encourage perseverance among their students. (Teachers might want to record themselves during a lesson to listen for how challenging and yet supportive their language is during critical instruction.) Teachers can also use cue cards (e.g., "This is a challenge we can accept" or "Trying is a part of triumph!") to prompt themselves and their students to use more productive language and practice more motivated perspectives during instruction. Tables 9.1 and 9.2 present some other ways to organize classroom instruction to develop student agency and for developing effective classroom rules and routines.

Establishing a positive and productive learning environment generally includes various participation structures, including whole group and cooperative learning. ELLs can benefit from small-group or partner configurations, especially, if paired

Table 9.1. Tips for Organizing Classroom Instruction to Develop Student Agency

1. Make classroom rules evident and focused on cooperative learning.
2. State expectations for individual participation and success (e.g., "I expect to hear some interesting ideas from you in this lesson.")
3. Structure classroom routines in order to focus on learning (not just student management).
4. Give clear directions that respect students as learners. (For example, "I know that we have done similar tasks before, but this time I want to see if you have mastered this concept, so please, take this seriously. It will show me if we are ready to move on to more advanced concepts.")
5. Use in-depth study of topics and thematic units so students feel challenged, not merely occupied.
6. Use interactive and cooperative classroom methods that strengthen community and collective agency (a "we can do this" mentality).
7. Model attitudes that reflect that students are academically able.
8. Create a classroom community that emphasizes responsibility and ownership.
9. Encourage effort and perseverance at every opportunity.
10. Foster self-regulation and time management.

Table 9.2. Tips for Developing Effective Classroom Rules and Routines

1. Classroom rules should respect the students.
2. Keep rules positive and succinct (e.g., Help others learn).
3. Rules should target: safety, self-control, personal responsibility, public courtesy, and a productive work ethic.
4. Post, explain, demonstrate, and rehearse rules; explain how the rules apply to various activities.
5. Revise rules as needed, but avoid confusing students about classroom expectations.
6. Praise students specifically as they learn and apply the agreed-upon rules.
7. Communicate the message that students are expected to be active learners.

with native speakers and trained to participate fully. However, students from some cultural backgrounds are not as familiar with typical ways of participating productively and may need to learn how to make contributions and to learn with and from other students. It is important that participation practices not be power based, where certain students tend to be in charge and tell others what to think and do. Successful group tasks are not easily managed; nor do they eliminate the need for strong, direct instruction. Teachers should acknowledge students' successful participation and indicate how their participation helps them and others learn. Group work and all classroom routines should maximize learning and "time-on-task" practice and application of what has been taught. Students should participate in carrying out various tasks as citizens of the classroom community and there is the possibility that such roles can grant ELLs some status with their peers (e.g., being assigned as group leaders). Finally, in a well-managed classroom, there should also be time to attend to social and personal problems that, left unattended, could detract from the focus on learning. Response or dialogue journals can sometimes communicate issues that might need the teacher's attention to keep a student on track.

Appreciate and Integrate Students' Prior Experiences

In middle and high-school classrooms, teachers are often most concerned with teaching their assigned subjects and they often assume that students have little interest or background knowledge to bring to the topics they need to cover. Presuming just the opposite, despite what students might confess, may be a much more productive approach. Expecting students to make connections between their background experiences and new learning requires that teachers learn more from and about their students and communicate to students that they should find ways to relate to the instruction, which is a way of developing ownership.

To better know students and their backgrounds, it can be fruitful to spend a little time surveying their interests and background experiences. Knowing who has a part-time job, or siblings living in another state or country, can be vital pieces of information. Table 9.3 lists steps that teachers can take to know and use students' prior knowledge and experiences:

Table 9.3.   Steps Teachers Can Take to Get to Know ELL Students

1. Use informal assessments (e.g., journal entries, checklists, personal reflections) to support each student's sense of self).
2. Design tasks for success and a sense of personal improvement. (Instructing in micro-steps requires careful, sequential planning.)
3. Give ongoing feedback so students are aware of their progress (e.g., lesson wrap-ups, journal comments, weekly updates on targeted tasks, conferences).
4. Acknowledge available internal and external resources, including school personnel, parents, and technology. (Promote an Information-Age mentality that encourages people to get answers from a variety of sources.)
5. Help students manage information for parents so that families are informed and involved. (Assume a positive stance on parents and extended family, realizing that it is not easy to keep up with the myriad, on-going activities in schools, especially if one is new to the American educational system.)

ACCESS

To those outside the classroom walls, schools can be viewed as providing equal opportunities for all students. In the American compulsory educational system, it is assumed that schooling is quite democratic. Unfortunately, however, there are great inequities and not all students have the same access to educational opportunities. Many students do not feel as if they even belong in school. Osterman (2000) found that, "students' experiences of acceptance influences multiple dimensions of their behavior but that schools adopt organizational practices that neglect and may actually undermine students' experience of membership in a supportive community" (p. 323). Educators should consider the ways that some students are denied access to education. For example, if students don't have personal computers at home, they are likely to be less adept in using computers and not as able to use the Internet to support their learning. If students' use of conversational English is still developing, they may not be able to ask questions or interact with other students and adults in ways that enhance their learning. If the only curriculum materials provided to students are from grade leveled textbooks, then an ELL who is struggling with language and reading skills will not have access to the content therein. If students are tracked into lower-level courses because they or their parents are not counseled about their curricular options, they do not get the same education as their more-informed, college-bound peers. Adolescent ELLs may be the first in the family to aspire to a high-school degree, and although their parents may support this goal, they might have limited understanding of what to do to manage the system.

While too many of the educational inequities that adolescent ELLs encounter are systemic, many are teacher specific. Individual teachers can more readily analyze their instruction and classroom policies for possible inequities. Perhaps the most fundamental way that teachers deny students to a quality education is by not providing solid, sequenced, high-level instruction. By improving their day-to-day teaching, teachers can immediately ameliorate their students' access to a better life in school and beyond. For ELLs, mastering English will afford incredible access to the printed word that is available via the Internet and prepare them for better jobs and post-secondary schooling. To overlook the development of their English literacy, even out of "niceness," is an insidious way to deny ELLs access to educational opportunities. Fortunately, there are ways to target and increase ELLs' access to educational opportunities.

Plan Purposeful Tasks That Use Language Productively

One aspect of social cognitive theory is the development of efficacy by proxy, which means that teachers can model productive thinking that helps their students to take academic risks. That is, teachers can "talk the talk" by using the language of learning strategies (Zimmerman & Cleary, 2006) and hope for the future (Snyder, 2000) so that students adopt them. For example, teacher think-alouds entail the teacher talking out loud about how he/she worked to make sense of a reading. In math, teachers might explain aloud how they worked through a problem. But, "talking the talk" should go beyond the heuristics and algorithms of subject matter. Teachers can vocalize a more positive approach to life by talking about their success or lack thereof on challenging tasks. Giroux (1995) argues for the development of "transformative intellectuals," which requires a discourse that "unifies a language of critique with a language of possibility" (Rossatto, 1994, p. 139). Attribution theory (Weiner, 1986) posits that beliefs about causes affect our motivation. Attributions for success and failure are categorized into four sources: ability, effort, task difficulty, and luck. In general, if we achieve success, it is more productive to attribute our success to our abilities as belief in our capacity motivates us to make future attempts. However, it is most productive to view failures as a result of a lack of effort or the difficulty of the task. If we attribute lack of success to our not having tried hard enough or in disproportion of the task, we are likely to exert more effort and not avoid similar tasks in the future. So, when adolescent students are ready to give up to avoid possible failure in front of their peers do teachers help them persevere by encouraging students to work smarter and to persevere because the task is challenging? Less-motivated students can be trained to use attributes that focus them in increasing effort, as well as appropriate strategy use (Mohr, 1998). In other words, students can be encouraged to work harder and smarter, rather than attribute academic difficulties to less-controllable factors, such as low ability or fate.

Attribution theory is an interesting and complex subject, but one that teachers and athletic coaches should understand enough to promote diligent effort among adolescents who want to make things look easy. (Mario evidenced some of this casualness in his interview.) Of course, failure is a part of life and students will encounter lack of success quite normally. However, some students are pessimistic about their lives and accept failure, while others are more optimistic and less defined by setbacks. In a study of optimism among Latino middle schoolers in a high-achieving school, Mohr, Robles-Goodwin, and Wilhelm (2009) found significant differences between genders and their perceptions of scholastic success. A key finding was that even in a very supportive and highly academic program, some ostensibly successful students are quite pessimistic about their futures. Assessing and monitoring students' perceptions about their abilities to learn and communicating that extra effort is the key to offsetting lesser ability or a more difficult task can help develop learning stamina among otherwise lethargic learners. In the classroom, teachers can coach students on how to use their time wisely, point out the more difficult parts of a task or test, remind students of test-taking strategies, or suggest ways to pace themselves in order to complete a demanding assignment. Students often need help to gauge the amount of effort needed for a task to increase persistence and increase the likelihood of success. This success coaching can include large group guidelines and rehearsed group-speak, but attribution training is more successful when applied with students in one-on-one comments made relative to specific performances. For example, do teachers talk to students to pinpoint why they might have done better or worse on one quiz in order to help them prepare better for the next?

Successful students tend to be more motivated and may not need praise or attribution training. But, to facilitate success, teachers should help students set specific goals that focus on the learning process, rather than outcomes. This is the crux of emphasizing mastery goals versus outcome goals (Schunk & Swartz, 1993). Students who focus on improving themselves in incremental steps tend to be more motivated than those focused on final products or performances, such as major tests. While they cannot do away with mandated tests, teachers can emphasize the day-to-day learning efforts and accomplishments of their students. Using mottos and mantras can help students focus on their immediate learning. For instance, to promote a hard-working focus on daily improvement, one teacher posted and had students recite the following:

Good, better, best—we shall never rest.
Until our good is better and our better is our best.

Another kind of classroom discourse that can support adolescents is future talk, which is, in part, a form of persuasion. If the teacher discusses students in the future tense, students begin to think more about their life trajectories. Connecting their classroom work with their tomorrow-opportunities provides incentive and a stronger sense of self. Assignments can often be easily adapted to include ways students might use their knowledge and skills in the real-world or in their futures. Reading about new jobs associated with the burgeoning technology field might help students realize the need for strong communication skills that are the foundation of many successful careers. Exploring ways that bilingualism relates to the job market might encourage ELLs to value their first or family languages and seek ways to maintain their native tongues. Classroom discourse is a vital part of any instructional program, yet teachers rarely analyze what dominates their own teacher talk for ways that could better motivate students. Table 9.4 lists ways to use language to increase student success in the classroom.

Table 9.4. Tips for Using Language to Increase Success on Tasks in the Classroom

1. Use language and routines to focus on quality instruction and productive interactions.
2. Keep directions brief, positive, and courteous.
3. Monitor your language for tone and clarity.
4. Repeating directions and acting them out can help ELLs comprehend more.
5. Do not talk down or sound irritated when students do not understand your English.
6. It can be helpful to explain how following directions will improve learning opportunities. (For example, point out key aspects of a text or assignment or highlight the segments that might be especially challenging or which are worth more points in the grading.)
7. Schools typically communicate both competitive and cooperative expectations; use them appropriately to support the classroom community and personal effort. Point out to students when and how they are to be cooperative and when and how they are to do their own work.
8. Teacher talk should include: *I believe you can; you're getting it; that's good thinking; we need you to help others; what should happen next; so, how can you put that knowledge to good use?*
9. Promote a sense of community by using community-oriented language (e. g., *we, let's, together, helpers, please, thank you,* etc.)
10. Show appreciation of and acknowledge student effort and the use of learning strategies (e.g., taking notes, asking questions) because these are elements of success that students can and should regulate.
11. Plan learning activities that encourage interaction between teacher and student and among students. Group students for problem solving activities and expect them to blend conversational and academic English through meaningful practice.

Another potentially powerful instructional tool that teachers across content areas should employ is the use of literature and writing that help students sustain or increase hope. Teachers can use literacy in ways that help students become protagonists in their own personal narratives. Middle schoolers "should be exposed to stories about goal pursuit activities, including biographies involving people [from various nationalities and occupational fields] who set difficult goals and grappled with obstacles to attain" them (Snyder, 2000, p. 34). Using narratives—even comic books and graphic novels—that portray high-hope protagonists (e.g., *A Gathering of Days,* 1979; *Esperanza Rising,* 2000; *Tangled Threads: A Hmong Girl's Story,* 2003, etc.) can help students to distance themselves from bad past outcomes and focus on routes to future goals. In fact, recent studies show that graphic novels help struggling readers to participate more in discussion, teach critical reading and thinking skills, and support comprehension for ELLs (Chun, 2009; Frey & Fisher, 2004). Teachers can also choose texts and curriculum materials that reflect the learner. These "identity texts" showcase the cultures, interests, and positive identities that will mirror back to an ELL a positive reflection of learning (Cummins, 2011). Storytelling, journal entries, or personal narratives can help ELLs position themselves in the future is a way of developing scripts for moving forward ". . . a kind of memory for our futures (Marcel, 1962, p. 53). Likewise, adolescents can hold online, interactive, conversations with family, friends, and other ELLs or create digital stories of themselves or family members on websites such as http://coasttocoast.pbworks.com/w/page/15273075/ Conversations and http://nativehealth.org/gallery/video/view/93.

ACCELERATED ACQUISITION

The all-too-typical approach to teaching ELLs is to "remediate" them by offering less, slower, or simpler instruction. Unless their instruction is rich and accelerated, many ELLs may never catch up to their peers. In addition to discriminating against ELLs, a remedial approach contributes to a lack of self-efficacy and personal agency to do well in school. Too many students don't feel as if they are wanted or belong in school and eventually drop out. Those who stay in school need and deserve a high-powered approach (Mohr, 2004) and access to the full curriculum. An accelerated approach to teaching ELLs entails providing a rich language environment and well-sequenced instruction that supports student success. Moreover, effective teachers of ELLs know that English is a language of power and access and make its acquisition a priority. Although other languages should be valued, respected, and developed, U.S. school children need high-levels of English proficiency to succeed in school, especially under the Common Core State Standards. ELLs also need access to all the social and economic opportunities available to them. Although most teachers intend to support students' language development, most could do more to support ELLs' acquisition of English. Here are some particular ways to do so.

Promote English as a Vital and Viable Socio-cultural Language System

As noted previously, modeling can provide vicariously induced efficacy, increase persistence, and promote transfer to related tasks. Teacher modeling of standard and academic English is the foundation of instruction. In one high-performing school (Mohr, et al., 2009), the teachers were observed for ways that their instruction supported the large majority of Latinos. Coding of the observation transcripts and classroom realia confirmed that the school implemented an inquiry approach, but further analysis indicated that the observed practices fell into three broad categories: Student and Situation Sensitivity, Forward-Moving Instruction, and Future-Mindedness. While sensitivity toward students and their community was expected, instruction that seemed to be flexible and forward moving was a pleasant surprise, as were the many ways that the school helped students move toward productive futures. The curriculum was fluid, focusing on problem-solving and critical thinking, including many instances of student choice, control, challenge, collaboration and creativity, all known contributors of motivation. The Future-Mindedness category included coding ascribed to shared goals, accountability associated with becoming independent, building connections to the real-world and contributing to the community via field trips and service projects. Students were very successful and teacher turn-over at this school was extremely low, in part due to the use of English as a way to connect to the curriculum, community, and the future.

Provide Rich Exposure to English Vocabulary and Scaffold Its Use

It is critical for ELLs that teachers target key vocabulary and relevant concepts in every lesson. Lessons should target language and content objectives and develop English language use and use it to learn subject matter. Vocabulary knowledge is primarily developed via wide reading (Nagy, Herman, & Anderson, 1985), so reading aloud and sharing picture-supported text (e.g., books and online resources) should be regular parts of the academic diet. When reading is organized around text sets, ELLs have the chance to delve deeper into selected topics or themes and use new vocabulary repeatedly. Again, using books and stories about overcoming challenges and facing difficulties can help highlight the diligence of heroes. Journey tales, adventure stories, historical accounts, current events, and hero quests can provide inspiration and a wide range of vocabulary.

In addition to diversified reading, ELLs need some focused instruction in English morphology and the use of cognates. ELLs don't necessarily recognize how their first language might be related to English, but given the large corpus of Greek and Latin morphemes in academic English, all students benefit from deliberate study of affixes and base words. Not understanding critical vocabulary is a main deterrent to reading comprehension.

Reading comprehension tasks for ELLs should include a lot of talk and then some kind of writing, so that ELLs can develop both their oral and written English use. Planning for interactive group work can support ELLs, but they must also be expected to read and write independently. Graphic organizers can facilitate the process of moving language and knowledge from talk to written text, but some designs expect language, rather than support its development, so teachers should analyze or customize any charts or tables that they use or expect students to complete for what is expected. For example, the KWL (Ogle, 1986) is well-known among teachers, but if teachers use this format they should use it for the right purpose—to access background knowledge and pose and answer questions from informational texts. Teachers should also support ELLs in completing the three columns, perhaps by using sentence starters (e.g., I know that . . ., I wonder about . . ., Now, I know that . . .) or posting the spellings of key terms and allowing students to work in groups to talk and complete the assignment. In other words, academic language use should not just be expected, but supported in daily applications.

Share Insights into How the Educational System Works and Can Be Maximized

It is only fair that educators teach students—especially those who are not from middle-class, English-speaking homes—how school is organized and how to do well therein. Communicating to students and parents the reasons for homework, parent-teacher conferences, open houses, etc. helps to make schooling more transparent. More specifically, teachers should carefully consider what they assign as homework. Homework should allow students to practice and extend what they have already been taught. But, homework can also be used to help students to set and monitor personal goals, especially if typical assignments are augmented with a personal reflection component that asks how the learning might be used in the future.

To students whose families are not familiar with American school practices, knowing what to do to get the most out of school is not automatic. Even at the college level, students frequently are unfamiliar with how to be successful. Students commonly need guidance on how to study for tests, how to avoid being dropped from a class, and how to access support services when needed. At all levels, students should be given guidance on how to do well and examples of excellent work. Most students need explanation and demonstration to do what good students do with regards to note-taking, help-seeking, recall strategies, reading and writing connections, and test preparation. Teachers should not withhold this kind of information from the students who may need it most or assume these competencies as the responsibilities of students. See Table 9.5 for tips for accelerating academic achievement among ELLs.

Table 9.5. Tips for Accelerating Academic Achievement Among ELLs in the Classroom

1. Curricular outcomes for ELLs should include language development, content knowledge, and student agency.
2. Tell students that learning is "their job" because learning helps them "construct their futures."
3. Ask students to explain how their behaviors help or hinder their learning or others' learning.
4. Model and expect students to produce high quality work.
5. It is the teacher's responsibility to help students master the basic skills and to learn to think critically, but do not do for students what they should do for themselves.
6. Key vocabulary can be introduced and rehearsed over several days of study of a unit.
7. Focus projects on inquiry, problem-solving, real-world application, and social interaction.
8. Unit activities can cross subject areas, but should connect students to their pasts, presents, and futures.
9. Explain the goals and roles of both independent and cooperative tasks; don't expect students to discern these details.
10. Utilize choral responses and response cards to keep students engaged and responsible.
11. One goal of cooperative grouping is to increase the opportunities for student talk, both conversational and academic; model the kinds of talk that are expected.
12. Mix the grouping assignments (e.g., dyads, triads, quads, etc.) and group roles.
13. Minimize "busy work"; review assignments for ways to "sophisticate" learning processes, even with limited-English speaking students.
14. Praise students for asking questions.
15. Build relationships with the students and assess interests and needs to utilize student interest for material selection, instructional decision making, and engagement strategies.

CONCLUSION

Adolescents need to commit themselves to goals that give them purpose and a sense of accomplishment. Without personal commitment to something worth doing, they become unmotivated, bored, or cynical. They become dependent on extrinsic sources of stimulation. A vision of a desired future helps to organize their lives, provides meaning to their activities, motivates them, and enables them to tolerate the hassles of getting there. Teachers serve a pivotal role in engaging students in learning and developing their sense of possible selves for the future (Cantor, Markus, Niedenthal, & Nurius, 1986; Markus & Nurius, 1986). For adolescent ELLs, it can be especially difficult to develop the self-efficacy that will sustain them. If teachers broaden their role to include that of learning-life coach, they can upgrade their instruction in ways that promote agency, access, and accelerated learning that could contribute to hopeful, life-long success. To function as learning coaches, teachers should reconsider their view of students, especially the capacity of their ELLs, and then change the way they think about and talk to students. By supporting their English language development during vibrant and relevant instruction, teachers help students enlarge their sense of selves. In a sense, effective teachers teach to their students' potentials—even when the students do not yet see the possibilities themselves.

QUESTIONS FOR REFLECTION AND DISCUSSION

1. What can teachers do to improve their own efficacy for teaching and their ELLs' efficacy for learning?
2. What does productive teacher talk entail? How can teachers use their classroom discourse to support the academic achievement of ELLs? What kind of teacher talk should be eliminated?
3. How are adolescent ELLs different from their native-English-speaking peers? How do their needs challenge teachers to be life- or learning-coaches while covering the grade-level curriculum?
4. How do the topics addressed in this chapter relate to the Mario Ramos case study? In what ways, might Mario need the kind of teacher/teaching described in this chapter?
5. What kinds of texts or reading and writing tasks could be used in Mario's classroom to increase his engagement and enhance his learning?

REFERENCES

August, D., & Shanahan, T. (Eds.). (2008). *Developing reading and writing in second-language learners: Lessons from the Report of the National Literacy Panel on language-minority children and youth*. New York, NY: Taylor & Francis.

Ballantyne, K. G., Sanderman, A. R., & Levy, J. (2008). *Educating English language learners: Building teacher capacity.* Washington, D.C. National Clearinghouse for English Language Acquisition. Retrieved September 16, 2010, from http://www.ncela.gwu.edu/files/uploads/3/EducatingELLsBuildingTeacherCapacityVol1.pdf.

Bandura, A. (2006). Toward a psychology of human agency. *Perspectives on Psychological Science, 1*(2), 164–80.

Bandura, A. (2005). Adolescent development from an agentic perspective. In F. Pajares & T. Urdan (Eds.). *Adolescence and Education, Volume V: Self-Efficacy Beliefs of Adolescents* (pp. 1–43). Greenwich, CT: Information Age.

Bandura, A. (1977). Self-efficacy: Toward a unifying theory of behavioral change. *Psychological Review, 84*(2), 191–215.

Birch, B. M. (2006). *English L2 reading: Getting to the bottom.* Mahwah, NJ: Lawrence Erlbaum.

Blos, J. (1979). *A gathering of days.* New York, NY: Avon.

Brozo, W. G. (1991). Hiding out in content classrooms: Coping strategies of unsuccessful readers. *Journal of Reading, 33*, 324–28.

Cantor, N., Markus, H., Niedenthal, P., & Nurius, P. (1986). On motivation and self-concept. In R. M. Sorrentino & E. T. Higgins (Eds.), *Motivation and cognition: Foundations of social behavior* (pp. 99–127). New York, NY: Guilford.

Carhill, A., Suárez-Orozco, C., & Páez, M. (2008). Explaining English language proficiency among adolescent immigrant students. *American Educational Research Journal, 45*(4), 1155–79.

Chun, C. (2009). Critical literacies and graphic novels for English-language learners: Teaching *Maus. Journal of Adolescent & Adult Literacy, 53*, 144–53.

Coleman, R., & Goldenberg, C. (2010). Part III: Promoting literacy development. *Kappa Delta Pi Record,* Spring, 106–11.

Cordova, D. I., & Lepper, M. R. (1996). Intrinsic motivation and the process of learning: Beneficial effects of contextualization, personalization, and choice. *Journal of Educational Psychology, 88*, 715–30.

Cummins, J. (2011). Literacy engagement: Fueling academic growth for English learners. *The Reading Teacher, 65*, 142–46.

De Jong, E. J., & Harper, C. A. (2005). Preparing mainstream teachers for English-language learners: Is being a good teacher good enough? *Teacher Education Quarterly, 32*, 101–24.

Dutro, S., & Kinsella, K. (2010). English language development: Issues and implementation in grades 6–12. In *Improving education for English learners: Research-based approaches.* Sacramento, CA: California Department of Education.

Eun, B., & Heining-Boynton, A. (2007). Impact of an English-as-a-second-language professional development program. *Journal of Educational Research, 101*, 36–48.

Frey, N., & Fisher, D. (2004). Using graphic novels, Anime, and the Internet in an urban high school. *English Journal, 93*(3): 19–25.

Gersten, R. (1996). Literacy instruction for language minority students: The transition years. *Elementary School Journal, 96*, 228–44.

Giroux, H. A. (1995). Border pedagogy and the politics of postmodernism. In P. McLaren (Ed.). *Postmodernism, postcolonialism and pedagogy, 37–64.* Albert Park, Australia: James Nicholas Publishers.

Hart, B., & Risley, T. E. (1995). *Meaningful differences in the everyday experience of young children.* Baltimore, MD: Brookes.

Lehtinen, E., Vauras, M., Salonen, P., Olkinuora, E., & Kinnunen, R. (1995). Long-term development of learning activity: Motivational, cognitive, and social interaction. *Educational Psychologist, 30*, 21–35.

Marcel, G. (1962). *Homo viatur* (E. Crawford, trans.). New York, NY: Harper & Rowe.

Markus, H., & Nurius, P. (1986). Possible selves. *American Psychologist, 41*, 954–69.

McGraner, K. L., & Saenz, L. (2009). *Preparing teachers of English language learners.* Washington, D.C.: National Comprehensive Center for Teacher Quality.

Mohr, K. A. J. (2004). English as an accelerated language: A call to action for reading teachers, *The Reading Teacher, 58*, 18–26.

Mohr, K. A. J. (1998). Teacher talk: A summary analysis of effective teachers' discourse during primary literacy lessons. *Journal of Classroom Interaction, 33(2)*, 16–24.

Mohr, K. A. J., Robles-Goodwin, P. J., & Wilhelm, R. W. (2009). A study of optimism among Latinos in a successful urban elementary school. *Tapestry Journal, 1*(1), 1–14. Accessed online at http://tapestry.usf.edu/journal/documents/v01n01%20%20Mohr%20et%20al.%20%20Study%20of%20Optimism.pdf.

Munoz-Ryan, P. (2000). *Esperanza rising.* New York: NY: Scholastic.

Nagy, W. E., Herman, P. A., & Anderson, R. C. (1985). Learning words from context. *Reading Research Quarterly*, 233–53.

National Center for Education Statistics (2013). *The nation's report card: Executive summary 2013.* Washington, D.C.: National Center for Education Statistics, Institute for Education Sciences, U.S. Office of Education. Retrieved from http://nationsreportcard.gov/reading_math_2013/#/executive-summary.

National Clearinghouse for English Language Acquisition and Language Instruction Educational Program (NCELA). (2007). Fast Facts. Retrieved from www.mcela.gwu.edu/expert/fastfaq/4.html.

National Council of Teachers of English. (2013). The NCTE Definition of 21st Century Literacies. Retrieved on November 13, 2013 from http://www.ncte.org/positions/statements/21stcentdefinition.

National Governors Association for Best Practices & Council of Chief State School Officers (2010). *Common Core State Standards for English language arts & history/social studies, science, and technical subjects, Appendix A.* Washington, D.C. Author. Retrieved from http://www.corestandards.rg/the-standards.

Ogle, D. M. (1986). KWL: A teaching model that develops active reading of expository text. *The Reading Teacher, 39*, 564–70.

Osterman, K. F. (2000). Students' need for belonging in the school community. *Review of Educational Research, 70*, 323–67.

Pajares, F., & Urdan, T. (Eds.). (2006*). Adolescence and education, Volume V: Self-efficacy beliefs of adolescents.* Greenwich, CT: Information Age.

Pintrich, P. R., & Schunk, D. H. (2002). *Motivation in education.* Upper Saddle River, NJ: Merrill.

Ramirez, J. D., Yuen, S. D., & Ramey, D. R. (1991). Longitudinal study of structured English immersion strategy, early-exit, and late-exit transitional bilingual education programs for language-minority children. San Mateo, CA: Aguirre International.

Rossatto, C. A. (1994). *Engaging Paulo Freire's pedagogy of possibility: From blind to transformative optimism.* New York, NY: Rowman & Littlefield.

Shea, P. D. (2003). *Tangled threads: A Hmong girl's story.* New York, NY: Clarion Books.

Short, D. (1999). Integrating language and content for effective sheltered instruction programs. In C. Faltis & P. Wolfe (Eds.). *So much to say: Adolescents, bilingualism, and ESL in the secondary school* (pp.105–37). New York: NY: Teachers College Press.

Snyder, C. R. (2000). *The handbook of hope: Theories, measures, and applications.* San Diego, CA: Academic Press.

Sternberg, R. J. (1996). *Cognitive psychology.* Fort Worth, TX: Holt, Rinehart, & Winston.

Tracey, D. H., & Morrow, L. M. (2006). *Lenses on reading: An introduction to theories and models.* New York, NY: Guilford.

Voigt, C. (1982). *Dicey's song.* New York, NY: Fawcett.

Weiner, B. (1986). *An attributional theory of motivation and emotion.* New York, NY: Springer-Verlag.

Wigfield, A., & Eccles, J. S. (2000). Expectancy-value theory of achievement motivation. *Contemporary Educational Psychology, 25,* 68–81.

Wigfield, A., Eccles, J., & Pintrich, P. R. (1996). Development between the ages 11 and 25. In D. Berliner & R. Calfee (Eds.), Handbook of educational psychology (pp. 148–85). New York, NY: Macmillan.

Zimmerman, B. J., & Cleary, T. J. (2006). Adolescents' development of personal agency: The role of self-efficacy beliefs and self-regulatory skill. In F. Pajares & T. Urdan (Eds.). *Adolescence and Education, Volume V: Self-Efficacy Beliefs of Adolescents* (pp. 45–69). Greenwich, CT: Information Age.

III

TALK AND TEXTUAL CONSIDERATIONS

10

Multimodality in Children's School-Based Texts

Roberta Linder

Students live in a media-saturated society, surrounded by print, images, and sounds of messages being communicated on both the printed page (i.e., books, magazines, newspapers) as well as on the screen (i.e., television, computer, movie). As readers/viewers of an array of media, students are accustomed to engaging with texts that are multimodal in their construction, utilizing not only the printed word but also images and sounds (Hull & Nelson, 2005; Kress, 2003). However, once these children pass through the doorways of their schools and classrooms, they enter an environment in which print-based texts are privileged as the primary means for the presentation (e.g., novels, worksheets) and the production (e.g., written essays, reports) of information (Faulkner, 2005; Hull, 2003; Hull & Nelson, 2005; Jewitt; 2005; Kress, 2003; Luke, 2004). In addition, the current proliferation of standards-based assessments and related instructional material has continued to further the privileged status of print. It is important for educators to develop an understanding of multimodality and its increasing presence in school-based texts, become familiar with the literature and research related to the use of multimodal texts in today's classrooms, and be aware of the implications for pre-service and practicing teachers, consistent with recommendations offered by literacy professional associations (International Reading Association [IRA], 2012; National Council of Teachers of English [NCTE], 2005) and outlined in the Common Core State Standards (National Governors Association Center for Best Practices [NGA] and the Council of Chief State School [CCSS] Officers, 2012), specifically Reading Anchor Standard 7 stating that students will read and critique a variety of print and non-print media composed of words, images, and numbers.

Increasingly, textbooks and other instructional media (i.e., CD ROMs, Internet websites) are utilizing multimodal formats requiring readers to construct meaning from the various visual, textual, and aural components on the page or screen. Readers need to be able to synthesize information from the text's linguistic, visual, gestural, spatial, and audio design elements (Kress, 2003; New London Group, 2000). Although these multimodal texts present information in a very appealing format, they require the readers to utilize complex, strategic reading skills (Afflerbach & VanSledright, 2001; Jacobs, 2007; Walsh, 2006). Multimodal texts also present challenges to the teachers who use them, for they cannot assume that students are attending to or correctly interpreting all the various words and images on the page or screen.

Teachers themselves must now become proficient readers of multimodal texts and begin to recognize the potentials and challenges these texts present to their students. Multimodal texts will provide new learning opportunities for some students, and at the same time they will also present barriers to the learning of others. Print-based texts no longer dominate students' school-based and out-of-school literacies. Messages are communicated through various elements of text (font type, color, size), images (i.e., proximity, movement, angle, color, space, gestures), and sound (music, special effects, voice-overs). As students and their teachers engage with multimodal texts within their classrooms, they will need to read these texts in a manner that enables them to derive meaning from the texts and to also evaluate them critically (Reed & Stavreva, 2006; Serafini, 2012; Walsh, 2006).

Today's students are confronted with the challenges of comprehending print and digital texts that merge lexical, visual, and sometimes aural elements to communicate narrative or informational material. Not only must students be able to comprehend the multiple messages conveyed by these elements, they must also be able to critique the construction of the texts and personal, social, and cultural factors that mediate their interpretations of the texts. Today's teachers are faced with the tasks of identifying, reading, and comprehending the various modes present in multimodal texts. They must also be able to guide their students in the comprehension and critique of print and digital multimodal texts. In her discussion of screen-based texts, Walsh (2006) noted, "As educators we need to determine the specific features of reading that occur and that are needed for the synchronous function of the modes of print, image, movement, colour, gesture, 3D objects, music and sound on a digital screen" (p. 36). The next sections define and describe elements of multimodality and emphasize the importance of design in an individual's production of and participation with multimodal texts.

MULTIMODALITY AND DESIGN

Multimodal texts are ubiquitous in the lives of today's students, both within and outside of the school setting. They exist in print and digital format, and their authors and creators design them to entertain, inform, and persuade their readers and viewers. Advances in technology have profoundly altered the manner in which these texts are produced, distributed, and read. In order to effectively help students comprehend and critique multimodal texts, educators should possess a foundational knowledge of multimodality and the concept of design.

Multimodality. *Multimodality* is a field of study that examines "how human beings use different modes of communication, like speech, writing, image, gesture, and sound, to represent or make meaning in the world" (Stein, 2008). *Multimodal texts* are print and non-print texts that communicate using a complex design composed of words, visuals, sounds, and movement. A mode is a "system of signs created within or across various cultures to represent and express meanings. Modes were developed by humans to express ideas and communicate with one another" (Serafini, 2012, p. 153). Modes can take a variety of forms in print and non-print texts. In print-based texts, the dominant modes may be words and pictures. However, the author can manipulate these modes to emphasize certain content to the reader in order to inform, persuade, or entertain. Font size and color can draw the reader's attention to specific text; picture selection, size, and placement can signal the importance of its content; word choice communicates the author's purpose and point of view as well as the content that is included or omitted from the text (Serafini, 2011; Walsh, 2010). In screen-based texts, the visual mode may dominate, but the reader must also attend to multiple visual design elements such as placement on the screen, size, camera angle, gaze of the character (i.e., directly at the reader, away from the reader or at another person), gestures, facial expressions, movement, close ups, or distance shots (Kress & van Leeuwen, 2006; Serafini, 2011).

Design. The concept of design is central to individuals' production of and participation with multimodal texts (Hassett & Curwood, 2009; Kress & van Leeuwen, 2006; Serafini, 2012; Stein, 2008; Walsh, 2008, 2010). In the production of multimodal texts, "the idea of design means that people choose how to represent meaning from a range of possible options" (Stein, 2008, p. 875). Individuals' design choices are influenced by their cultures and the resources available to create representations for communication, therefore, words and images that carry a specific meaning for one culture may mean something entirely different to members of a different culture. In addition, the textual and visual design elements contain value-laden messages; they are not "neutral, objective representations of reality" (Serafini, 2012, p. 156). The design gives form to the motivations and interests of a message's originator and, using the semiotic resources that are available, matches the message with the interests of the intended audience (Kress, 2010).

In their participation with multimodal texts, readers use different approaches to navigate through and interpret these print and non-print texts; they are *designers*, actively constructing meaning as they engage with the texts. Given the nonlinear format of some textbooks, picture books, and websites, readers design the individual and unique pathways they take to navigate through the visual and textual elements of the text. As noted by Serafini (2012), factors such as a student's interests, needs, and motivations influence the selection of the reading pathway. In addition, a student's interpretation of a multimodal text is affected by the information included in or omitted from the selected reading path as well as the student's background knowledge, life experiences, and culture. Due to the constant transformations taking place in society and within each individual reader, design is seen as fluid and continually changing (Kress & van Leeuwen, 2006). Designers of texts must periodically change the designs of their messages in order to produce texts that effectively communicate to the intended audience, and readers design different pathways and interpretations over time as they participate with the multimodal texts.

Print and non-print multimodal texts are becoming more prevalent in today's classrooms. These texts communicate meaning through a variety of modes, such as words, visuals, sounds, and movement. Central to the production of and participation with multimodal texts is the principle of design. Creators design texts that effectively communicate through visual and textual elements, and readers design the pathways they follow and interpretations they form as they participate with the multimodal texts. Educators are faced with the challenge of helping students comprehend these non-traditional texts that demand new ways of making meaning from both the textual and visual elements of the multimodal texts.

COMPREHENSION OF MULTIMODAL TEXTS

Although print texts may still dominate school-based literacy, multimodal texts are being integrated into classroom instruction on a more regular basis as educators recognize their value. Multimodal texts can be used as models for writing projects in which students not only write the words of the text but they also design and include visual or aural elements (Frey & Fisher, 2004; Hassett & Curwood, 2009; Hughes, King, Perkins, & Fuke, 2011; Walsh, 2008, 2010). Multimodal texts can be used as supplements to textbooks, making content area information more interesting and accessible to students (Guzzetti, 2009, 2010; Jewitt, 2002; Jewitt, Kress, Ogborn, & Tsatsarelis, 2001; Sweeny, 2007; Walsh, 2010). Comic books can help young students begin to notice and understand elements of visual design in multimodal texts (Yannicopoulou, 2004), and e-readers can physically engage students during the reading of a text through the use of tools such as annotating and highlighting (Larson, 2009). Because today's society surrounds students with multimodal texts and will continue to do so throughout their lives, school use of these texts can motivate students (Frey & Fisher, 2004; Harris, 2011; Larson, 2009; Schwartz & Rubinstein-Avila, 2006) and also prepare them for a future in which they will need to be able to comprehend and critique these texts (Crovitz, 2007; Hughes, King, Perkins, & Fuke, 2011; Schwartz & Rubinstein-Avila, 2006; Serafini, 2005). Comprehension of multimodal texts will require teachers to recognize the similarities and differences in reading and understanding print-based texts and multimodal texts. Although they were originally established to aid the comprehension of print-based texts, current models of the comprehension process can serve as a starting point for understanding how teachers can support students' comprehension of multimodal texts.

Existing conceptualizations of reading comprehension of print-based texts have served as foundations for understanding the comprehension of multimodal print-based and digital texts. One such model of reading comprehension has been proposed by the RAND Reading Study Group. The RAND Reading Study Group (2002) defined reading comprehension as "the process of simultaneously extracting and constructing meaning through interaction and involvement with written language. It consists of three elements: the reader, the text, and the activity or purpose for reading" (p. xiii). These three elements occur within "a larger sociocultural context that shapes and is shaped by the reader and that interacts with each of the elements iteratively throughout the process of reading" (p. xiii). Coiro (2003) has expanded upon this heuristic in order to include comprehension of online texts that require additional reading and comprehension skills from students. For example, when examining the textual aspect of online reading, Coiro noted that the nonlinear, interactive, multimedia format demanded more inferential reasoning and decision-making in order for students to successfully navigate and draw meaning from the hyperlinks, video clips, audio recordings, virtual environments, and electronic text environments students encounter.

A second model that has been adapted to the reading and comprehension of multimodal texts is Luke and Freebody's (1997) four resources model. The model articulated the four roles of successful readers, focusing on the reading of printed text: (a) code breaker, (b) text participant or meaning maker, (c) text user, and (d) text analyst or critic. Serafini (2012) expanded upon this original framework to include visual images and design elements in addition to written text. In his alternate model, the roles of the reader in reading multimodal texts are (a) navigator, (b) interpreter, (c) designer, and (d) interrogator. As *navigator*, a reader must understand how to move through the spaces of a print-based or digital text by not only decoding the words but also by understanding the visual structures and designs of the text. As an *interpreter*, the reader constructs meaning from the images and written texts, noting various perspectives and the author's purpose, and generating responses shaped by personal experiences and sociocultural contexts. A reader of a multimodal text is considered to be a designer because the individual constructs, or designs, the manner in which the text is read, the reading path that is selected, and the items that are attended to. As an *interrogator*, the reader considers the social, historical, political, and cultural aspects of text production and interpretation, adopting a critical stance as a reader.

Classroom teachers and researchers have been examining a wide array of multimodal texts in their literacy instruction and investigations. Multimodal texts utilized in classrooms can be categorized as either print-based (e.g., textbook, picture book, graphic novel), digital (e.g., CD ROM, website) or a combination of both (e.g., series such as *Skeleton Creek* and *39 Clues*). As noted by Walsh (2008), "To read and produce multimodal texts, students need to be able to combine traditional literacy practices with the understanding, design and manipulation of different modes of image, graphics, sound and movement with text" (p. 106). Thus, teachers incorporating multimodal texts into their classroom instruction need to be aware of the comprehension demands of the various types of texts and be prepared to provide instruction and guidance that enable their students to comprehend and critique these texts. The next sections first provide a comparison of comprehension similarities and differences when reading print-based and multimodal texts, then present three sets of frameworks for helping students comprehend and critique the textual, visual, and aural elements of multimodal texts, both print-based and digital.

Comprehension similarities and differences. Walsh (2006) analyzed the content of two print-based texts and one digital text related to the topic of wolves: a children's novel, a narrative picture book, and an informational website. The novel contained words only, the picture book contained words and images, and the website contained words, images, and sounds. Although the formats for the three texts varied, Walsh concluded that there were a number of similarities and differences in the comprehension processes required for each format of text.

Walsh (2006) noted numerous similarities in the reading processes used by readers in comprehending print-based and multimodal texts. For example, readers need to determine the purpose for reading, utilize strategies such as activating schema and making predictions, understand the influences of culture, ideology, point of view, and apply skills such as skimming and scanning when reading both types of texts. Comprehension of both print-based and multimodal texts also requires the reader to transact with the text, identify the genre of the text, and understand, analyze, and critique the texts.

Differences in comprehending the texts occur due to the different modes used within the texts and the manner in which the reader makes meaning from the modes. Whereas print-based texts rely on words that readers follow in a primarily linear manner, multimodal texts are composed of an interconnected combination of words, visual images, and sounds that readers navigate in a non-sequential, non-linear manner. Verbal imagery (e.g., symbolism, metaphor, simile, poetic devices) creates pictures in the minds of the readers of print-based texts, but visual images and sound effects combine with words to communicate the messages of multimodal texts. Coiro articulated these differences in her discussion of online texts:

> I think one of the biggest differences between offline and online reading comprehension is that offline texts reside in familiar and bounded spaces that remain static over time, while online texts are part of a dynamic and unbounded information system that changes daily in structure, form, and content. (Coiro & Moore, 2012, p. 552)

When English language arts teachers understand the similarities and differences in reading print-based and multimodal texts, they can help their students make connections in reading the different types of texts and also help them learn the skills necessary to read the messages contained in the images, sounds, and structures of multimodal texts. Several instructional strategies have been developed to teach students how to comprehend and critique multimodal texts.

Here-hidden-head questions. In order to develop an effective tool for assessing his 10- and 11-year-old students' comprehension of digital multimodal texts, Harris (2011) modified the 3-tiered assessment system popularized by Fountas and Pinnell.

- **Thinking within the text:** searching for and using information
- **Thinking beyond the text:** making connections; synthesizing
- **Thinking about the text:** analyzing and critiquing (p. 21)

Harris implemented this assessment tool in the form of task sheets during his students' reading of the online series Inanimate Alice (http://www.inanimatealice.com). Table 10.1 provides descriptions of the three levels of questions as well as examples from a task sheet for Inanimate Alice.

After analyzing his students' responses to the here-hidden-head questions on task sheets for four episodes of Inanimate Alice, Harris noted improvement in comprehension of higher order questions from episode one to episode two. However, the inclusion of two games in episode three and a more complicated text in episode four lowered students' comprehension and task completion. Overall, Harris observed that the task sheets produced discussion among the students, that the online multimodal text was more demanding than a print-based text, and that traditional comprehension strategies and assessment could be used effectively with an online multimodal text.

Three-part framework for comprehending multimodal texts. Youngs and Serafini (2011) proposed a three-phase set of strategies for comprehending multimodal texts, relating their framework to the reading of historical fiction picture books. The framework is both cumulative and recursive. The model is cumulative based on the premise that readers must first identify various components of the multimodal text before they can interpret and then critique the text. The model is recursive because readers can return to components they initially noticed and interpretations they had originally developed in order to develop deeper analyses of the text.

The three phases of this framework (Youngs & Serafini, 2011) include (a) previewing, noticing, and naming, (b) interpretation, and (c) critical analysis. In the previewing, noticing, and naming phase, readers begin by attending to the peritextual features of the text (i.e., cover, character representation, setting, illustration style, end pages, book jacket, title page) and the visual and textual elements. Teachers can engage students in an examination of the text with a class discussion that follows the

Table 10.1. Here-Hidden-Head Assessment Tool

Type of Question	Description	Examples from Inanimate Alice
Here	Answer found in the text; sounds like the question	How old is Alice? Where in the world is Alice living?
Hidden	Parts of the answer may be found scattered around the text; may paraphrase the question	Why does a photo and a map of Alice's house help you understand where she lives?
Head	Answer not written on the page; requires me to make connections to my experiences or opinions	Why does Alice get frightened in the car when they are looking for her Dad?

first read-aloud of the text. The interpretation phase can be facilitated by the teacher through a second reading of the book, this time focusing on the point of view of the narrator, the composition of the text and visuals, and the relationship between the characters and the reader. Finally, in the critical analysis phase, the teacher and students will consider the historical background of the story and the cultural, political, and social symbols representing that historical period or event. The readers will also take note of motifs (i.e., images used repeatedly throughout a text), visual symbols that are embedded in the text's illustrations, and the manner in which characters are placed within the illustrations.

Serafini (2011) offered an additional instructional strategy to assist students with their comprehension of multimodal texts. To focus students' attention on the visual elements of a text and to begin to consider their connection to sociocultural contexts, the author devised a "Noticings-Meanings-Implications" chart. In the first column, students record and describe "What We Notice" about visual images in a text. In the second column, students connect to their prior experiences and knowledge to speculate "What It Might Mean." In the final column, students must consider what the "Implications" of the image might be outside its inclusion in the text. Serafini also provided guiding questions for analyzing visual and design elements of picture books, analyzing visual structures, and analyzing advertisements. Teachers considering the implementation of visual analysis into their reading of historical fiction picture books or other multimodal texts might find the "Noticings-Meanings-Implications" chart a helpful strategy for closer examinations of images in texts.

Readers of historical fiction texts must also consider other factors when reading this genre. First, the readers must determine the type of historical fiction text being read. Youngs and Serafini (2011) identified four types of historical fiction texts.

1. Fictionalized memoirs
2. Fictionalized family history
3. Fiction based on research
4. Time travel back to the historical event

Second, the readers of historical fiction must also be able to distinguish between the factual and fictional elements of the text. These additional comprehension demands and the need to attend to the multimodal elements of an historical fiction picture book require teachers and students to closely examine the messages of both the words and images and historical origins of the content.

Four step online reading plan. Coiro (2011) offered a model for guiding students in reading online resources effectively and critically. The four steps of the model include (a) approaching the online reading task, (b) navigating and negotiating the online text, (c) monitoring the comprehension of and the pathways through the texts, and (d) responding to the online text. Using thoughtfully designed lessons involving explicit think-alouds, teachers are able to model effective use of online texts and guide students in the critical analysis of these texts. Coiro provided two sample lessons, one designed to teach students how to effectively find information online and a second lesson in reading critically across multiple texts on a single subject. Throughout the lessons, familiar comprehension strategies such as establishing a purpose for reading, determining importance, evaluating, and summarizing were aligned with the various steps of the model and connected to the teacher's think-alouds. The online reading comprehension lessons provide students with models for their own online reading and also connect to comprehension strategies they had previously used with print-based texts.

As print-based and digital multimodal texts have gained acceptance in language arts classrooms, literacy researchers have sought to understand if, and how, traditional models of reading comprehension for print-based monomodal texts could be adapted to print and digital multimodal texts. Many reading comprehension strategies are utilized across print and digital formats, but additional reading skills are necessary for navigating and critiquing digital texts. Multimodal texts offer the potential to motivate and engage reluctant, disinterested, or struggling readers, but teachers need to ensure that these students are also able to comprehend the contents of these texts.

INSTRUCTIONAL CONSIDERATIONS FOR MARIO

Mario is a sixth grade student reading two to three years below grade level and struggling with his writing skills. He does not feel like he is a good reader, but he does value reading and understands how important it is outside of school. Mario speaks both Spanish and English at home, and he reports that he enjoys reading comic books, fantasy books, and gaming magazines. Multimodal texts can be used by teachers to address Mario's areas of need, but at the same time, teachers need to be aware of the comprehension difficulties Mario may experience when reading multimodal texts.

Supporting Mario with multimodal texts. Mario stated a preference for reading comic books and gaming magazines, both examples of print-based multimodal texts. He mentioned that the illustrations in his comic books facilitated his understanding of the text. Mario's teachers could integrate supplemental nonfiction texts that utilize a graphic format (Frey & Fisher, 2004; Schwartz & Rubinstein-Avila, 2006). For example, Capstone Press publishes a number of nonfiction series based on topics related to middle school science and social studies. The graphic format of series such as Stories of War, Graphic Science and Engineering in Action, and Graphic Expeditions would appeal to Mario, and the topics would connect to his content area classes. The printed text in these books is kept to a minimum, the illustrations support the text, and struggling and reluctant readers can use both the textual and visual modes to comprehend the information in the text. Mario's teachers could also provide him with illustrated versions of classic literature that may be required reading. Teacher's Discovery is a company that distributes a variety of instructional materials, including classic literature adaptations retold in graphic novel and manga editions. Professional resources such as *Teaching Graphic Novels* (Monnin, 2010), *Teaching Visual Literacy* (Frey & Fisher, 2008), or *Building Literacy Connections with Graphic Novels: Page by Page, Panel by Panel* (Carter, 2007) provide teachers with information, activities, and book lists that will enable them to integrate this popular genre into their language arts curriculum. Picture books could also serve as a resource for Mario and his teachers, providing him with information related to topics being studied in his classes, using both the illustrations and words to communicate relevant material to him (Serafini, 2011; Youngs & Serafini, 2011).

Mario might also benefit from the use of digital multimodal texts such as interactive and enhanced e-books (Larson, 2009). Publishers such as Capstone Press who publish print-based graphic texts also offer interactive versions of their titles. As part of the Stories of War series, the title *True Stories of the Civil War* (Yomtov, 2013) is offered as both a print-based text and as an interactive e-book. Other publishers such as Scholastic and Benchmark Education also offer e-texts for students. The features of the interactive texts would allow Mario to listen to the text or search for definitions in a pop-up glossary. Some Internet websites would provide Mario with print texts but would also include audio and graphic support for him. For example, adolescents can read about health topics of interest on the website KidsHealth (http://kidshealth. org/teen). Mario could choose the article on safety tips for football, select the font size, select English or Spanish, and then click on the icon to listen to the audio version of the article. Mario can follow along with the reader because the words are highlighted as they are read. The article could also be printed for Mario to read and reread at later times.

Potential challenges for Mario. Even though Mario is motivated by reading comic book formats and using computer games and Internet sites, he may need to be scaffolded in using these texts for educational rather than recreational purposes. First, teachers would want to determine Mario's ability to derive meaning from the various elements comprising his textbooks, picture books, graphic novels, or informational texts. For example, is Mario taking the time to read the sidebars, graphs, maps, photographs, primary documents, and captions in textbooks and informational? Does he take note of the information being presented in the illustrations and the text in picture books? Is Mario reading and understanding all of the words and illustrations presented on the pages? When reading graphic novels, is Mario attending to the characters' facial expressions, gestures, movements, and verbal expression? If it appears that Mario is having difficulty comprehending the information in these texts, his teachers may need to use a graphic organizer such as the "Noticings-Meanings-Implications" chart (Serafini, 2011) to help him focus on the messages being communicated through the images of the text. Mario might also benefit from using a textbook prereading strategy such as THIEVES (Zwiers, 2010) that would guide him to preview the various elements of a textbook chapter before reading it. Mario's teachers would need to ensure that he is comprehending all textual and visual elements in his printed multimodal texts.

Second, Mario's teachers would need to determine his proficiency at reading Internet websites and comprehending the information presented in those digital multimodal texts. Does Mario attend to the relevant information on the website or is he distracted by advertisements and other irrelevant links? Can Mario determine which links will contribute to his understanding and which will not? Can Mario navigate the audio and visual components of the website? Is he able to synthesize the information he obtains from the visual and aural components of the website? Is he able to critique the website for authenticity and the author for credibility? Reading Internet websites demands a complex set of reading skills, and even though Mario reported that he spent time reading on the Internet, he may need to have his teachers model the reading comprehension strategies necessary to effectively make meaning from these digital multimodal texts (Coiro, 2011).

Print-based and digital multimodal texts have the potential to motivate and support struggling readers such as Mario. Texts with visual supports and minimal text (e.g., picture books, graphic novels) can provide Mario and other struggling readers with comprehensible information related to content areas. These texts also appeal to his interest in reading comic books. Some digital multimodal texts offer Mario features such as an audio reading of the text, pop-up glossaries, or video clips. However, Mario's teachers need to ensure that he is actually comprehending the information contained in the texts, deriving meaning from all the modes composing the texts, and choosing an efficient and effective reading pathway.

CONCLUSION

Although printed, word-based texts have been the privileged format in most school settings and have served as the basis for previous models of reading comprehension, multimodal print and digital texts are becoming more prominent in twenty-first century classrooms. They are already the preferred text of many students for their out-of-school reading, and educators are beginning to envision and enact the use of multimodal texts for their students. School-based multimodal texts are available in a variety of appealing, motivating formats, and they provide teachers with the opportunity to address the unique needs of both their capable and struggling readers. In order to effectively integrate the use of multimodal texts into their existing curricula, teachers must not only be able to read and comprehend the multiple messages being communicated by the various modes in the texts, but they must also be able to assist students in their navigation through and comprehension of these complex texts. For students such as Mario, multimodal texts may provide a means to comprehend subject-area content through their use of words, images, and sound. However, Mario may need the support of knowledgeable teachers to help him derive information from multimodal texts, reading them for academic rather than recreational purposes. School-based multimodal texts require both educators and their students to comprehend and critique a variety of print and digital texts, reading not only the words on the page or the screen but also the images, sounds, movements, and other modes that communicate the messages of the author.

REFERENCES

Afflerbach, P., & VanSledright, B. (2001). Hath! Doth! What? Middle graders reading innovative history text. *Journal of Adolescent & Adult Literacy, 44*(8), 696–707.

Carter, J. B. (Ed.) (2007). *Building literacy connections with graphic novels: page by page, panel by panel.* Urbana, IL: National Council of Teachers of English.

Coiro, J. (2003). Reading comprehension on the Internet: Expanding our understanding of reading comprehension to encompass new literacies. *The Reading Teacher, 56*(5), 558–64.

Coiro, J. (2011). Talking about reading as thinking: Modeling the hidden complexities of online reading comprehension. *Theory into Practice, 50,* 107–15. doi:10.1080/00405841.2011.558435.

Coiro, J., & Moore, D. W. (2012). New literacies and adolescent learners: An interview with Julie Coiro. *Journal of Adolescent & Adult Literacy, 55*(6), 551–53. doi:10.1002/JAAL.00065.

Dalton, B., & Proctor, C. P. (2008). The changing landscape of text and comprehension in the age of new literacies. In J. Coiro, M. Knobel, C. Lankshear, D. J. Leu (Eds.), *Handbook of research on new literacies* (pp. 297–324). New York, NY: Lawrence Erlbaum.

Drovitz, D. (2007). Scrutinizing the cybersell: Teen-targeted web sites as texts. *The English Journal, 97*(1), 49–55.

Faulkner, V. (2005). Adolescent literacies within the middle years of schooling—A case study of a year 8 homeroom. *Journal of Adolescent & Adult Literacy, 49*(2), 108–17.

Frey, N., & Fisher, D. (2004). Using graphic novels, anime, and the Internet in an urban high school. *The English Journal, 93*(3), 19–25.

Frey, N., & Fisher, D. B. (2008). *Teaching visual literacy: Using comic books, graphic novels, anime, cartoons, and more to develop comprehension and thinking skills.* Thousand Oaks, CA: Corwin Press.

Guzzetti, B. J. (2009). Thinking like a forensic scientist: Learning with academic and everyday texts. *Journal of Adolescent & Adult Literacy, 53*(3), 192–203.

Guzzetti, B. (2010). A content analysis of forensics comic books and graphic novels: Implications for science instruction. In R. T. Jimenez, V. J. Risko, M. K. Hundley, & D. W. Rowe (Eds.), *59th Yearbook of the National Reading Conference* (pp. 90–101). Oak Creek, WI: National Reading Conference.

Harris, A. (2011). How effective are print-based comprehensions models for reading assessing multimodal texts? *Literacy Learning: The Middle Years, 19*(3), 19–32.

Hassett, D. D., & Curwood, J. S. (2009). Theories and practices of multimodal education: The instructional dynamics of picture books and primary classrooms. *The Reading Teacher, 63*(4), 270–82. doi:10.1598/RT.63.4.2.

Hughes, J. M., King, A., Perkins, P., & Fuke, V. (2011). Adolescents and "autographics": Reading and writing coming-of-age novels. *Journal of Adolescent & Adult Literacy, 54*(8), 601–12. doi:10.1598/JAAL.54.8.5.

Hull, G. (2003). Youth culture and digital media: New literacies for new times. *Research in the Teaching of English, 36*(2), 229–33.

Hull, G., & Nelson, M. E. (2005). Locating the semiotic power of multimodality. *Written Communication, 22*(2), 224–61.

International Reading Association (2012). *Adolescent literacy* (Position statement, Rev. 2012 ed.). Newark, DE: Author.

Jacobs, D. (2007). More than words: Comics as a means of teaching multiple literacies. *English Journal, 96*(3), 19–25.

Jewitt, C. (2002). The move from page to screen: The multimodal reshaping of school English. *Visual Communication, 1*(2), 171–95.

Jewitt, C. (2005). Multimodality, "reading", and "writing" for the 21st century. *Discourse: Studies in the Cultural Politics of Education, 26*(2), 315–31.

Jewitt, C., Kress, G., Ogborn, J., & Tsatsarelis, C. (2001). Exploring learning through visual, actional and linguistic communication: The multimodal environment of a science classroom. *Educational Review, 53*(1), 5–18.

Kress, G. (2000). Multimodality: Challenges to thinking about language. *TESOL Quarterly, 34*(2), 337–40.

Kress, G. (2003). *Literacy in the new media age.* New York, NY: Routledge.

Kress, G., & van Leeuwen, T. (2006). *Reading images: The grammar of visual design* (2nd ed.). New York, NY: Routledge.

Larson, L. C. (2009). e-reading and e-responding: New tools for the next generation of readers. *Journal of Adolescent & Adult Literacy, 53*(3), 255–58. doi:10.1598/JAAL.53.3.7.

Luke, A. (2004). The trouble with English. *Research in the Teaching of English, 39*(1), 85–95.

Luke, A., & Freebody, P. (1997). Shaping the social practices of reading. In S. Muspratt, A. Luke, & P. Freebody (Eds.), *Constructing critical literacies: Teaching and learning textual practice* (pp. 185–225). Cresskill, NJ: Hampton Press, Inc.

Monnin, K. (2010). *Teaching graphic novels: Practical strategies for the secondary ELA classroom.* Gainesville, FL: Maupin House.

National Council of Teachers of English (2005). *NCTE position statement on multimodal literacies.* Retrieved from http://www.ncte.org/positions/statements/multimodalliteracies.

National Governors Association Center for Best Practices and the Council of Chief State School Officers (2012). *Common Core State Standards for English language arts & literacy in history/social studies, science, and technical subjects.* Retrieved from http://www.corestandards.org/ELA-Literacy.

Reed, S. L., & Stavreva, K. (2006). Layering knowledge: Information literacy as critical thinking in the literature classroom. *Pedagogy: Critical Approaches to Teaching Literature, Language, Composition, and Culture, 6*(3), 435–52.

Schwartz, A., & Rubinstein-Avila, E. (2006). Understanding the manga hype: Uncovering the multimodality of comic-book literacies. *Journal of Adolescent & Adult Literacy, 50*(1), 40–48. doi:10.1598/JAAL.50.1.5.

Serafini, F. (2005). Voices in the park, voices in the classroom: Readers responding to postmodern picture books. *Reading Research and Instruction, 44*(3), 47–64.

Serafini, F. (2011). Expanding perspectives for comprehending visual images in multimodal texts. *Journal of Adolescent & Adult Literacy, 54*(5), 342–50. doi:10.1598/JAAL.54.5.4.

Serafini, F. (2012). Expanding the four resources model: Reading visual and multi-modal texts. *Pedagogies: An International Journal, 7*(2), 150–64.

Serafini, F., & Blasingame, J. (2012). The changing face of the novel. *The Reading Teacher, 66*(2), 145–48. doi:10.1002/TRTR.01113.

Smolkin, L. B., & Donovan, C. A. (2005). Looking closely at a science trade book: Gail Gibbons and multimodal literacy. *Language Arts, 83*(1), 52–62.

Stein, P. (2008). Multimodal instructional practices. In J. Coiro, M. Knobel, C. Lankshear, & D. J. Leu (Eds.), *Handbook of research on new literacies* (pp. 871–98). New York, NY: Lawrence Erlbaum.

Sweeny, S. M. (2007). Reading for technology savvy students: Utilizing choice of multi-modal texts to engage students in content literacy. *The NERA Journal, 43*(1), 15–22.

Walpole, S. (1998/1999). Changing texts, changing thinking: Comprehension demands of new science textbooks. *The Reading Teacher, 52*(4), 358–69.

Walsh, M. (2006). The "textual shift": Examining the reading process with print, visual and multimodal texts. *Australian Journal of Language and Literacy, 29*(1), 24–37.

Walsh, M. (2008). Worlds have collided and modes have merged: Classroom evidence of changed literacy practices. *Literacy, 42*(2), 101–108.

Walsh, M. (2010). Multimodal literacy: What does it mean for classroom practice? *Australian Journal of Language and Literacy, 33*(3), 211–39.

Yannicopoulou, A. (2004). Visual aspects of written texts: Preschoolers view comics. *L1 Educational Studies in Language and Literature, 4,* 169–81.

Yomtov, N. (2013). *True stories of the Civil War.* Makato: MN: Capstone Press.

Youngs, S., & Serafini, F. (2011). Comprehension strategies for reading historical fiction picturebooks. *The Reading Teacher, 65*(2), 115–24. doi:10.1002/TRTR.01014.

Zwiers, J. (2010). *Building reading comprehension in grades 6–12: A toolkit of classroom activities* (2nd ed.). Newark, DE: International Reading Association.

11

Addressing Adolescents' Need for Voice and Interaction

Jill Lewis-Spector and Mary McGriff

I met Marissa when she was eleven years old while I was consulting in a high poverty urban school. She gravitated towards me each time I visited her classroom, reaching for my hand, touching my wedding band, asking about the clothes I was wearing. She treated me as though I were special, but in reality she was the special one. She was in the process, as were her classmates, of becoming a teenager—that mysterious mix of an individual who so wants to be independent and, yet, who is so needy of adult assistance, guidance, and care, that contradiction of an individual who is on Wednesday the moody, brooding, explosive child and who on Thursday is the sweet, cooperative student. Marissa's classmates and their teachers would have to connect to achieve academic goals, and it was largely up to their teachers to make this happen.

What would Marissa's teachers need to know about identity development during adolescence and what activities might her teachers incorporate into their literacy instruction that would contribute to academic achievement while also developing Marissa's confidence, maturity, and identity?

IDENTITY CHALLENGES DURING ADOLESCENCE

Fortunately, Marissa's middle school teachers understood the nature of early adolescence and that during the next decade Marissa and her classmates would be struggling with issues of identity and independence and were sure to present and experience challenges. Lewis and Jones (2009) explain, "We can observe adolescents experimenting with identities, shifting peer groups, and sometimes totally rejecting societal norms only to embrace them at other times" (p. 8). Some young adolescents actively seek to establish a unique identity, perhaps through their personal dress style (e.g. tattoos, hair color, etc.), behavior (star scholar, class clown, risk taker). Others may deliberately exclude themselves from social activities and try to avoid being noticed (sitting in the back of the classroom; not initiating new friendships). Most have difficulty communicating their thoughts to friends, family, and teachers. Students' explorations of identities are reflected in choices they make about friends, values, media preferences, language use, personal appearance, and cultural practices as they seek to clarify who they are and to address questions of gender, intellectual, spiritual, moral, and ethnic identity. It is perhaps this last aspect, ethnic identity, which deserves special note because as our public school population grows more diverse, it becomes more likely that teachers' own ethnic and cultural norms may diverge from those of their students (Papanastasiou, 2001). And since the teachers that students encounter can dramatically impact the process of adolescent identity formation, it is important that educators remain mindful of these potential differences as they seek to provide supportive, efficacious instructional experiences for their students.

Research Evidence and Theoretical Framework

The climate teachers create in their classrooms is affected by the process and content of instructional decisions and classroom conversations, classroom norms, and models and attitudes teachers either knowingly or not encourage students to emulate; teachers who are responsive to students often witness greater academic achievement. A nurturing environment that promotes positive relationships among members of the classroom community is essential for creating a sense of belonging, which "may have an energetic function, awakening enthusiasm, interest, and willingness to participate in academic activities" (Furrer & Skinner, 2003, p.158). Multiple theoretical frameworks inform what we understand about adolescent identity development and offer perspectives for considering best practices for promoting adolescent literacy that will yield positive identities and teacher-adolescent interactions in classrooms.

Cross-cultural perspective. Students whose at-home cultures differ considerably from that of the traditional classroom, such as students from Middle Eastern, Hispanic, or Asian families, may struggle to incorporate competing values and expectations of the different groups with whom they interact.

According to Phinney, Horenczyk, Liebking, & Vedder (2001), students may choose one of four paths as they seek resolution to this conflict: assimilation, wherein they adopt the majority culture's norms and standards thus sacrificing those of their native group; marginalization wherein they live within the majority culture but feel estranged; separation, wherein they essentially limit their associations to members of their own culture and reject the majority culture; and integration—maintaining ties both to the majority culture and one's own ethnic culture by intermixing the two. This last approach may be the most satisfying to adolescents (Chen, Benet-Martínez, & Bond, 2008), and, through effective and ongoing communication, students may be able to integrate their ethnic identity into a larger sense of self. What makes such communication particularly challenging for teachers is the wide gap between most teachers' cultures and those of their students. As Papanastasiou (2001) notes, most American teachers are white, middle class, and female, but our student population has become increasingly diverse.

Teacher expertise in adolescent development, especially being adept at helping students with exploring identities and communicating, including identities that teachers find unfamiliar or in stark contrast to their own, will be essential for successful instruction and students' academic growth.

Psychosocial perspective. While early in life children recognize themselves as separate beings, differentiated from others (*individuation*) (Jung, 1989, p. 209), it is during adolescence that we see greater abstract reasoning and children begin to experiment with different identities. We can assist students with exploring alternatives and making commitments to particular identities, thus establishing identity coherence and avoiding identity confusion (Erikson, 1968). As Clark & Justice (n.d.) note, established identities yield "higher self-esteem, increased critical thinking, and advanced moral reasoning." Effective teachers of adolescents are able to help students with finding their voices, especially with those students who seem most silenced.

Schools and classrooms can help students establish solid identities while they also maintain *connectedness* with others, by providing a safe, positive environment from which students can explore who they are. A body of research (Kirshner, O'Donoghue, & McLaughlin, 2003; National Research Council, 2002; Zeldin, 2004; Zeldin, Camino, & Mook, 2005) supports the importance of empowering students through greater participation in classroom and school decision making. As children mature, they are better able to express their opinions, make choices, and assume larger roles as members of democratic learning communities. They become more committed to education and integrate more successfully in intergenerational activities, better preparing them for citizenship and careers. As Kordalewski (1999) notes, "When students have a voice in classroom processes, they share in decision-making and the construction of knowledge. The teacher, consequently, becomes a co-learner and facilitator as well as a source of knowledge."

Sociocultural perspective. Perhaps even more important to adolescent development is the role social networking, including social interaction in classrooms, plays in identity formation. Lewis (2007) advises, "We can use their need for connection to instructional advantage by engaging students in collaborative projects" (p. 151). Faircloth & Hamm (2005) explain that students' sense of belonging in classrooms contributes to engagement in learning and achievement-related behavior. And Alvermann (2008) reminds us, "Young people are tirelessly editing and remixing multimodal content they find online to share with others, using new tools to show and tell, and rewriting their social identities in an effort to become who they say they are" (p. 10).

Classrooms contribute in important ways to identity construction. In their study of how the classroom social environment affected early adolescents' beliefs about themselves, Patrick, Kaplan, & Ryan (2007) find benefits to self-regulation and task engagement when students feel emotionally supported by their teachers and academically supported by their peers, and further, "When students perceive the classroom as respectful, we expect that they will be most likely to suggest and explain their ideas about schoolwork, even when tentative, without feeling constrained by concerns about what others might think or say if they are incorrect" (p. 85).

A key concept related to this perspective is that our identities are socially situated. That is, every individual has a core identity that is recognizable by actions that are fairly consistent and predictable across all communities in which he or she interacts e.g. school, church, peer group, family. However, to some degree an individual also modifies his/her behavior within each community in accordance with the particular group's norms and expectations and in response to the level of validation he/she receives by the group, overall (Gee, 2000). School-based norms and expectations often include the ability to generate and respond to questions, the ability to work in cooperative groups, and the ability to delay gratification. Therefore, a student who effectively modifies his/her behaviors and language to align with these expectations will likely have his or her membership in the learning community validated by teachers and peers. By contrast, the students who have been less successful at effectuating school-based expectations will be less likely to incorporate these patterns of behavior within the identities they assume. Moreover, adolescents who struggle to enact the behaviors typically expected of students may even assume identities that incorporate academically maladaptive practices, and for this reason it is critical that educators devise means of validating all students' presence and participation in school-based learning communities as illustrated in later sections of this chapter.

But identity is not singular. Adolescents also have access to many affinity-based extracurricular, neighborhood, and online groups, and as they interact with others in these communities, they become more adept at modifying their own identities in accordance with each group's norms and expectations. In fact, this ability to shift identity is commendable. As Gee (2001) suggests, "people who are adept at taking on new identities, interacting within affinity groups, and are well connected in networks will flourish" (p. 8).

When language arts literacy teachers planning for instruction consider multiple perspectives as well as students' varied and diverse community memberships, they can create dynamic classroom environments that respect individual voices, allow for expression of multiple cultures, and facilitate productive and respectful interactions with peers. Within such classrooms, students like Marissa and her peers will thrive.

LITERACY OPPORTUNITIES TO PROMOTE POSITIVE IDENTITIES FOR ADOLESCENTS

Adolescents' identity formation involves both looking inward, to learn more about themselves, as well as looking outward, to better understand others. Here we suggest three broad approaches that teachers can take to facilitate inward/outward investigations of self and others, beginning with activities to promote critical literacy.

Exploring Multiple Perspectives through a Critical Literacy Lens

Teachers understand the need to promote critical thinking with their students, but critical literacy goes even beyond that. Shor suggests that "Critical literacy challenges the status quo in an effort to discover alternative paths for self and social development" (1997, p. 1). Lewison, Flint, and Van Sluys (2002, p. 382) suggest four dimensions of critical literacy: "(1) disrupting the commonplace, (2) interrogating multiple viewpoints, (3) focusing on sociopolitical issues, and (4) taking action and promoting social justice." Significantly, enacting critical literacy within the classroom also enables students to develop English language arts proficiencies consistent with the Common Core State Standards (CCSS).

In the classroom, students can consider texts from different content fields through a critical lens by analyzing stereotypes in portrayals of gender roles, race, ethnicity, and socioeconomic status. Through discussion, students can evaluate biases, and determine whether actions of particular characters or historical figures reflect social justice. They can examine language as a reflection of power relationships, bias, stereotyping, or discrimination.

Teachers may wonder how, with limited resources, critical literacy can be advanced with their students. But discussion is, in fact, more important in promoting critical literacy than the availability of texts (McLaughlin and DeVoogd (2004). For instance, Elizabeth Sky-McIlvain (n.d.) provides an example of how this can be done in her post-reading lesson plan for *The Sign of the Beaver* that she designed for middle grade students. As she explains, "This lesson requires students to read for stereotypes, comparing their response to a published essay praising the novel" (n.p.). As students examine the stereotypes of Native peoples in the passages, they also consider whether these stereotypes are appropriate for today and whether the book should be used in today's classrooms. They discuss how young readers might be affected by the stereotypes and whether the author's work "rises above the stereotypes it contains" (n.p.).

Critical literacy discussions often focus on how some individuals' voices are privileged over others, perhaps due to status (e.g. student/teacher; parent/child), or race (e.g. majority/minority). The daily effects of one kind of privilege are described in depth by Peggy McIntosh (1988) in her article, *White Privilege: Unpacking the Invisible Knapsack*. She describes her advantages explaining, "I can arrange to protect my children most of the time from people who might not like them. I can swear, or dress in second hand clothes, or not answer letters, without having people attribute these choices to the bad morals, the poverty, or the illiteracy of my race" (n.p.).

As students read texts they want to ask whose voice is heard, whose is not, and then to explore the extent to which under what circumstances their own voices may or may not be privileged. In fact, adolescents often feel their voices are marginalized, that is, no one listens to them. Through the use of *response journals,* their teachers can counter this feeling while simultaneously giving students opportunities to establish and confirm their identities. In these journals, students respond to text, perhaps agreeing with or disputing an author's ideas, or commenting on some of its features, such as language, photographs or other visuals, examples, and making text-to-self connections. Students might also raise questions or offer suggestions. Students might wonder why the author framed an argument in a certain way, used a particular example, or holds a certain point of view. Texts might be ones that concern significant issues, or perhaps that can engage students in critical literacy analysis. They can examine such aspects of the text as the audience or context. Teachers usually have students create two columns in their journals, one column for the author's text and the other for their own. Others suggest three columns, with the third for the teacher to respond to the student's comments, ensuring that the student has, indeed, been heard. Response journals allow teachers and students to get to know each other better and can provide the basis for successful and stimulating peer interactions and personal essays. They also offer teachers a means for assessing how well students employ critical literacy as they interpret texts, identify subtleties, make judgments, and support their ideas. Teachers can also use response journals to evaluate how well students are able to express their thoughts through writing.

When students have opportunities to examine text through a critical literacy lens, they are also deepening their own understanding of their personal values and biases, hence contributing to individual identity formation. In this process of discovery, their own self-worth is validated and they learn how to respect and value others who may differ from them significantly. Adolescents also need experiences that strengthen positive identities. Here, too, classroom teachers can be effective. Table 11.1 illustrates how critical literacy discussions and response journals also address the Common Core State Standards.

Table 11.1. Common Core State Standards—English Language Arts Anchor Standards Addressed through Critical Literacy Discussions and Response Journals

English Language Arts Anchor Standard	Skills and Knowledge	Critical Literacy Discussions and Response Journals
CCSS.ELA-Literacy. CCRA.R.3	Analyze how and why individuals, events, or ideas develop and interact over the course of a text	Analyze gender, race, ethnic, and socioeconomic stereotypes present in reading materials
CCSS.ELA-Literacy. CCRA.R.4	Interpret words and phrases as they are used in a text, including determining technical, connotative, and figurative meanings, and analyze how specific word choices shape meaning or tone.	
CCSS.ELA-Literacy. CCRA.L.3	Apply knowledge of language to understand how language functions in different contexts, to make effective choices for meaning or style, and to comprehend more fully when reading or listening.	Analyze how the use of language in texts does/ does not reflect biases, discrimination, or the privileging or one group over another
CCSS.ELA-Literacy. CCRA.SL.3	Evaluate a speaker's point of view, reasoning, and use of evidence and rhetoric.	
CCSS.ELA-Literacy. CCRA.R.8	Delineate and evaluate the argument and specific claims in a text, including the validity of the reasoning as well as the relevance and sufficiency of the evidence.	Evaluate gender, race, ethnic and socioeconomic stereotypes from a socio historical perspective

PROMOTING PERSONAL AGENCY
WITHIN A LITERACY DEVELOPMENT CURRICULUM

More than 100 years ago, G. Stanley Hall (1904) referred to adolescence as a period of "sturm and drang," a turbulent period during which children feel conflicted by the constraints imposed on them by adults on whom they also depend for their basic needs, and their desire for independence. As they struggle through this stressful period, some find satisfaction within peer groups where they can exert leadership and feel more in control of outcomes.

Literacy Activities to Promote Personal Agency

Teachers can organize classroom literacy opportunities such that more students assume leadership roles and experience personal agency. Such literacy experiences also align well with the English Language Arts CCSS.

Jigsaw Strategy. Utilizing the Jigsaw strategy is one avenue for giving leadership opportunities to all students. According to jigsaw.org, a website dedicated to discussion of the Jigsaw instructional strategy, Jigsaw is "a cooperative learning technique that reduces racial conflict among school children, promotes better learning, improves student motivation, and increases enjoyment of the learning experience." All of this is true, with research to support these contentions (Perkins & Saris, 2001; Hanze & Berger, 2007). What is also true of Jigsaw is that it has the promise of being a powerful tool for building student leadership abilities among those students whom teachers might not have considered as having leadership potential.

Jigsaw was developed in 1971 by Eliot Aronson and his graduate students to help public schools in Austin, Texas address negative student behavior. He explains that Jigsaw helped to "defuse an explosive situation" (Aronson, 2000–2008). Teachers can use the strategy for single articles, text chapters, or research projects. During Jigsaw, students participate in *Home* groups as well as in *Expert* groups. If a single article or chapter is used, the teacher typically selects text that contains new material having some complex or unfamiliar ideas. The selected material should have information divided clearly, perhaps indicated by subtitles or by divisions teachers have created. Further, each section of the article or chapter should be able to be understood fairly well without the reader knowing the information within the other sections. For instance, an article or chapter about classical Greece might be divided into sections that discuss wars, art, politics, life in Athens, etc. To begin Jigsaw, the teacher organizes students into *Home* groups, with each group having as many students as there are sections of the article. Students in each group count off; each number represents a section of the article to be read. Next, students will leave their *Home* group to form their *Expert* groups, which are comprised only of students with the same number, e.g. all 2's come together as an *Expert* group.

A similar organizing approach is used for research projects. Here all *Home* groups might have similar topics to research (e.g. John F. Kennedy's presidency). The teacher assigns subtopics and each *Home* group member selects one to research, the one for which that student will become an expert, e.g. JFK's presidential election, foreign policy, domestic policy, assassination. *Expert* groups are formed for each subtopic, and individuals in these work together to locate sources and share information. When students return to their *Home* group, each student's information is shared. *Home* group members work as a team to determine how they will finalize and present their project.

Thus, within the *Expert* groups, students work cooperatively to help each other learn the material in their assigned section of a reading selection or subtopic for a research project. Here is where leadership potential is realized. Peers assist struggling readers, but all students in the *Expert* group, including struggling readers, become experts of their assigned part. Students can ask each other questions to test their knowledge, assist with creating demonstrations they plan to present to their *Home* groups, practice demonstrations, and offer constructive critiques. When the experts complete their task of learning their part, they return to their *Home* group where each expert shares what s/he has learned from the reading selection or research material reviewed. Collectively, then, the *Home* groups learn the content of the entire article or key ideas about all aspects of the research topic being studied. As Chang (2009) explains, "No matter what kind of jigsaw approach is used, group members can make separate contributions to a joint product" (p. 228). Further, Jigsaw lends itself to learning a wide variety of content fields. Chang (2009) and Pozzi (2010) have both been successful using jigsaw with students in online communities.

Observant teachers will notice how engaged the struggling readers are during all phases of Jigsaw. Because these students are experts on whom their *Home* group will depend for information, they are motivated to remain focused on the task. Their accomplishments as experts generate feelings of self-efficacy. As they instruct their *Home* group peers about what they have learned, they assume positive leadership roles. Jigsaw opportunities build confidence for struggling readers. For them, and for others, it promotes positive social skills, reduces boredom, and encourages supportive behaviors. In addition to the numerous benefits of Jigsaw already noted, Table 11.2 illustrates how this strategy addresses the Common Core English Language Arts Anchor Standards.

Booktalks. Comparing a booktalk to a movie trailer, Nancy Keene aptly observes that, "the purpose of a booktalk is to 'sell' the book" (http://nancykeane.com/booktalks/faq.htm). Structured as brief presentations that highlight a book's most compelling features, booktalks have traditionally been used by librarians and classroom teachers to encourage students to read selected texts by offering students enticing, strategically-selected glimpses at the plots, characters, and/or authors' rhetorical devices. However, *student-prepared, student-delivered* booktalks empower adolescents to assume responsibility for supporting the literacy engagement of other learners. Additionally, adolescent-run booktalks enable students to develop leadership skills as they promote well-selected texts that they have read to other students, either peers or younger students with whom they may be paired in cross-age partnerships.

Table 11.2.   Common Core State Standards—English Language Arts Anchor Standards Addressed through Jigsaw

English Language Arts Anchor Standard	Skills and Knowledge	Jigsaw Activity
CCSS.ELA-Literacy. CCRA.R.1	Read closely to determine what the text says explicitly and to make logical inferences from it; cite specific textual evidence when writing or speaking to support conclusions drawn from the text.	Students in Expert groups work collaboratively to understand/interpret assigned reading material; ask and answer questions to test their knowledge of reading material.
CCSS.ELA-Literacy. CCRA.W.7	Conduct short as well as more sustained research projects based on focused questions, demonstrating understanding of the subject under investigation.	
CCSS.ELA-Literacy. CCRA.SL.1	Prepare for and participate effectively in a range of conversations and collaborations with diverse partners, building on others' ideas and expressing their own clearly and persuasively.	Create demonstrations or presentations about assigned reading materials to present to *Home* groups.
CCSS.ELA-Literacy. CCRA.W.2	Write informative/explanatory texts to examine and convey complex ideas and information clearly and accurately through the effective selection, organization, and analysis of content.	
CCSS.ELA-Literacy. CCRA.SL.5	Make strategic use of digital media and visual displays of data to express information and enhance understanding of presentations.	
CCSS.ELA-Literacy. CCRA.SL.4	Present information, findings, and supporting evidence such that listeners can follow the line of reasoning and the organization, development, and style are appropriate to task, purpose, and audience.	Expert group members share what they learned from assigned reading material with *Home* group members.

Booktalks serve as potent agency-building mechanisms, particularly when they are prepared for and delivered to peers, because they encompass a wide range of content and delivery options that adolescents must carefully consider when seeking to promote a text to classmates. For example, students must consider how much of the plot to share, what to disclose about the author's writing style, and whether excerpts from the text should be read during the presentation. Also, students must carefully consider how to deliver their booktalks. Should the booktalk be delivered live, or would the audience respond more effectively to a prerecorded or digitally created variant? Which modality would enable the presenter to optimize his or her creative and linguistic strengths? As adolescents gain greater proficiency in preparing and delivering booktalks, they better understand the function and impact of each component feature and therefore become better able to make decisions about the approaches to use in preparing and delivering the most effective booktalks possible. When preparing booktalks for their own classmates, adolescents can use their knowledge of peers' interests, current fads, and common concerns to guide their decision-making.

Cross-age literacy experiences enable middle and high school students to serve as literacy mentors to younger students, and booktalks offer an ideal opportunity for adolescents to positively influence their mentees' engagement with text. When adolescents are preparing booktalks for younger students, they would need to take intentional steps to learn more about younger students' interests and texts that match those interests. Shiflett (1998) describes this process as a market analysis.

The market analysis process is ideal for teens. Adolescents gather information about the general interests of the younger students by conferring with classroom teachers and also noticing the topics the younger students discuss among themselves. School media specialists can contribute information about the most popular titles, genres, and/or series of books for students in this age range. Adolescents then generate a profile of literature preferences for their mentees, perhaps refining it further by conducting individual interviews. Equipped with general and specific information about the reading interests of the younger students, adolescents will be able to work together to prepare and deliver booktalks for the whole class, and conduct one-on-one or small group booktalks for the targeted interests of individuals. They may also follow up with classroom teachers and students to learn how effective their booktalks were!

The adolescent's level of preparation will, of course, dictate the overall effectiveness of the booktalks they deliver. But well-planned, well-delivered booktalks have the potential for adolescents to positively influence the reading habits of their audiences; they allow adolescents to *lead* other students to greater levels of engagement with text. All leaders must actively consider the interests and goals of those they lead. As such, cross-age and peer-oriented booktalks enable adolescents to develop leadership skills while supporting the literacy growth of other students. Booktalks contribute to reaching the Common Core State Standards Anchor Standards for English Language Arts, as illustrated in Table 11.3.

Literacy Circles. Literature circles denote an instructional framework in which students read independently and learn collaboratively though structured, yet authentic and free-flowing discussions about text. Within this framework, students select books from a range of titles which may share a common theme, and they are formed

Table 11.3.   Common Core State Standards—English Language Arts Anchor Standards Addressed through Booktalks

English Language Arts Anchor Standard	Skills and Knowledge	Booktalk Activity
CCSS.ELA-Literacy. CCRA.W.7	Conduct short as well as more sustained research projects based on focused questions, demonstrating understanding of the subject under investigation.	Research/analyze audience interests in order to select appropriate texts.
CCSS.ELA-Literacy. CCRA.R.2	Determine central ideas or themes of a text and analyze their development; summarize the key supporting details and ideas.	Identify and summarize compelling features of a text based upon audience interests.
CCSS.ELA-Literacy. CCRA.R.4	Interpret words and phrases as they are used in a text, including determining technical, connotative, and figurative meanings, and analyze how specific word choices shape meaning or tone.	Strategically select text excerpts based on audience interests.
CCSS.ELA-Literacy. CCRA.SL.5	Make strategic use of digital media and visual displays of data to express information and enhance understanding of presentations.	Strategically select presentation mode and format to optimize audience engagement.
CCSS.ELA-Literacy. CCRA.W.1	Write arguments to support claims in an analysis of substantive topics or texts using valid reasoning and relevant and sufficient evidence.	Prepare booktalk outline or script with the goal of "selling the book" to a specific audience.
CCSS.ELA-Literacy. CCRA.SL.6	Adapt speech to a variety of contexts and communicative tasks, demonstrating command of formal English when indicated or appropriate.	
CCSS.ELA-Literacy. CCRA.SL.4	Present information, findings, and supporting evidence such that listeners can follow the line of reasoning and the organization, development, and style are appropriate to task, purpose, and audience.	Deliver a carefully prepared booktalk to a specific audience.
CCSS.ELA-Literacy. CCRA.L.1	Demonstrate command of the conventions of standard English grammar and usage when writing or speaking.	

into small discussion groups based on these selections (Daniels, 2002; Moeller & Moeller, 2007). *Literacy circles* is an adapted version of this process that incorporates expository text formats and that may be applied across content areas (Lewis, 2006). The literacy circle framework calls for students to take turns assuming a variety of defined roles as they prepare for and take part in small group discussions. While roles can be added or adjusted according to literary genre and student needs, there are four basic roles that are typically included in group discussions: discussion director, connector, passage master, and illustrator. By assuming different roles, students read for different purposes and contribute distinct reflections or analyses of text that enhance all group members' understanding of the literature. Additionally, the discussion director, connector, passage master, and illustrator roles offer authentic, substantive opportunities for students to exercise leadership within their groups.

The discussion director holds overall responsibility for ensuring that the group remains actively and specifically engaged in discussing the text. To this end, the discussion director comes to discussions prepared with open-ended questions and potential follow-up questions to pose to the group. Additionally, the director monitors interactions as those in other roles lead their segments, and directors encourage all group members to actively join in the conversation. It is important that the climate within literacy circles remains accepting and constructive, and the discussion director takes the lead in maintaining this atmosphere, redirecting digressions and recasting potentially insensitive comments by using cues and other linguistic tools. Teachers model and scaffold students' understanding of how to use these cues and tools in this context. Overall, the discussion director carries out leadership functions that require advance preparation, in-the-moment responsiveness, and a concern for the learning of others.

The connector is responsible for identifying and sharing ways that the text relates to life. These can include links to values, lived experiences, current events, or other readings. Additionally, these should be links that the connector has a sincere interest in exploring with other group members since genuinely thought-provoking connections add a measure of enthusiasm and investment in the discussion. At the same time, the connector attempts to elicit participation in discussion from all group members and must therefore consider their experiences, interests, and dispositions when selecting text excerpts and related life experiences to bring before the group. Leading this component of the group discussion provides students with the opportunity to purposefully balance the needs and interests of all group members in order to optimize collaborative analyses of text during discussions.

The passage master holds responsibility for selecting noteworthy passages of text and for facilitating the groups' examination of these excerpts. In leading this segment of the small group discussion, the passage master must exercise careful judgment in determining which excerpts will add the greatest value to the group's understanding of the text. In addition to selecting the text, the passage master also decides how it should be shared with the group. In some instances, silent reading of the text allows group members to appreciate its noteworthy aspects. Other passages may be best experienced when read by one group member or by the book's author on an audio recording. The passage master, therefore, must purposefully consider a range of options in determining what and how to guide his or her peers' analysis of the reading. This role gives students control over the discussion's content and format, and it provides them with important opportunities to reflect on the learning needs of others as they plan and lead their discussion segments.

The illustrator provides the group with a visual response to the reading, and this nonlinguistic element provides a particularly unique means of guiding the group's understanding of the text. The illustrator may create a pencil sketch, diagram, or computer generated design. The illustration may depict an event from the text, or it can represent something that the illustrator was reminded of while reading. The illustrator may also opt to represent an emotion or idea generated while reading. Creating this type of visual representation requires that the illustrator call upon his/her personal reactions to the reading. The illustrator's perspectives, therefore, will be foregrounded in the group discussion, and this enables students who express themselves more effectively through nonverbal modalities to contribute meaningful, thought-provoking content to the group's discussion. Additionally illustrations may be interpreted in a wide variety of manners, and the group's consideration of an illustration typically evokes a broader range of responses than those elicited by linguistic prompts. Like the passage master, the illustrator must plan how to share his or her work with the group. For example, the illustration may be silently displayed while the group members reflect on its message or make connections to their own ideas about the reading. Alternatively, the illustrator may opt to explicitly share the message conveyed in the illustration. Overall, the illustrator is empowered to lead the group in exploring a diverse array of literal, abstract, and affective responses to the text. It is a leadership role that gives a distinctive voice to the illustrator's perspectives, and it is a role that challenges group members to venture beyond the use of words in constructing meaning from text.

Overall, literacy circles prioritize student voices. They enable students to recognize that, through their direct leadership, supportive contributions and critical analyses, they have the ability to broaden their own learning and to richly enhance the learning experiences of others. Literacy circles help adolescents cultivate a sense of agency around literacy-related activities, and they support adolescents' positive identity development. Additionally, as Table 11.4 illustrates, literacy circles offer ample opportunity for development of many of the Common Core English Language Arts Anchor Standards.

Teachers can promote classroom-based book clubs to extend experiences in literacy circles. Clubs can be initiated and managed completely by the students. They give book talks to suggest books classmates might enjoy reading, and students join the club of their choice. Club members can alternate turns as discussion leader, but participants do not have designated roles in clubs. Teachers provide time for clubs to meet to respond to the text, which may extend to written responses or even creative projects. Some teachers use their observations during book club time to identify

Table 11.4. Common Core State Standards—English Language Arts Anchor Standards Addressed through Literacy Circles

English Language Arts Anchor Standard	Skills and Knowledge	Literacy Circle Activity
CCSS.ELA-Literacy. CCRA.R.1	Read closely to determine what the text says explicitly and to make logical inferences from it; cite specific textual evidence when writing or speaking to support conclusions drawn from the text.	Read and interpret reading material according to the specific requirements of the assigned role— discussion director, connector, passage master, illustrator, etc.
CCSS.ELA-Literacy. CCRA.R.2	Determine central ideas or themes of a text and analyze their development; summarize the key supporting details and ideas.	
CCSS.ELA-Literacy. CCRA.W.2	Write informative/explanatory texts to examine and convey complex ideas and information clearly and accurately through the effective selection, organization, and analysis of content.	Prepare written, visual, or audiovisual interpretation(s) of assigned reading.
CCSS.ELA-Literacy. CCRA.W.4	Produce clear and coherent writing in which the development, organization, and style are appropriate to task, purpose, and audience.	
CCSS.ELA-Literacy. CCRA.L.1	Demonstrate command of the conventions of standard English grammar and usage when writing or speaking.	
CCSS.ELA-Literacy. CCRA.SL.5	Make strategic use of digital media and visual displays of data to express information and enhance understanding of presentations.	
CCSS.ELA-Literacy. CCRA.R.4	Interpret words and phrases as they are used in a text, including determining technical, connotative, and figurative meanings, and analyze how specific word choices shape meaning or tone.	Analyze and respond to author's use of language.

English Language Arts Anchor Standard	Skills and Knowledge	Literacy Circle Activity
CCSS.ELA-Literacy. CCRA.R.5	Analyze the structure of texts, including how specific sentences, paragraphs, and larger portions of the text (e.g., a section, chapter, scene, or stanza) relate to each other and the whole.	
CCSS.ELA-Literacy. CCRA.SL.1	Prepare for and participate effectively in a range of conversations and collaborations with diverse partners, building on others' ideas and expressing their own clearly and persuasively.	Share analyses/interpretations with other literacy circle members in a manner that facilitates their understanding of the assigned reading.
CCSS.ELA-Literacy. CCRA.SL.4	Present information, findings, and supporting evidence such that listeners can follow the line of reasoning and the organization, development, and style that are appropriate to task, purpose, and audience.	
CCSS.ELA-Literacy. CCRA.L.1	Demonstrate command of the conventions of standard English grammar and usage when writing or speaking.	

student needs and plan mini lessons; others may evaluate student discussion and participation, although using book clubs for evaluation may diminish student enthusiasm for what could be a completely student-controlled experience.

Self-assessment and goal setting. The practices of self-assessment and goal setting can fuel adolescents' sense of agency as readers and writers. As pedagogical processes, they challenge the notion that teachers alone control the assessment of students' work, and they provide adolescents with mechanisms to effectively control their literacy learning. Rubrics, checklists, and student-teacher conferences offer valuable structures that facilitate self-assessment and goal setting among adolescent learners. Additionally, these structures explicitly support literacy achievement since they heighten students' knowledge of specific outcomes within the CCSS, and they help students understand their individual progress toward these outcomes.

Both rubrics and checklists demystify the assessment process by identifying the criteria by which a task or product is appraised (Bromley, 2007). Rubrics include descriptions of specific levels of performance under each criterion. Checklists are simpler variants that delineate criteria for assessment that students "check off" when completed. Both enable students to plan and assess their performance in specific areas, and both affirm students' identities as learners.

Regularly scheduled student-teacher conferences offer opportunities for informative, individualized discussions about students' growth related to specific dimensions of literacy (Galda & Graves, 2007). During conferences students and teachers examine work samples and share observations about students' engagement in literacy processes, such as literacy circle participation, booktalk preparation or essay revision. Prior to a scheduled conference, students have the opportunity to assess their work relative to fixed criteria. Additionally students reflect upon and assess their progress toward personal goals set at preceding conferences. Significantly, during conferences students can reflect upon their affective responses to literacy practices and products, such as aspects of a recent and challenging literacy circle discussion. Or they might identify the elements of what they consider to be one of their best essays or poems. During conferences, students and teachers share their respective feedback, taking care to link observations back to specific writing pieces, literacy circle role sheets, booktalk notes, or other process-related artifacts. Students can also set new measurable goals and corresponding action steps that they will take before the next scheduled conference. Teachers use their understanding of each student's instructional needs and their broader knowledge of curriculum standards to guide students in this practice. It is essential, however, that students' voices remain prominent throughout the process.

As students grow increasingly adept at using rubrics, checklists, and conferences to assess their progress and inform their goal-setting, they learn more about the processes used by successful readers and writers and how to refine the products they generate. Ultimately, they develop a greater sense of control over their literacy development.

Literacy Opportunities That Build Positive Identities as Community Members

You may have witnessed adolescents often exhibiting contradictory behaviors, sometimes acting cruel and callous towards their peers (e.g. cyber bullying, street fighting, name-calling) while at the same time demonstrating altruism and showing deep empathy for others. Adolescents' exuberance for life can give way to deep depression; their egoism to self-abasement. In their efforts to untangle this tumultuous, confusing time in their lives, teens may lose their connectedness to others, leading to complete disengagement from families, friends, and society. They do not recognize that in addition to the small world in which they participate every day, they are citizens of a much larger universe, which gives them both rights and responsibilities as they become adults.

By using literacy opportunities to engage students in civic conversations and activities while also increasing students' literacy achievements across disciplines, teachers will contribute to "developing a citizenry that can participate in decision making and in new knowledge production" (Moje, 2007, p. 31). As students learn what is considered responsible and respectful citizen behavior, their identity as citizens is confirmed, and they will be better equipped to act constructively to further the public good. They will demonstrate attitudes that respect values essential to democratic citizenship such as political tolerance, trust in the democratic process, respect for the rule of law, and compromise. Such dispositions are essential for U.S. citizens today, and as Michael Edwards (2005) notes,

> In its role as the "public sphere," civil society becomes the arena for argument and deliberation as well as for association and institutional collaboration, and the extent to which such spaces thrive is crucial to democracy, since if only certain truths are represented, if alternative viewpoints are silenced by exclusion or suppression, or if one set of voices are heard more loudly than those of others, the "public" interest inevitably suffers. When all politics are polarized, public policy problems become embedded, even frozen, in polities that cannot solve them—think health care and welfare reform in the US, for example. Breaking the resulting gridlock requires the creation of new publics in support of broad-based reform—exactly what is missing in the US right now. (10)

While teachers may not foist their political opinions on their students, they can create literacy activities by which students become more aware of such concepts as ethical behavior, the common good, compromise, volunteerism, and community. Many teachers and students enjoy a feeling of community within their own classrooms. In these spaces, all members have respect for classroom rules (often created by students), for the rights of individuals, and for the rights of other students or groups of students to express their interests and opinions, even when they differ from those of the majority.

Researching other communities. Students researching the communities in which they live will have ample opportunity to build personal connections and to identify and/or reaffirm their values. Students can work as teams using literacy skills to locate available information about their communities, and evaluating sources, especially those found in newspapers and on the Internet. As they work, students learn more about the ethnic and religious minorities, seniors, and the disabled who live nearby. They may find evidence of support as well as intolerance of these groups. Their findings can be used as a basis for discussion and debate as well as ideas for community initiatives that will serve all residents. Students can choose how to share their concerns and ideas with others, such as disseminating them by writing persuasive letters to newspaper editors, contacting local radio stations, or contributing to community websites or blogs that facilitate resident communication. They can work together to share common goals, or independently to pursue individual ones. Some students might wish to produce a film or website illustrating their concerns or suggestions. Others might map community assets to identify local organizations that can help to implement students' ideas. They might learn about organizations in their community that work to maintain a civil society, such as charities, clubs, community foundations and organizations, churches, food cooperatives, professional associations, and nonprofits.

Student identities can thus develop positively through classroom literacy experiences that engage students in looking both inward and outward.

REVISITING MARIO

As we learned earlier in this text, Mario Ramos is a sixth grade, Hispanic student whose primary language is English. Mario describes himself as someone who does not like reading *books*, who reads poorly, and who has friends with equally limited literacy-related interests and proficiencies. In school, Mario performs inconsistently below grade level in all of his content area classes, and he receives forty minutes of remedial reading instruction daily. Overall, this sketch of Mario depicts a struggling, disengaged reader and writer. However this is a sketch that contrasts with the results of Mario's assessment data. It is a sketch that fails to recognize the literacy practices Mario does engage in or to consider how these might be effectively utilized to promote Mario's school-based literacy development.

Mario's *Adolescent Motivation to Read Profile and Analytical Reading Inventory* assessments reveal a clear discrepancy between his content area performance and his ability to comprehend text. From Mario's assessment interview with his teacher, we also know that he has developed a noteworthy repertoire of out-of-school literacy practices, literacy practices that can be harnessed in order to support his academic literacy development. The theoretical perspectives described at the opening of this chapter provide important lenses through which we may view and interpret Mario's literacy development. Taken together, these perspectives also point to measures his teacher may take so that her instructional approaches and the overall classroom learning environment can more effectively foster Mario's academic literacy development as well as his sense of agency and a positive identity.

Mario's Self-efficacy and Adolescent Identity

The messages students receive from teachers and others about their competency as readers and about their ability to achieve literacy goals, often referred to as self-efficacy, naturally have the potential to influence their motivation and identity. These messages are especially influential during adolescence since this is a critical period of intense identity exploration and development (Lewis, 2007). Through daily instruction, curricular decisions and individual interactions, educators must bolster students' self-efficacy so their students can view themselves as capable, reflective readers and then integrate this self-perception into the identities that they adopt (Alvermann, 2002). To cultivate self-efficacy in adolescent readers and writers, it is critical that we attend to the subtle and direct messages we send adolescents about their abilities and potential in these areas (Alvermann, 2002; Tatum 2004).

Statements Mario makes as his teacher administers the Adolescent Motivation to Read Profile illustrate his low self-efficacy as a reader. Early in the assessment,

Mario shares that he does not read books often, and that he has difficulty figuring out unfamiliar words. Mario further explains that his group of friends does not view reading as an enjoyable activity, and he shares his disinterest in reading and in discussing books with them. Later in the interview, Mario plainly states, "I am not very good at reading." This sixth grader holds a distinctly negative self-appraisal of his abilities and interests in reading. It is also significant that he associates with peers whose limited interest in reading appears to match his own. Information included within Mario's profile, as well as additional data gathered during his assessments point to salient school-based factors that contribute to his reduced literacy-related self-efficacy. Once identified, teachers can eliminate these factors and help Mario develop a healthier and more accurate estimation of his abilities as a reader.

A major consideration is that Mario was placed in a resource room setting for forty minutes of daily remedial reading instruction, and it is worthwhile to consider the impact that this ability-based separation from his peers has on his self-efficacy as a reader. Adolescence is a developmental period in which a sense of membership in the classroom community heavily influences the beliefs students develop about themselves and their academic capabilities. (Faircloth & Hamm, 2005; Lewis, 2007; Patrick, Kaplan, & Ryan , 2007). Mario's placement in this pull-out reading support program sends the message that, when it comes to reading, he has no place within the larger learning community. When considering the range of reading support models and program options currently available, schools must remain mindful of the negative impact that ability-based separation can have upon the very students that such programs are intended to help (Alvermann, 2002; Xu, 2008), and teachers can serve as effective advocates in this regard.

In addition to supporting school-based programs that promote a sense of belonging within the classroom community, Mario's teacher can further support his literacy-related self-efficacy by implementing processes that enable him to engage in self-appraisal and goal setting within the classroom by using rubrics that describe assessment criteria for processes such as literacy circle participation or Jigsaw reading. If used consistently, rubrics will enable Mario to gain an understanding of the individual practices and attributes that, when applied together, lead to reading and writing proficiency. Additionally, Mario's teacher can hold regular reading and writing conferences with him to guide Mario in selecting goals and in tracking his progress throughout the year. Such practices would allow Mario to strengthen his literacy-related self-efficacy within his classroom environment.

To be effective, instructional approaches that promote classroom inclusion, self-assessment and goal setting first require that teachers hold high expectations for their students' literacy achievement. It is a well-established fact that teachers can impact adolescents' literacy-related self-efficacy with the expectations that they hold for and communicate to their students (Alvermann, 2001; Nieto & Bode, 2008). Unfortunately, as Mario's teacher administers the Analytic Reading Inventory, her statements communicate her belief that the fifth grade passage she asked Mario to read will be difficult for him. The following exchange after Mario read the passage reflects these low expectations, despite the fact that he needed help with pronouncing just two words.

Teacher: That was a hard one but you got through it. Very good. Okay. Let's ask some questions. Who was the main character?

Mario: Sheila.

Teacher: Yes, that's right. And now you remember her name right? That was a hard one.

Mario's comprehension of the passage was at the independent level, which is acceptable given that he is in sixth grade. His score on the Inventory suggested that he did not find the fifth grade passage hard, yet this was the message he received from his teacher at different points during the assessment. In this instance, Mario's assessment response, "I am a poor reader," appears more reflective of his teacher's comments about the difficulty of the reading than of his actual ability to read and respond to the passage. Mario's low estimation of his in-school literacy provides a potent reminder of the impact that teachers' messages can have on identity construction.

During the assessment session, Mario received other messages, including messages about the value of his cultural heritage, which would affect most adolescents as they wrestle with identity issues.

Mario's Cultural Resources Identity

Mario identifies himself as Hispanic during his assessment interview, and he provides information about his family's culturally-based knowledge and practices that can inform his teacher's use of culturally responsive instructional practices. Mario's cultural background is not unique in schools today. In fact, America's public school population has never been more culturally and linguistically diverse, and students whose language, race, and/or ethnicity differ from the school's dominant culture bring an abundant range of resources and opportunities for fostering academic literacy. Through culturally responsive instruction, teachers acknowledge the value of diverse, culturally-rooted practices, interests, and guiding beliefs and integrate these into school-based learning experiences (Au, 2000; Ladson-Billings, 2009; Nieto & Bode, 2008; Rios-Aguilar, Marquez Kiyama, Gravitt, & Moll, 2011). Since the majority of American teachers are white, middle class, and female, these resources may differ markedly from those encountered in teachers' own educational and cultural experiences (Papanastasiou, 2001), and cultural responsiveness may require that teachers examine their own preconceptions of what "counts" as an educationally valuable resource. It also necessitates that teachers learn about the communities, interests, and culturally-distinct practices of their students. With this knowledge and with these grounding dispositions, teachers will be well-poised to create learning experiences and on-going instructional practices that explicitly draw upon aspects of their students' cultures.

Students like Mario will benefit greatly as their self-worth is acknowledged. Affirming students' cultural practices within an academic setting breaks down the perception of a dichotomy between home-based and school-based norms. Culturally responsive instruction also facilitates bi-culturalization (Chen, Benet-Martínez, & Bond, 2008) since it provides ways for students from all linguistic and cultural backgrounds to develop integrated identities in which reading and writing hold personal relevance both in and outside of school. There is much that Mario's teachers can do to provide recognition and appreciation of his cultural heritage.

Harnessing Mario's cultural resources. Mario shares that he primarily speaks English at home but that his parents teach him Spanish on a consistent basis, "[B]oth of my parents know how to speak Spanish so I just get good teaching lessons from them 24/7." His parents' concern that Mario continue to develop his knowledge of Spanish should lead Mario's teacher to incorporate elements of Hispanic culture into her instruction. Research-based strategies that appear in professional literature document examples of teachers using culturally-based knowledge of herbal remedies, building construction, and environmental health to create academically rigorous units of study (Moje, et al., 2004; Rios-Aguilar, Marquez Kiyama, Gravitt, & Moll, 2011). Other research includes examples of teachers making use of students' languages and rhetorical patterns to promote their text comprehension and writing proficiency (Risko & Walker-Dalhouse, 2007). Mario's teachers would have much to draw upon for ideas.

For instance, in a social studies unit focusing on the branches of government his teacher might invite Mario's parents to discuss government structures in their native country and to share Spanish translations of vocabulary related to the unit. This lesson could readily lead to a research project in which Mario and his classmates investigate the governmental structures of their ancestral countries and analyze them in relation to those of the United States. In a science unit, the teacher might use community members such as Mario's parents to teach Spanish translations of scientific terms. In fact, many scientific terms are Spanish-English cognates; they share a common Greek or Latin root and appear similar in print or when spoken and thus offer a prime opportunity for Mario's teacher to make strategic use of his heritage language in order to cultivate academic learning.

Mario's teacher could also use her administration of the Adolescent Motivation to Read Profile as an opportunity to probe for further data regarding Mario's culturally-based knowledge and practices, and there were several occasions during this assessment when she might have sought out such information. For example, during one exchange, Mario's teacher clarified that he speaks English as a primary language at home, and then she promptly moved on to her next question:

Teacher: Well, do you speak at home all the time in Spanish?

Mario: English.

Teacher: When you are at home you speak English?

Mario: Yeah, except when my dad's friends come back. We speak Spanish to some of them.

Teacher: Okay, so here's another thing. Let's see, I will ask these questions. Tell me about a book that you have read recently that you think is really good.

In this instance, she could have affirmed Mario's use of Spanish to communicate with his father's guests, and she might have then continued to inquire about the interests that arise during these discussions. In this case, the discussion might have unfolded in the following manner:

Teacher: Well, do you speak at home all the time in Spanish?

Mario: English.

Teacher: When you are at home you speak English?

Mario: Yeah, except when my dad's friends come back. We speak Spanish to some of them.

Teacher: I think it is fantastic that you can speak Spanish with your dad's friends. When your dad's friends come back, do you enjoy discussing anything in particular? Tell me more about that. What about topics that you talk about with your family, whether in English or in Spanish?

Mario's response to these questions can provide leads to designing projects that capitalize on the Ramos family's culturally-based knowledge and practices. However in order for these opportunities to present themselves, Mario's teacher must first be aware that they exist. She must also be disposed to asking the kinds of questions and completing the needed legwork that would convert these practices and interests into academically substantive, culturally responsive instructional practices.

Students' cultural and linguistic backgrounds provide potent tools for adolescent literacy and content area learning. They also provide students with the means to effectively integrate school-based practices and elements of their cultural backgrounds into their developing identities. There are additional out-of-school experiences adolescents have that teachers can draw upon to create dynamic classrooms to help students with developing satisfying and coherent identities.

Mario's Out-of-School Literacies and Identity

Examining Mario's out-of-school literacy practices and the possibilities they hold for in-school literacy growth provides educators with an example of how adolescents' enthusiasm for these modalities may be harnessed within an academic context.

Drawing from psychosocial research (Kirshner, O'Donoghue, & McLaughlin, 2003; National Research Council, 2002; Zeldin, 2004; Zeldin, Camino, & Mook, 2005) and from the sociocultural body of literature (Au, 2000; Moje, et al., 2004), we know that adolescent identity development and literacy development mutually support one another when literacy experiences incorporate occasions for social interaction and when students are afforded greater opportunities to decide what and how they will read and write. Typically the developmental needs for social interaction and increased agency manifest themselves through the out-of-school reading and writing activities that adolescents take part in. Researchers document tremendous growth in adolescents' use of graphic and electronic text formats, including interactive online gaming, social media outlets, downloadable literature, and text messaging (Alvermann, 2001; Moje, et al., 2004; & Xu, 2008). Teachers can make use of their students' pervasive use of these text formats and accompanying literacy practices in order to bolster academic literacy development (Alvermann, 2001). Mindful of this research, Mario's teachers could utilize his out-of-school literacy practices advantageously.

Capitalizing on Mario's out-of-school literacies. Mario's assessments offer important information about his recreational reading and writing practices. During the assessment interview he tells his teacher that his out-of-school reading interests include materials related to online gaming, comic books, and fantasy books. To build Mario's academic literacy, his teacher could affirm these literacy practices for their inherent value, and then explicitly describe how these practices are like the reading and writing tasks that are required in his classes. Additionally, his teacher could use this interview as an opportunity to probe for further information about Mario's literacy practices since additional information can provide insights into how she might further refine her instructional practices in order to optimize Mario's learning in the classroom. The following excerpt from Mario's assessment interview offers one example of an opportunity Mario's teacher might have taken to learn about his extracurricular literacy practices and to validate these for their intrinsic worth and for their in-school applications.

Teacher: Okay, so here's another thing. Let's see, I will ask these questions. Tell me about a book that you have read recently that you think is really good.

Mario: Well, I like animations so I am guessing possibly my favorite book I like to read is this animation that I downloaded for free. I forgot the title but it's on my PSP. It's like this magical boy and this book, the most recent one I liked was The Return of King I forgot his name but it's The Return of King—

Teacher: Okay, and where did you read that?

Mario: At the library. I checked it out.

Teacher: This library?

Mario: Mmm-hmm.

Teacher: And how did you find it?

Mario: I looked in the fantasy space, so yeah.

Teacher: So you looked it up for it, you went looking for one.

Mario: Yeah, and each time I read a fantasy book, it's kind of like giving me thousands of ideas in my mind.

Teacher: Oh, that's good. Okay. And it was interesting to you because you liked the—

Mario: I like reading fantasy books that make my ideas faster and faster so if I ever write a book, I know how to write a book like that.

Teacher: Okay, do you ever talk about the books you read with your friends?

In this exchange, Mario describes his engagement in literacy practices in a manner that reveals him as an engaged, thoughtful reader. He discusses the fact that he enjoys reading books within the fantasy genre and that he actively reflects on the concepts in these books, using them to generate ideas for his own fantasy writing. Additionally, the fact that he expresses interest in authoring a fantasy novel is significant in that Mario reveals himself as someone who has the agency to use literacy (writing) as a medium for self-expression. This segment also reveals Mario's proficiency in accessing library resources that support his interests. He knows where the fantasy books are located, and he knows how to download free online fantasy animations. The following adapted version of this exchange illustrates how Mario's teacher might have used this discussion to validate these practices and to learn more about his interests.

Teacher: Okay, so here's another thing. Let's see, I will ask these questions. Tell me about a book that you have read recently that you think is really good.

Mario: Well, I like animations so I am guessing possibly my favorite book I like to read is this animation that I downloaded for free. I forgot the title but it's on my PSP. It's like this magical boy and this book, the most recent one I liked was The Return of King I forgot his name but it's The Return of King—

Teacher: The Return of the King. Great. That is based on the Lord of the Rings, a very important book in English literature. Okay, and where did you read that?

Mario: At the library. I checked it out.

Teacher: This library?

Mario: Mmm-hmm.

Teacher: And how did you find it?

Mario: I looked in the fantasy space, so yeah.

Teacher: Good. Being able to locate the books that you want or need in the library is a very important skill for readers like you to have.

Mario: Yeah, and each time I read a fantasy book, it's kind of like giving me thousands of ideas in my mind.

Teacher: Yes, and that is exactly what good readers do; they constantly think about what they are reading, and they use the ideas in books to create ideas of their own. What do you like about the fantasy books?

Mario: I like reading fantasy books that make my ideas faster and faster so if I ever write a book, I know how to write a book like that.

Teacher: Well you are definitely taking the right steps to learn how to write fantasy books, and there are lots of authors your age that write in all kinds of genres. I am sure that there are ways that you can read and write fantasy books right here in school. Tell me more about your ideas for fantasy books. Do you have a place where you write down your different ideas?

Learning of Mario's interest in reading and writing within the fantasy genre could have been an exciting discovery for Mario's teacher. Young adult book lists are replete with examples of well-written, high interest fantasy novels (including graphic and online varieties), and these could be strategically utilized during the school day (Tomlinson & Lynch-Brown, 2010). For instance, with the help of the school's media specialist, Mario's teacher could teach students how to prepare and deliver booktalks for their classmates or for younger "reading buddies" in the school. This practice would place Mario in a leadership role by empowering him to broaden the reading interests and cultivate the reading engagement of others. He would need to analyze fantasy literature through the lens of those less familiar with the genre and actively consider how to foster enthusiasm for the genre based on their interests. Interested students could then select texts for independent reading projects or structured literature circle experiences. Mario's motivation to read fantasy material could be further developed by creating an audio book listening station in the classroom, and writing workshop would provide an ideal opportunity for Mario to pursue his interest in fantasy writing. These pedagogical approaches allow for peer interaction, choice, and leadership, and they therefore accommodate adolescents' growing interest in sharing perspectives and making decisions about their reading and writing practices. It is important to note that, while Mario expresses a keenness for fantasy, other students in the class may favor fiction, poetry, or other literary genres. Therefore, Mario's teacher should plan to employ a variety of genres during the school year so that students may benefit from developmentally ideal instructional approaches using content that they are already well-motivated to study.

CONCLUDING THOUGHTS

Effective literacy instruction does more than give students the tools for academic success. The texts we choose and the dialogue we have with our students impact their personal development as well. Overall self-efficacy, cultural connections, and out-of-school literacies are critical factors to consider when cultivating academic literacy during adolescence, a period of concentrated identity exploration and development. Taken together, they add relevancy, agency, and validation to the content area literacy experiences that students encounter in school. When used consistently, they enable students like Mario to construct identities for themselves that incorporate the practices of critical reading and confident, purposeful writing.

REFERENCES

Alvermann, D. E. (2002). Effective literacy instruction for adolescents. *Journal of Literacy Research*, 34(2) 189–208. doi: 10.1207/s15548430jlr3402_4.

Alvermann, D. (2008). Why bother theorizing adolescents' online literacies for classroom practice and research? *Journal of Adolescent & Adult Literacy, 52*(1). doi:10.1598/JAAL.52.1.2.

Alvermann, D. E. (2001). Reading adolescents' reading identities: Looking back to see ahead. *Journal of Adolescent & Adult Literacy*, 44(8), 676–609. Retrieved from EBSCO*host*.

Aronson, E. (2000–2008). "History of the Jigsaw." Jigsaw Classroom website, http://www. jigsaw.org/history.htm. Date accessed November 2, 2011.

Au, K. (2000). A multicultural perspective on policies for improving literacy achievement: Equity and excellence. In M. L. Kamil, P. B. Mosenthal, P. D. Pearson, & R. Barr (Eds.), *Handbook of reading research*, Vol. 3 (pp.835–52). Mahwah, NJ: Lawrence Erlbaum Associates.

Bromley, K. (2007). Assessing student writing. In J. R. Paratore, J. R. & R. L. McCormack, R. L. (Eds.). *Classroom literacy assessment: Making sense of what students know and do.* (pp. 210 –24) New York, NY: The Guilford Press.

Chang, C. (2009). Using jigsaw collaborative learning strategy in online discussion to foster a project-based learning community on the web. *International Journal of Instructional Media, 36*(2), 221–33.

Chen, S. X., Benet-Martínez, V., Bond, M. H. (2008). Bicultural identity, bilingualism, and psychological adjustment in multicultural societies: Immigration-based and globalization-based acculturation. *Journal of Personality,* 76:803–38.

Clark, E. G. & Justice, E. M. (n.d.) http://social.jrank.org/pages/322/Identity-Development. html.

Daniels, H. (2002). *Literature circles. Voice and choice in book clubs and reading groups,* 2nd ed. Portland, ME: Stenhouse Publishers.

Edwards, M. (2005). Civil Society. Retrieved November 26, 2011 from http://www.infed.org/ association/civil_society.htm.

Erikson, E. (1968). *Identity: Youth and crisis.* New York, NY: Norton.

Faircloth, B. S., & Hamm, J. V. (2005). Sense of belonging among high school students representing four ethnic groups. *Journal of Youth and Adolescence, 34,* 293–309. doi: 10.1007/ s10964-005-5752-7.

Furrer, C. &Skinner, E. (2003). Sense of relatedness as a factor in children's academic engagement and performance. *Journal of Educational Psychology, 95*(1) 148–62. doi: 10.1037/0022-0663.95.1.148.

Galda, L. & Graves, M. F. (2007). *Reading and responding in the middle grades: Approaches for all classrooms.* New York, NY: Pearson.

Gee, J. P. (2000). Identity as an analytic lens for research in education. In W. Secada (Ed.), *Review of research in education, 25.* Washington, D.C.: American Educational Research Association.

Gee, J. (2001). New times and new literacies: Themes for a changing world. In B. Cope and M. Kalantzis (Eds.), *Learning for the future: Proceedings of the Learning Conference, 2001.* Melbourne: Common Ground Press.

Hall, G. S. (1904). *Adolescence: Its psychology and its relations to physiology, anthropology, sociology, sex, crime, religion, and education.* New York, NY: Appleton.

Hanze, M., & Berger, R. (2007). Cooperative learning, motivational effects, and student characteristics: An experimental study comparing cooperative learning and direct instruction in 12th grade physics classes. *Learning & Instruction, 17,* 29–41. doi:10.1016/j.learn-instruc.2006.11.004.

Jung, C. G. (1989). *Memories, Dreams, Reflections* (Rev. ed., C. Winston & R. Winston, Trans.).

Keane, N. (2011). *Booktalks—Quick and Simple.* Retrieved from http://nancykeane.com/ booktalks/faq.htm.

Kirshner, B., O'Donoghue, J. L., & McLaughlin, M. W. (Eds.). (2003). *New directions for youth development: Youth participation improving institutions and communities.* San Francisco, CA: Jossey-Bass.

Kordalewski, J. (November 1999) [ED440049] Kordalewski, John. 1999. *Incorporating student voice into teaching practice.* Retrieved from http://www.ericdigests.org/2000-4/voice.htm.

Ladson-Billings, G. (2009). *The dreamkeepers: Successful teachers of African American children.* San Francisco, CA: John Wiley & Sons.

Lewis, J. & Jones, B. (2009). How can what we know about adolescent learners be used to benefit our literacy instruction? In J. Lewis (Ed.). *Essential questions in adolescent literacy: Teachers and researchers describe what works in classrooms* (pp. 3–34). New York, NY: Guilford Press.

Lewis, J. (2006). Strategies for developing academic literacy with struggling adolescent readers. Paper presentation. International Reading Association Annual Convention, Chicago: IL.

Lewis, J. (2007). Academic literacy: Principles and learning opportunities for adolescent readers. In J. Lewis & G. Moorman (Eds.). *Adolescent literacy instruction: Policies and promising practices* (pp.143–66). Newark, De: International Reading Association.

Lewison, M., Flint, A. S., & Sluys, K. V. (2002). Taking on critical literacy: The journey of newcomers and novices. *Language Arts, 79*(5), 382–92.

McIntosh, P. (1988). This essay is excerpted from Working Paper 189. "White Privilege and Male Privilege: A Personal Account of Coming to See Correspondences through Work in Women's Studies." Retrieved from www.nymbp.org/reference/WhitePrivilege.pdf.

McLaughlin, M., & DeVoogd, G. L. (2004). *Critical literacy: Enhancing students' comprehension of text.* New York: Scholastic.

Moje, E. B. (2007). Developing socially just subject-matter instruction: A review of the literature on disciplinary literacy teaching. *Review of Research in Education, 31,* 1–44. DOI: 10.3102/0091732X07300046.

Moje, E. B., Ciechanowski, K. M., Kramer, K., Ellis, L., Carrillo, R., & Collazo, T. (2004). Working toward third space in content area literacy: An examination of everyday funds of knowledge and discourse. *Reading Research Quarterly, 39*(1), 38–70. Retrieved from http://draweb.njcu.edu:2078/docview/212137068?accountid=12793.

Moeller, V. J. & Moeller, M. V. (2007). *Literature circles that engage middle and high school students.* Larchmont, NY: Eye on Education, Inc.

National Research Council (2002*). Community programs to promote youth development.* Washington, D.C.: National Academy Press.

Nieto, S. & Bode, P. (2008). *Affirming diversity: The sociopolitical context of multicultural education,* 5th ed. New York, NY: Pearson.

Papanastasiou, E. C. (2001). *Multicultural transformations through LATTICE: An evaluation of professional development for teachers.* Michigan State University. (ERIC Document Reproduction Service No. ED453182.)

Patrick, H., Kaplan, A., & Ryan, A. (2007). Early adolescents' perceptions of the classroom social environment, motivational beliefs, and engagement. *Journal of Educational Psychology, 99*(1), 83–98. doi: 10.1037/0022-0663.99.1.83.

Perkins, D. V. , & Saris, R . N. (2001). A "Jigsaw Classroom" technique for undergraduate statistics courses. *Teaching of Psychology, 28,* 111–13.

Phinney, J., Horenczyk, G., Liebking, K., & Vedder, P. (2001). Ethnic identity, immigration and well-being: An interactional perspective. *Journal of Social Issues, 57*(3) 497–510. Retrieved from cretscmhd.psych.ucla.edu/events/PhinneyPaper.pdf.

Pozzi, F. (2010). Using Jigsaw and Case Study for supporting online collaborative learning. *Computers & Education, 55*(1), 67–75. doi: 10.1016/j.compedu.2009.12.003.

Rios-Aguilar, C., Marquez Kiyama, J., Gravitt, M., & Moll, L. C. (2011). Funds of knowledge for the poor and forms of capital for the rich? A capital approach to examining funds of knowledge. *Theory and Research in Education, 9*: 163–84. doi: 10.1177/1477878511409776.

Risko, V. J. & Walker-Dalhouse, D. (2007). Tapping students' cultural funds of knowledge to address the achievement gap. *The Reading Teacher*, 61(1), 98–100. doi: 10.1598/RT.61.1.12.

Shiflett, A. (1998). Marketing literature: Variations on the book talk theme. *Journal of Adolescent & Adult Literacy, 41*(7), 568.

Shor, I. (1997). What is critical literacy? *Journal for Pedagogy, Pluralism & Practice.* Retrieved November 20, 2011 from www.newhavenleon.org.

Sky-McIlvain, E. (n.d.). Stereotypes in *The Sign of the Beaver*: A post-reading lesson for Middle School. NY: Freeport Middle School, Retrieved from http://www.leasttern.com/Wabanaki/Lessons/SOB/SOBStereotypes.pdf.

Tatum, A. (2008). A road map for reading specialists entering schools without exemplary reading programs; Seven quick lessons. *The Reading Teacher, 58*(1), 28–39. doi: 10.1598/RT.5313.

Tomlinson, C. M. & Lynch-Brown, C. (2010). *Essentials of young adult literature,* 2nd ed. New York, NY: Pearson.

Xu, S. H. (2008). *Rethinking literacy learning and teaching: Intersections of adolescents' in-school and out-of-school literacy practices.* In K. Hinchman & H. K. Sheridan-Thomas (Eds.). Best practices in adolescent literacy instruction. New York, NY: The Guilford Press.

Zeldin, S. (2004). Youth as agents of adult and community development: Mapping the processes and outcomes of youth engaged in organizational governance. *Applied Developmental Science, 8*(2), 75–90. doi: 10.1207/s1532480xads0802_2.

Zeldin, S., Camino, L., & Mook, C. (2005). The adoption of innovation in youth organizations: creating the conditions for youth-adult partnerships. *Journal of Community Psychology*, 33(1), 121–35.

12

From Resistance to Engagement— The Importance of the Digital Literacies for Struggling Readers and Writers

Peter McDermott and Kathleen A. Gormley

The term *digital literacies* refers to the many ways that meaning is composed, viewed, and shared with others through electronic environments (McKenna, Conradi, Lawrence, Jang, & Meyer, 2012). These environments include desktop and laptop computers, tablet computers, smart phones, and classroom digital display boards. The development of digital literacies entails effective reading/viewing and composing of meaningful text, drawings, images, sound and/or video. Students develop expertise with the digital literacies through rigorous reading, composing, and viewing of online and other digital texts. Throughout this chapter we argue that students, such as Mario, will become more engaged in literacy learning and improve their literacy skills, both conventional and digital, through careful and thoughtful use of online viewing, reading, and composing activities.

THE DIGITAL LITERACIES

The last decade has experienced a revolution in how reading and writing are used in everyday life. Today people are more likely to read and write with digital devices than with books and paper, at least this is so outside of school (Jacobs, 2012; O'Brien & Scharber, 2008). We posit that the lack of digital literacies in K–12 classrooms will remain problematic until teachers learn to integrate them into their classroom lessons (Gormley & McDermott, in-press).

The digital literacies are transforming the ways we read and write in everyday life, but they are infrequently seen in schools and classrooms. There are multiple reasons for their absence from academic settings: (1) the digital literacies are not yet assessed on statewide exams, although NAEP plans to implement testing of technology in 2014 (NAEP, http://nces.ed.gov/nationsreportcard/about/); (2) many schools lack adequate resources for purchasing computers and providing access to the Internet—particularly in rural areas (Sundeen & Sundeen, 2013); and (3) teachers often lack knowledge of how to integrate digital literacies into their lessons (Carpo & Orellana, 2011; Gormley & McDermott, in-press). Yet despite these challenges we believe the digital literacies offer great promise for improving classroom teaching and engaging Mario and other resistant learners in literacy learning.

The digital literacies have characteristics that provide users with more information and support than conventional ways of reading and writing. While conventional reading relies entirely on the alphabet to convey information, the digital materials offer multiple ways of communicating content—text, audio, visual (images and video) with color and possibly animation. Stated another way, print is very linear in organization, while digital materials are non-linear allowing choice of direction that is based on the interests or needs of the individual. When reading a newspaper's website, for instance, readers can quickly change from text-based (alphabetic) reading, to listening to a podcast, or viewing slideshows and videos. Readers can do all of this within a few moments of time, clicking back and forth as they choose. Similarly when composing with digital devices, users can compose by starting with the alphabet or with images, photos, sound, and video to create media productions; moreover users can collaborate with others who physically present as well as those in distant spaces and separated by time.

The digital literacies and their associated tools have affordances that distinguish them from conventional alphabetic texts. That is, digital productions are multimodal (New London Group, 1996) participatory (Jenkins, 2006) and social (Coiro, Knobel, Lankshear, & Leu, 2011) in nature, and they involve more self-directed choices than conventional reading (Leu, et al., 2011).

There is accumulating evidence that the digital literacies are more engaging for struggling readers and writers than conventional literacy (Leu, et al., 2011; O'Brien, Beach, & Scharber, 2007; Wood, 2011). Our own experiences with after-school literacy programs suggest that students who resist reading and writing in school are often the very same ones who love to read and write digitally. It has long been our belief, which is aligned with research findings (Allington, 1977; Krashen, 2011 & 2013; Taylor, Pearson, Peterson & Rodriquez, 2003), that the more time that students spend reading and writing, regardless of whether it occurs with conventional books, comics, or today's digital devices, the better their overall literacy achievement will be.

EDUCATIONAL REFORM AND THE DIGITAL LITERACIES

National reform efforts (e.g., *No Child Left Behind Act*, 2001; *Race to the Top*, 2009) have attracted extensive attention to increasing student achievement, yet the same reforms have mostly ignored the digital literacies and their importance in everyday life. Yet the two most prominent professional organizations in literacy education, the International Reading Association [IRA (www.reading.org)] and the National

Council of Teachers of English [NCTE (http://www.ncte.org/)] have called attention to the new literacies and have recommended that they be integrated into classroom teaching methods.

IRA (2009) argues that students should have access to teachers who know and can use the new digital literacies in their classroom literacy lessons. Similarly, NCTE (2007) recommends that: (1) teachers integrate the new literacies into their methods of teaching; (2) students have regular access to technology; (3) teachers have professional development to learn strategies for integrating digital literacies into their teaching.

The Common Core State Standards (CCSS) (National Governors Association, 2010) include the digital literacies in its expectations for student learning. Anchor Standard 7 in Reading asks students to *Integrate and evaluate content presented in diverse formats and media* (CCSS, 2010, p. 18). Anchor Standard 6 in Writing requires students to *Use technology, including the Internet, to produce and publish writing* (CCSS, 2010, p. 18). Anchor Standard 8 in Writing asks students to *Gather information from print and digital sources and assess the credibility and accuracy of each source, and integrate the information while avoiding plagiarism* (CCSS, 2010, p. 18). Clearly, the digital literacies are explicitly woven into the CCSS. Other Anchor Standards imply support for students learning digital literacy skills and tools. For example, collaboration is noted in Anchor Standard 6 in Writing: *Use technology, including the Internet, to produce and publish writing and to interact and collaborate with others* (CCSS, 2010, p.18) as well as in Anchor Standard 2 in Speaking and Listening: *Integrate and evaluate information presented in diverse media and formats, including visually, quantitative and orally* (CCSS, 2010, p. 22), which we maintain can be done through the incorporation of digital tools.

Digital literacy proponents argue schools will be transformed for the better when the new literacies and technologies are integrated into classroom teaching. They proclaim that digital whiteboards, laptops, and tablet computers will improve teaching and learning. The "Flipped Classroom," for example, represents a popular teaching model where students use technology (screencasts and podcasts) to acquire curricula content at home and use classroom time for discussion, analysis, and application of the concepts (Millard, 2012; Sams & Bergmann, 2013).

The digital literacies should not be viewed as a panacea for educational reform—the work of Cuban (2003) as well as Philip and Garcia (2013) have clearly argued the limitations of technology for transforming classroom teaching. Yet no one denies that twenty-first century students must know how to use the new literacies tools and skills to acquire, analyze, and share information with others. Without doing so they will be shortchanged in their ability to fully and effectively participate in the world of work and higher education.

When thoughtfully used, the digital literacies can improve the literacy achievement of all students, especially those who resist learning to read and write in school. Engaged readers are those who are motivated to read, strategic in their use of reading and writing, and socially interactive when reading or composing (Guthrie & Wigfield, 2000; Guthrie, Wigfield, & You, 2012). Web tools for composing podcasts, scre-

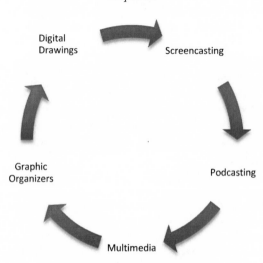

**Figure 12.1.   Supporting students who resist read-
ing and writing with digital literacy.**

encasts, multimedia compositions (electronic posters), graphic organizers and drawings can be effectively used to motivate and engage as well as improve their literacy
achievement. In the pages that follow we describe strategies for integrating the digital
literacies via various web tools into classroom teaching so that students like Mario will
succeed in school. Figure 12.1 displays the digital literacies examined in this chapter.

Podcasting

Before television our grandparents and great grandparents gathered around cabi-
net size radios to listen to their favorite broadcasts. These broadcasts were often family events when adults and children listened to the daily news, variety shows, dramas,
and comedies. Today podcasts are similarly used, although they are more likely to be
heard individually on iPods and other digital devices.

Podcasts are audio recordings (typically mp3s) that can be composed with web
tools or recorded with software on a digital device and later shared with others.
Podcasts have many educational uses—wherever the human voice is used, podcasts
can be successfully employed.

There are many ways that podcasting can be integrated into classroom teaching
and help resistant learners. For example, Owens (2013) describes how eighth graders
used podcasting for composing their own radio shows. Wilson, Chavez, and Anders
(2012) explain how podcasting can be used to reflect students' identities, values, and
cultural heritage in composing narratives and poetry. Vasinda and McLeod (2011)
describe podcasting as enhancing classroom readers' theater, which is highly dependent upon multiple reads and, thus, develops fluency in word reading with prosody.

Davis and McGrail (2009) explain how podcasting can be used to improve students' understanding of their composing processes. We have seen podcasting used in the primary grades as an assigned "job"; just like tidying the book area or watering the plant, young students can send a quick podcast to parents/families summarizing the new content they learned while using academic vocabulary [another emphasized point across the CCSS; specifically Anchor Standard 5 in Language: *Acquire and use accurately a range of general academic and domain-specific words and phrases . . . important to comprehension or expression* (CCSS, 2010, p.25)]. We know of classroom teachers who communicate with their students' families by regularly posting podcasts on classroom blogs and websites.

Children can record interviews with people in their community, and these recordings can be converted into podcasts. We remember, for instance, a second grade teacher who taught community history by having her children interview adults from a local senior center. The children interview the seniors about community life fifty years ago. During the learning unit children learned how to prepare interview questions, take notes, and use oral language to clearly communicate their findings into audio recordings. Interviews such as these could easily be converted into podcasts and shared with others. For example, middle school children might interview Vietnam War veterans about their service to their country, or they might conduct interviews about the kinds of employment that adults have had during their lives.

"Two-voice" poems are frequently used in elementary teaching (e.g., Fleischman, 2004). Two-voice poems can be recorded and converted into podcasts. Afterwards students might reflect in writing what the poems meant to them. This way, students are learning conventional and digital literacies! Furthermore, we believe that combining literacies and digital composing further enriches students' understanding that clear communication undergirds all literacies.

Process descriptions are often used in school and are part of the Common Core State Standards (Anchor Standard #2—Writing: *Write informative/explanatory texts to examine and convey complex ideas and information clearly through the effective selection, organization of content*, CCSS, 2010, p. 18). Process descriptions, such as making peanut butter and jelly sandwiches, can be converted into podcasts. Students might record their process description, and then a volunteer from the class might be invited to literally follow the steps identified in their peer's podcast and critique its accuracy. Often the peanut butter and jelly lesson results in laughter about how important details contribute to the success of a step-by-step description. Students enjoy process descriptions, and informational writing such as this directly pertains to the Common Core State Standards. Similarly, older students might compose directions for conducting science experiments.

Fluency is a reading skill that many struggling learners, such as Mario, need to acquire (Rasinski, 2012). Podcasts are effective for improving students' fluency, and particularly so with students with learning difficulties (Ring, et al., 2013). Students can compose podcasts of themselves reading a text, and then after repeated practice they can make other recordings with the same text to document their improvement with fluency. Fluency progress (e.g., word identification accuracy, speed, intonation) can be closely monitored (Marcell, 2011) and charted onto graphs and Excel sheets. We have found that students enjoy plotting their fluency growth over time as displayed in podcasts where time and accuracy can be easily measured and displayed onto their graphs.

Oral reading fluency is essential for English language learners' (ELLs) (Baker, Stoolmiller, Good, & Baker, 2011). Podcasting can be used when teaching ELLs because their production requires multiple reads to assure correct pronunciation, phrasing, and ultimately prosody. ELLs can record their podcasts and afterwards hear their pronunciation, rate, and intonation. These podcasts can be used to provide awareness of their fluency as well as providing awareness of how they sound to others. (They have another benefit for teachers and families—they can document a student's progress over time.) Podcasts might also be used as models with the teacher reading and the learner echo reading.

Podcasts can be effectively used for helping students, who have difficulties with fine motor coordination. Instead of struggling with cursive or manuscript writing (even with using keyboards) students with special needs can compose their ideas by dictating them into podcasts. By doing so they successfully accomplish the composing task, and they are not restricted by their fine motor challenges. Such adaptations are very much in line with Universal Design for Learning (www.cast. org) that explains multimodal considerations a teacher should employ prior to lesson development and offers opportunities of leveling the playing field so that students can demonstrate what they know.

There are two general methods to composing podcasts. The first is to use websites that record, post, and provide URL addresses and embed codes. One podcasting site that we have found particularly useful for beginning podcasting is Audioboo (https://audioboo.fm/). Audioboo is simple to use and appealing, and can be used (online with computer, iPad, and mobile devices) for recordings up to ten minutes. It is free, a factor that is helpful for many schools and families in times of economic challenge. Students can record, save, and hyperlink or embed their recordings into a digital essay for others to hear. An embed code is provided so the "boo" (Audioboo calls their mp3s "boos") can be hosted to a blog or emailed to the teacher to share in class or post on their website. A beginning basic checklist for using podcasts that we have used in our own teaching is seen in the figure below (Figure 12.2).

Although editing is not possible with Audioboo, we have found that students are willing to re-record if they are not satisfied with their "boo."

VoiceThread (VT) (https://voicethread.com/) is a website where audio files can be recorded and posted by students. Mobile apps are available for smartphones and tablet devices, which makes it a very flexible tool for users. Although VT also allows for video recordings, we only address audio here because it is so easy to respond by voice alone.

VoiceThreads can be composed in two ways. Teachers can develop a VT (typically images, text, and voice are incorporated) and provide access to it by sending

Questions   **Student Evaluation**

Questions		
1. The podcast is one minute in length.	Yes	No
2. The podcast pertains to the assigned topic.	Yes	No
3. It is audible and in normal speed.	Yes	No
4. It is accompanied with a written reflection.	Yes	No

Figure 12.2.   Podcast checklist for students.

its URL to students. Students then click the hyperlink, log onto the site, and open the VoiceThread. There they can upload a photo of themselves or simply let VoiceThread assign an icon, such as a car. If students are young we suggest they NOT upload their image, though they could create avatars if they so wish (e.g., Voki, http://www.voki.com/) and contribute their recorded voice about the posted topic. Their voice can be recorded via a microphone or they can use a phone and call in their comments.

An alternate way to use VoiceThread is to have students post their own "threads," and then they invite others to listen and post responses. We make note of caution here. We think it's important to teach students to attribute work appropriately, so when they select images from the Internet they must be required to include the image and the associated URL into a Word document and then "capture" *both* the image and URL as one image. This strategy forces students to think about copyrighting and attribution, which we think is a critical habit to develop.

Users are allowed three free "threads" at any given time. Teachers can remove "threads" that are no longer needed, so that only three are simultaneously posted. An annual fee allows users to post multiple threads, but we have found the basic free version is satisfactory for most teachers.

Another way for composing podcasts is to use recording software on your computer or digital device. Audacity (http://audacity.sourceforge.net/) is a podcasting tool that we recommend. While it can be used on Macs, we typically use it only on PCs because we very much like Mac's Garageband (see later section). Audacity can be downloaded without cost from the Internet and installed on classroom computers and other digital devices. We have frequently used Audacity in after-school literacy programs, and students find the program easy to use and are amazed with the visual display of their voice while composing. We have found the visual display helps students think about pacing, prosody, tone, and loudness of voice, though we don't typically use this vocabulary with younger students. An added advantage of Audacity is that it permits editing so that an audio segment can be easily deleted if a student sneezes or is interrupted during a recording. More advanced features include white noise considerations and removal of background noises, for example.

Audacity involves two downloads: One is of the Audacity program itself and the second is an ancillary program (LAME) that is used to convert the audio recording to mp3 files, which can be transferred to digital devices, attached to emails, or embedded on websites and blogs.

Garageband is preinstalled as a program application on Macs and it is intuitive for student users. Users open Garageband by clicking on its icon; if the icon is not available, then search for Garageband under Mac Applications.

Click on "Create New Podcasting Program," write a title for it and decide where it will be saved (e.g., desktop folder); we suggest using children's initials and include the date of the recording for ease of locating. Next a screen with choices appears and the user picks voice (Male or Female); then the user clicks on the red dot and the recording begins (see arrow in the screenshot below). The same button is clicked to stop the recording. Students enjoy seeing their voices displayed on the Garageband screen (much like the Audacity screen, though it is visually more complex). We teach learners to save their Garageband podcasts into iTunes for easy retrieval. They can change their podcast title if they wish to do so. Figure 12.3 depicts Garageband's recording screen. Garageband includes editing features, but we do not initially teach these to children because there would be too many steps to recall.

We have used podcasting tools with elementary and secondary students who experience difficulties in reading and writing. Our experience is that students, such as Mario, love to podcast. They enjoy hearing their voices, using the digital devices, and are eager to learn what listeners think of their podcasts.

Students who enjoy podcasting display characteristics that are associated with engagement and success in literacy. That is they enjoy literacy activities, they use

Figure 12.3.   Garageband's recording screen.

specific strategies for composing their podcasts, and they are socially interactive when using them (Guthrie, Wigfield, & You, 2012). In the long term podcasting will not only improve students' engagement in reading, it will develop their fluency and composing skills. These skills can be used to address the Common Core State Standards and develop real world participatory skills for the digital age.

Graphic Organizers

Many teachers use graphic organizers in their teaching. Concept mapping, Venn diagrams, KWL charts, tree-charts, body biographies (Smagorinsky & O'Donnell-Allen, 1998), mind-maps (Margulies & Naal, 2002), and timelines are examples of graphic organizers that help students "see" the ideas they are studying and learning. The KWL strategy (Ogle, 1986) is a widely used visual organizer, and with it students use a visual chart to guide their thinking both before and after completing their learning activities. Middle school students sometimes complete body biographies (Smagorinsky & O'Donnell-Allen, 1998), which is another graphic organizer for composing text, drawings, and symbols to represent the personalities, challenges, and accomplishments of protagonists they have read about in literature. Students often prepare story maps and storyboards about narratives they have read or plan to compose (Bruce, 2011; Gambrell & Jawitz, 1983; Reif, 2007; Robb, 2000). Story maps are graphic organizers that illustrate episodic structures (single episodic structure—setting, characters, problem, attempts to solve problem and resolution, among others) and are designed to help students better comprehend narratives they have read; storyboards are visual frames for helping students visualize the sequence of narratives they have read (Narkon & Wells, 2013; Smith, 1990) or ones they want they want compose.

Web tools can be successfully used to compose graphic organizers, story maps, and storyboards, and resistant learners, such as Mario, will enjoy working with them. One of the earliest digital programs for composing graphic organizers was Inspiration (www.Inspiration.com), which is paid software, and is still widely used by teachers and students. Many schools purchase site licenses for this program, and teachers eagerly adopt it into their instruction. Inspiration allows teachers and students to create visual and text displays of ideas with color, graphics, and photos that can be hyperlinked to websites and exported as a Word document in an outline format that represents the hierarchical graphic. It remains one of our favorite programs, even though it is not free; we encourage teachers to subscribe for a trial for a month to determine how helpful it might be for them. Figure 12.4 provides an example of a graphic organizer that was developed by a student attending an after-school literacy program—defining the vocabulary word, "livid," in Inspiration. This graphic organizer includes text and rays that can be color-coded for emphasis and design.

There are many other programs for creating graphic organizers. Many of these programs are free and readily available by accessing them from a website with a user ID and password. A favorite graphic organizer tool is Popplet (www.popplet.com), which incorporates multimodal forms of communication. Audio and video files

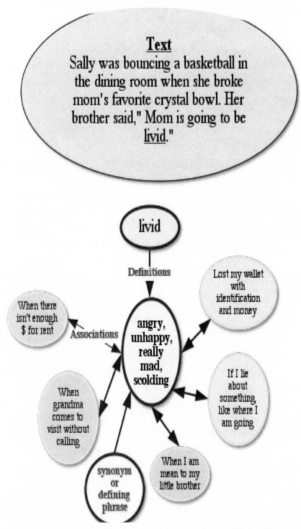

Figure 12.4.   Example of a graphic organizer with inspiration.

can be integrated with text into its graphic organizers. Popplets have the potential of making graphic organizers exciting for students to compose, and certainly more dynamic than those that might be created with pencil and paper or with a conventional word processing program. Students can email links to their graphic organizers or insert embedded codes directly into their blogs and webpages. (Embedded codes hyperlink the first frame of a video or image from a podcast, and they provide an attractive way of posting video and audio files onto webpages or in this case a Popplet.) Students can change the background color of their organizer, and sketches and photos can be inserted into the Popplets. Figure 12.5 displays a sample Popplet with

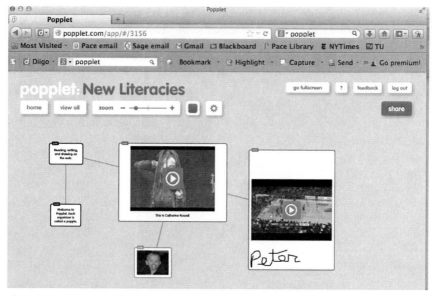

Figure 12.5. Sample Popplet (http://popplet.com/app/#/3156).

alphabetic text, cursive writing, photos, and video, which are activated when the viewer clicks on the red arrows.

Drawings

Visualization is another form of representation that has been widely used in teaching for hundreds of years. Personal slate boards and classroom chalkboards attest to teachers' beliefs in the importance of having students visualize the ideas they are studying. Overhead transparencies and newer digital whiteboards affirm the continuing importance of visualization as a way to display information to learners. Some classrooms now have document cameras for projecting written ideas, images, and opaque objects for students to see (Hennessy, 2011).

Although the usefulness of visualization for study and memory has often been overlooked (Foer, 2011), research indicates that it facilitates memory, and the more meaningful and detailed a mental image, the easier it is to retrieve the information it represents (Pressley, Levin, & Delaney, 1982). Well-known thinkers, such as Dostoevsky and Einstein (Foer, 2011), are reported to have used visualization as a strategy for constructing their ideas. Dostoevsky liked to doodle in the margins of his notebooks before composing his novels, whereas Einstein is reported to have used visual images to help him conceptualize ideas that he later transformed into mathematical formulas. Einstein's theory of relativity, for example, is said to have originated from a picture in his mind about riding a bolt of lightning through the universe.

Other educational research affirms the importance of visualization strategies on students' learning (Sadoski & Paivio, 2001). The National Reading Panel (2000) emphasized the importance of using empirical research to support classroom practices, and one of its recommendations was to use visualization strategies to develop children's comprehension of text. Allington (2006), a widely known expert in children's literacy development, similarly identifies visualization as a research-based reading strategy to help struggling readers.

Drawing offers an effective way for many students to visualize their learning (Leigh, 2012), and there are many instructional strategies where drawing has been effectively used in classroom lessons. It can be used to represent what students have learned from reading, viewing, or listening to texts, regardless of text forms used (e.g., multimedia productions). "Sketch-to-Stretch" (Short, Harste, & Burke, 1996; Kauffman, 2006) requires students to draw images about what they have learned and then share their sketches with others to elicit their responses; after others have been heard, the artist confirms or disconfirms why he/she drew the sketch the way they did.

Web tools can make drawing engaging and helpful for Mario and all students who experience learning difficulties. Drawing does not have to be limited to the primary grades, though we often see more drawing at that level. Digital drawing tools can be selected depending on their complexity and age appropriateness for their student users. Intermediate grade students might compose basic sketches of what they read, but older and more advanced readers might integrate text and detailed texts and graphics into their drawings. Digital drawing tools can involve sophisticated and complex thinking about ways to visually represent ideas in the intermediate and middle grades.

Digital drawing tools can be used to extend students' content area learning. For example, students can sketch and label a concept they are learning in science, or they can illustrate the mental steps they have taken to answer a math story with one of the digital drawing tools. The Common Core State Standards emphasize reading informational text [Anchor Standard 7 in Reading—*Integrate and evaluate content presented in diverse media and formats, including visually and quantitatively, as well as in words* (CCSS, 2010, p. 10)], and digital drawing tools can be used to help students visualize their learning with sketches of concepts and ideas.

Drawings provide an alternate way for students to share their learning with others. Many children who are learning to write and those with writing difficulties find drawing a productive way to compose and share their ideas (Miller, 2013). Drawings can be used for students to display what they see in their "mind's eye," and these drawings can be shared with others via the URL's or embed codes for response, interpretation, or analysis. A teaching strategy that we like for visualization is "Save the Last Word for Me" (Short, Hartse, Burke, 1996). With it groups of students might read a text or listen to a podcast. Then they compose digital drawings representing their interpretations of what they read or hear. Next they can participate in a discussion forum about their drawings with each artist remaining silent until the discussion ends. At the end each artist can present his or her reasons for drawing their ideas the way they did.

Digital drawing programs can be used for students to illustrate their comprehension of texts they have read, heard, or viewed (Bruce, 2011). For example, after reading a text, students might sketch the setting and each of the episodes in the narrative they read.

There are a variety of drawing programs that we have found helpful with students. Two online drawing programs that are particularly useful for literacy teachers are draw.to (www.draw.to.com) and Tux Paint (www.tuxpaint.com). Draw.to provides users the opportunity to compose sketches with basic line strokes and use of digital brushes for inserting color. Figure 12.6 is an example of a drawing made with the draw.to program.

Tux Paint provides a variety of options for inserting color and shape and is especially appealing to children in the elementary grades because it provides sound to each of the keystrokes that is used. In addition it uses many icons and templates for inserting pre-drawn images and graphics into it.

There are many other drawing programs offering greater versatility in their composition, but the learning curve for mastering the more advanced drawing programs requires additional effort and attention to detail than the casual user might want to spend. We find that basic programs, such as Draw.to and Tux Paint work well for learners who struggle in school.

Another effective way to use drawing, although less digital, is to have learners summarize their learning with crayons/colored pencils. Then their drawings can be scanned, saved into jpegs, and published books online. For example, suppose that students are reviewing the Civil War. As a class they might develop an outline, select pieces for individuals to illustrate and then comprise a book for review. These images can be inserted in a PPt and then voice recorded while recording a screencast. Students will be thrilled to share their books online, and they can make these books audio books by selecting a free screencasting tool, such as Screencast-o-matic (http://www.screencast-o-matic.com/), and recording their understandings to make the book come alive (see *Screencasting* section below). Likewise, teachers of young students can scan students' drawings; if the class had taken a field trip to the firehouse, children's drawings could be scanned as images (jpegs) and used to develop a book, which they could narrate.

Figure 12.6.   Quick sketch of a Big Wheels bike—DrawTo.

Digital Media Productions

Experienced teachers know that their lessons are almost always more effective when ideas are presented in multiple modalities. That is, saying something is not as good as saying and showing it. It is even more effective to say it, show it, and have students interact or simulate a concept, event, or process. Media production—the combination of text, audio (voice/music), and visual images—enables the viewer a richer experience than text alone.

Digital media production offers exciting opportunities for supporting students' learning (e.g., Considine, Horton, & Moorman, 2009; O'Brien & Voss, 2011; Turner, 2011), and it can be particularly effective for engaging resistant learners, such as Mario, in reading and writing. There are many websites using multimedia forms of communication. Users can select text, upload photos and select/upload royalty free music and then determine a presentation style for sharing the information with others. Support for the creation of media productions is also found in the Common Core [Anchor Standard 5 in Speaking and Listening—*Make strategic use of digital media and visual displays of data* (and other material) *to express information and enhance understanding of presentations* (CCSS, 2010)].

Media creations allow students to integrate information with their favorite music and images. Such ways of presenting information can be engaging, exciting, and stimulating. In many ways multimedia presentations are analogous to a SuperBowl advertisement in which content is shared and presented with music, images, text, narrative, and video.

Animoto (www.animoto.com) is a multimedia website that works well across disciplines. Animoto involves the uploading of images, insertion of optional text and selection of design presentation. The free version enables the creator to make a thirty second video, but Kay has subscribed to the pro-version (three minute maximum) and we think teachers may find it more useful in the long run. We have used this site for students to compose introductions of themselves, to share essential knowledge with others, and to communicate family stories. In effect, media presentations can be used whenever narrative is needed. It personalizes learning, and the end product is very professional.

Glogster is a tool that allows students to create online digital whiteboards that incorporate images, symbols, video, text, and audio files. We recommend that teachers use the free educational version (http://edu.glogster.com/) that allows for more controls in terms of access, which is quite important with younger students. The regular Glogster (http://www.glogster.com/) has an age requirement (must be thirteen or older) and often incorporates questionable content, such as alcohol use or scantily clad images. For that reason, we encourage teachers to sign up for the educational version. The beauty of Glogster is that students can create glogs from many starting points, and the end product is very engaging. For example, suppose as part of a unit of study on the Harlem Renaissance a student wanted to do a review of Zora Neale Hurston's writing, they might upload an image of *Their Eyes were Watching God* (1937), link to videos on YouTube (maybe one as background to the

Harlem Renaissance and another on Zora Neale Hurston), incorporate images from the Internet, record their own voice on the importance of Hurston's contribution in terms of folklore and select background colors, symbols, and quotes to develop a one-page summary. We find that students who struggle with reading and writing will spend hours creating glogs to showcase their understandings, and they are almost always delighted to share their work with others. Our experience has been that initially creating glogs in dyads encourages personal interaction as well as learning from each other in a collaborative situation. Again, such expectations find clear support in CCSS [Anchor Standard 1 in Speaking and Listening: *Prepare for and participate effectively in a range of conversations and collaborations with diverse partners, building on others' ideas and expressing their own clearly and persuasively* (CCSS, 2010, p. 22)]. Glogster is a superb web tool for learners, and we recommend it with enthusiasm.

Screencasting

Screencasting provides a recording of a computer screen while an author-producer narrates what is displayed. We have observed that screencasting offers many opportunities for resistant learners, such as Mario, to become more engaged in classroom learning. Screencasts are an especially effective digital tool for learning. They are typically quick and easy videos that are developed for specific purposes—often answering questions, providing information, or presenting a point of view. Screencasts can be helpful and exciting in classroom teaching and learning activities. We often compose screencasts of our own mini-lessons so that our students can view them at home. We use them for online teaching to introduce students to concepts and skills that are important for the topics they are studying. We also develop them for re-teaching concepts, which has much potential for classroom teachers, when we realized some students have struggled with specific content or have incomplete understanding as evidenced by quick exit checks (Owen & Sarles, 2012).

In our own teaching we have required undergraduate and graduate students to compose screencasts about their favorite literacy websites, including how to navigate the site and narrating their evaluation of the website's content and use for beginning teachers (e.g., www.ncte.org; www.reading.org). Our students have made screencasts of family stories with photographs of their members. They have asked their students in tutoring situations to develop screencasts on topics of interest (e.g., second graders exploring animals and animal habitats they have been studying), which are shown and celebrated at a share-chair.

Intermediate and middle school students eagerly create screencasts, too. Today's students often compose PowerPoint and Keynote (presentation software on Macs) slideshows, and these same slides can be used for screencasting. The challenge is for teachers to help students use screencasting programs that easily upload and record narration. Screencasts can be linked or posted onto school websites for students and parents to view at home. Intermediate grade and older students can create their own screencasts. For example, pupils might produce individual screencasts of book talks for others in their classrooms to view, while groups of students might display their summary learnings related to a topic of study. Students might compose screencasts retelling family stories, or they might make screencasts about a controversial topic in their community (e.g., nuclear energy, homelessness). There are countless other ways screencasts can be used to make school curricula interesting and engaging for students and their families.

Teachers can easily develop screencasts of PowerPoint or Keynote slides for introductions or reviews of units of study, which could be embedded on their class websites or included in their school's learning management system. They can develop screencasts to explain new content, elaborate on difficult concepts or for helping parents work with their children on nightly homework. Screencasts can be used to differentiate instruction by offering different levels of instruction (beginning, middle, advanced) for students studying particular topics and concepts.

There are a number of online programs that are very effective screencasting tools. Three of our favorites are Jing, Screencast-o-matic, and Knovio. These screencasting programs encourage sharing of content and thoughtful media productions with specific purposes, both important considerations in socially constructed participatory literacy interactions.

We recommend Jing for elementary and middle school students unfamiliar with media production. The program must be downloaded and installed on computers, so teachers will need to work with the school's technology folks. Because it was created by a well-known, reliable source (TechSmith, (http://www.techsmith.com/jing.html) and specifically developed student use, most schools allow its instillation. Jing allows the recording and sharing of whatever appears on the computer screen with narration, provided there is a microphone; it also allows easy screenshots, so students can "capture" a screen image to use in a PPt, for example. Jing screencasts can be saved on the computer or stored at screencast.org (http://www.techsmith.com/screencastcom.html) and shared via email or embedded. We know that with young students, teachers often worry about sharing broadly, so Jing screencasts can be stored in the school's storage drive, though some negotiation might have to occur because many districts restrict access to storage for a variety of reasons (e.g., size of videos that "eat" up much storage space). Jing screencasts are limited to ten minutes, which is a perfect size for young students (and often older ones too) because they discourage redundancy due to the short recording timeframe. While editing is not possible on the free version, students can define the portion of the screen to be captured and learn to pause the recording as they switch between websites and a PPt, for example. The end product is a fairly high quality video. Moreover, if they "flub" during recording, they are willing to re-do their media productions because of the short duration of recording.

Screencast-o-matic (http://www.screencast-o-matic.com/), also developed by TechSmith, is an online screencasting program that does not require downloads, so it can be used immediately. It is a simple click and record system; that is, the student/teacher clicks on the button to start the recording, pauses as s/he moves among websites or between PPt and website, and then renders the video saving it at screencast.org (http://www.techsmith.com/screencastcom.html). This tool records up to fifteen minutes, which we find is *FAR* too long, and we often limit students in time (e.g., seven minutes for middle level students and ten for high school students) to ensure that students avoid redundancies (e.g., "And like I said . . . "). Similar to Jing, Screencast-o-matic allows students to showcase their understanding (individually or in groups) and create videos to share with others or teach content, while educators find the screencasts helpful for teaching and re-teaching.

Knovio (http://www.knovio.com/) is the third free tool that we find helpful for teachers and older students. Knovio is actually a combination of the words "knowledge" and "vision" (http://www.knovio.com/about/) that is an editable screencasting tool. Basically the creator uploads a PPt and narrates with Knovio. After uploading a premade PPt, which will take a couple of minutes depending on the length of the PPt, the user then allows the tool to connect with their computer and microphone. The end result is that there is a video of the creator narrating in addition to the PPt; while this feature makes the video much more personalized, we recommend this feature for older students (upper middle level and high school) due to privacy and safety concerns. Once the PPt is uploaded, the user clicks on the first slide and records narration. When they click on the next slide, they repeat the process until the last slide and hit "stop recording." After the video is rendered, the creator can click the "play" button to review his/her presentation. If satisfied, the creator can send as an attachment in email, embed in a blog or website, or share via social media (e.g., Facebook). The final Knovio screencast is quite professional in appearance.

USING THE DIGITAL LITERACIES TO IMPROVE MARIO'S READING AND WRITING

In this section we discuss a variety of digital technologies that can be used to effectively improve Mario's reading and writing. Throughout the case study Mario reveals a concern about his spelling, and for this reason we first propose several digital literacy strategies that will improve his spelling and composing. His comments from the reading interview identified his interest in reading about video games, fantasy, sports, and comics, but it did not reveal his cognitive strategies for comprehending what he reads. For this reason we share digital tools that Mario can use to develop his reading comprehension.

Helping Mario with His Spelling and Composing

It is common for struggling learners to encounter difficulties in spelling. Teachers complain that students' texting on digital devices, such as is done on cell phones, table computers, and in Mario's case on video game devices (Playstation 3), interfere with their spelling and writing development. We suggest that the spelling that students use when texting should not be viewed as an obstacle to conventional spelling and composing. Instead texting and the inventive spelling that occurs with it are better viewed as systematic sound-to-symbol associations that are logical and complex in their own right. Inventive spellings are analogous to speakers' use of dialect in which they switch vernacular depending on the setting and participants involved. The challenge for struggling learners is that they often do not know when and how to switch from inventive spelling to conventional spelling. The digital literacies can help by having them write often.

The first principle for improving Mario's spelling is to have him write frequently. Too much attention to the surface structure and spelling rules, at the expense of content, will interfere with his writing and reading development. For this reason the first teaching strategy that we recommend is to have Mario compose frequently. One way to have Mario compose is to participate in electronic discussions with his peers. He already does this on his Playstation 3, but we recommend he participate in electronic discussions about academic issues, too. Wikispaces is a website that we have seen effectively used in middle schools. There is a school version that costs money, and it allows teachers much more control; we do recommend that option for discussion and rich interface options (http://www.wikispaces.com/content/classroom/about). We recall an integrated unit in which the social studies and English teachers in a particular middle school used Wikispaces for the students to respond to literature about the Civil War. The teachers emphasized responding in meaningful ways, and the spelling that occurred was never considered a problem providing it did not interfere with readers' understanding of what was written. Teachers viewed the students' electronic discussions as informal writing, and the focus of the wikis was for students to engage in sharing their thoughts about what they understood and inferred from the literature about the war. Having Mario write frequently with real audiences on a wiki is the first step in developing his spelling skills.

A second strategy for developing Mario's spelling is to have him maintain a blog. We find wordpress' free blog works well for students with many themes and options (https://signup.wordpress.com). Blogging represents more formal writing than digital conversations found on a wiki because blog entries are not contextualized in an interactive conversation with others. In addition, blogging is similar to journaling, but it also offers advantages to conventional journals. Bloggers can select templates that offer a variety of ways to frame their entries with colors and textures. They can insert photos, graphics, and videos into their entries, and of course the most important feature of a blog is that it can be shared with others via its URL and published for others to see. Blogging offers a digital strategy to engage Mario in frequent writing. Importantly it provides him a social context to write more publicly than the electronic discussions that would occur in the wiki. The more he writes, the more refined his spelling will become. Blogger.com and kidblog.com are two websites that are free and easy for Mario to learn and use.

A third digital strategy to improve Mario's spelling and composing is for him to develop his metalinguistic awareness about letter patterns and spelling principles. After participating in his ELA teacher's mini-lesson pertaining to a spelling pattern,

Mario might take the pattern, such as dropping the final /y/ to /i/ and adding *es* and compose a Knovio (http://www.knovio.com/) about it. He might compose three slides, one with the rule, a second with an example of its application, and a third with an explanation as to why spellers sometimes misinterpret the rule. His Knovio presentation could be placed on the classroom website, and its URL can be shared with others in the class.

Another tool that might be helpful to develop Mario's spelling is WordFind, a game from Spelling City (http://www.spellingcity.com/wordfind.html). Within WordFind words are leveled and divided by content (e.g., sight words, compound words, grades 6–8), and he can practice the level appropriate for him. We think this will appeal to Mario because of its game format and may make him more conscious of typical words he needs to master for effective communication. Kerpoof Studio (see also section on comics and graphica) also has a "spell a word" section that might be appealing to Mario (http://www.kerpoof.com/).

A fifth option, if he has an iPhone or access to iPads in school, is a phonetic word speller app (https://itunes.apple.com/us/app/american-wordspeller/id397617771?mt=8&ign-mpt=uo%3D4) that allows the user to phonetically spell a word with the automatic generation of correct possible spelling(s). It's a bit pricey ($4.99) but a potentially helpful tool for Mario and one that should be considered.

Finally a practical, final-edit spell check strategy might work well for Mario. The teacher and Mario need to analyze his frequent spelling errors. For example, in reading he mispronounced "*from*" as "*for*," and we have found that many struggling spellers make visually similar errors, such as "*form*" for "*from*" or "*posse*" for "*possess*." As a final spell check, Mario could use Microsoft Word feature and consciously search his writing for his typical errors, such as *for*, and double check that he intended to use "*for*" and not "*from*." This strategy encourages him to do a final careful editing addressing his most frequent errors. Over time, our experience has been that students are more conscious of personally challenging word spellings and make fewer transpositions or visually similar spelling errors.

Wikis, blogs, and audio video presentations offer engaging and exciting teaching strategies to improve students' spelling. We believe these strategies will in the long term help Mario become more confident, accurate, and fluent in his spelling and writing development.

Helping Mario Improve His Comprehension

Most literacy specialists know that comprehension is the most important component of the reading process. Comprehension is not only the goal of reading, but it improves the process of reading. That is, reading words is easier when students understand what they are reading.

We appreciate the way the teacher in the interview asks Mario questions about what he has orally read (*The Bicycle Race*) because the comprehension questions pertain to the text's narrative structure. Narrative structure is helpful for asking students about their comprehension, and in the long term by questioning them in this way students internalize text structure, which will help them when reading independently. It might be helpful for Mario to have a copy of narrative story structure provided by the International Reading Association and the National Council of Teachers of English jointly sponsored website, Read/Write/Think for review and reference (http://www.readwritethink.org/classroom-resources/printouts/narrative-pyramid-30845.html).

There are many ways that the digital literacies can be used to help Mario's use of text structure. Voicethreads (http://voicethread.com/) are a particularly exciting way for Mario to retell what he has read because the program offers the opportunity to integrate visuals, text, video, and audio in his retelling. Each slide of Mario's Voicethread could pertain to a different structural element of the narrative he has read. For example, Mario might compose five slides pertaining to a fantasy text he has completed reading: the first slide will consist of the title and author; the second slide will describe its setting and characters; the third will identify the story problem, the fourth will illustrate the protagonist's attempts to solve the problem, and the final slide could describe the story outcome and theme. Each Voicethread slide could consist of text and/or a visual that Mario composed on his computer screen with a screen capture command; on an Apple computer Mario could simultaneously press "command," "shift," and the number "4" keys to capture the selected screen segment for uploading to Voicethread. If his computer has a real time camera, he can record a video of himself speaking and incorporate that as well. He will enjoy hearing his voice and seeing the visuals that he created for each of the slides in his Voicethread. Others can respond to his work, and thus there's a social aspect that is very reinforcing.

A pre-reading comprehension activity is for Mario to brainstorm what he knows about a text before reading. Years ago researchers argued that reading is only "incidentally visual" to highlight the importance of the knowledge readers bring to the printed page. Before reading Mario might create a "wall" to identify what he knows about a topic. A good web tool for this is Padlet (http://padlet.com/) because Mario can post his ideas about the topic he is going to read, insert videos and photos about it, and then share his wall with others for discussion. For instance, if Mario were to read about a new game on his Playstation 3, he could first brainstorm all the games he has for his Playstation, their essential features, and even questions he has about being successful playing them. Mario could insert videos and photos onto his "wall" and then share it electronically by sending its URL or pasting its embed code into one of his blogs; he could also export it as a PDF file and send via an attachment to his friend and fellow readers. Activating prior knowledge about a topic to be read and setting purposes for reading, either as goals or questions, has long been shown to be an effective comprehension strategy. A digital pre-reading strategy such as Padlet is likely to help improve Mario's engagement and comprehension of text.

Readers need to learn how to monitor what they read, and this is an important strategy for Mario to use as well. The Common Core State Standards emphasize reading of informational text in the secondary grades, and an effective webtool that Mario might use for monitoring his reading is Popplet (http://popplet.com/). Popplet is a digital graphic organizer that allows readers to compose ideas using the alphabet, drawings, music, and/or video files. Mario might independently read an information text about the "Emancipation Proclamation," and as he read he could periodically stop, think, and react to its key ideas by inserting retellings, questions, drawings, photos, or videos into the digital graphic organizer. He could title each of these thought bubbles with an identifying number that corresponded to a particular section of text. Later these notes can be reviewed for study, shared with others via their URL's, embed codes, or posted onto social media networks, such as Facebook (https://www.facebook.com/), or Pinterest (http://www.pinterest.com/). The process of composing a graphic organizer while reading will improve Mario's comprehension, and by doing so he will learn that comprehension involves effort and thought while reading. As Mario uses this digital to monitor his reading, his comprehension will improve, and he will learn that understanding what one reads requires one to monitor what he reads.

Mario should also learn strategies for analyzing and reflecting on what he has read. Such strategies are often called unpacking or reflection strategies and are based on the principle that comprehension is best accomplished through conscious review and response to what has been read. There are many ways for Mario to use the digital literacies to reflect on what he has read. One webtool that we have found helpful with middle school students is glogster.edu. Glogster (http://edu.glogster.com/) is a digital poster that accommodates texts, videos, music (mp3's), and photos, and we particularly like the Glogster Edu website because of teacher controls. The regular Glogster may contain inappropriate language, for example, or worrisome topics. We think that Mario would enjoy responding to content or literature by making glogs and sharing them with his peers.

Since Mario likes video games, the teacher might consider free apps that build connections between his reading and what he considers fun activities. For example, building on *The Bicycle Race*, he might enjoy "Bike Race Free" (https://play.google. com/store/apps/details?id=com.topfreegames.bikeracefreeworld), which is a physics-based game that allows the user to race to the top of the mountain in multi-levels with various bikes and worlds.

Victoria Forester is the author of *The Girl Who Could Fly*, one of the few books that Mario mentions enjoying. Building on his enjoyment and engagement, his teacher may want to encourage him to explore the author's website (http://www. victoriaforester.com/home.html). In particular, he might find her "Diary" section interesting and develop a writer's lens (i.e., How does Forester approach journaling?) to assist him in writing his own blog. Unfortunately, this is her first book, but she is well-known for her featured films, including *Cry of the White Wolf* (Disney Channel), a story where two lost teenagers are befriended by a wolf who leads them back home. He could watch the film and write a review, which he could post online at The Student Center (http://www.student.com/allreviews.php). [As an aside, he could also publish game reviews on this same website, since video games are a strong interest of the learner.] Another possibility is writing an online review of the book for other students. Scholastic (http://teacher.scholastic.com/activities/swyar/write. asp) has an easy book review that would allow Mario to publish online, surely an authentic writing experience. He could use this resource to find other fantasy and science fiction books that students are reading to locate other books he might want to read. In a sense, he becomes a member of the online community, recommending and receiving recommendations for book choices. Kidsreads (http://www.kidsreads. com/) is another good book review site for students, and since Forester's book has not yet been reviewed on this site, it's a perfect opportunity for Mario to publish is review. Importantly, both websites provide resources to guide him to read more books in fantasy that he will enjoy.

Multimedia Composing

Comics are a type of reading that Mario appreciates and engages in willingly. While graphica (referencing comics and graphic novels) have become increasingly prevalent in mainstream books and include options for a variety of genres, he does not seem aware of these books. First the teacher might want to expose him to author studies of graphic novel writers. Good Reads, an online community that reviews books, has a superb listing of popular graphic novels for middle school (http://www.goodreads.com/list/show/24894.Best_Graphic_Novels_for_Middle_School), and this resource could be helpful to Mario and his teacher in book selection. We particularly like graphica because it include more involved storytelling than comics alone (uses speech, sound bubbles, illustrations, images to advance a fiction or informational storyline) and encourages students' to inference across panels with the words and images co-supporting understanding of what has happened in the gutter (the white space between panels). Additionally, graphica may lead Mario to read other genres. Moreover there are often content area graphic texts that might support discipline knowledge that he is learning in social studies or science classes. For more information on graphica we recommend Thompson (2008).

Writing comics will allow Mario to develop a deeper understanding of how graphica works and support his efforts at multimedia composing. There are several options that we have found popular and successful with preadolescents. Kerpoof Studio (http://www.kerpoof.com/) is a great starting point for writing comics. It allows the writer to insert images, speech and sound bubbles, and create a storyline. The appeal of this web tool is ease of use and ability to revise/edit, so we find it a great beginning point for writing comics. Mario can make comics with animation and music or complete digital storytelling projects. Comic Life (http://comiclife. com/) is the best option once Mario has mastered an easier online comic creator, like Kerpoof Studio. It produces very attractive professional looking panels with many options (e.g., layout, panel types, speech bubbles) and easy editing (e.g., rearranging slides). Mario could develop a summary of material he has learned in content area study, for example. We believe that online comic creators will engage Mario and help increase his stamina for multimedia composing and ultimately traditional writing.

CONCLUSION

Throughout the years others have proposed various intervention strategies for helping resistant learners, such as Mario, learn to read and succeed in school. These include systematic phonics instruction (Stahl, Duffy-Hester, & Stahl, 1998), one-to-one tutoring (e.g., Wasik, 1998), cross-age tutoring (e.g., Taylor, Hanson, Justice-Swanson, & Watts, 1997), motivation and engagement practices (Guthrie & Fox, 2001; Guthrie & Wigfield, 2000), cooperative learning (e.g., Slavin, Madden, Dolan, & Wasik, 1996) and metacognitive strategy instruction (e.g., Dole, Brown, & Trathen, 1996) among others. In this chapter we argued that the digital literacies offer much potential for helping students move from resistance to engagement in their classroom literacy activities.

Our argument for integrating digital literacies into classroom learning is first supported by our own observations that many resistant learners are fully engaged in literacy when using digital devices (e.g., computers, tablets, and smartphones) outside of school. Second, there is a long and rich history of research supporting the integration of community and school literacies (e.g., Moll, Amanti, Neff, & Gonzalez, 1993), which leads to culturally meaningful learning in school. Third, the new digital literacies offer multiple sources of information (alphabetic, visual, audio, social) for struggling readers, and this increases the likelihood of engagement and success with reading and writing regardless of whether it occurs in or outside of school.

The mismatch between learners' in-school and out-of-school literacies is one of the contributing factors which is often noted in discussions about the achievement gap in literacy education (McKown, 2013). Online web tools offer ways to address achievement gaps for non-engaged students, especially for students from historically underrepresented groups and those outside the mainstream school culture, by using active, culturally responsive techniques (Griner & Steward, 2013). The suggested web tools in this chapter are closely aligned to the Common Core State Standards and nudge students towards being fully literate in the twenty-first century. Teachers have a critical role in integrating the digital literacies into classroom instruction. Importantly, we believe the web tools discussed in this chapter will help resistant learners, such as Mario, become more engaged in literacy learning activities when the digital literacies are used.

REFERENCES

Allington, R. (2006). *What really matters for struggling readers: Designing research-based programs* (2nd Ed.). Boston: Pearson.

Animoto. http://animoto.com/. Retrieved September 1, 2013.

Audacity. http://audacity.sourceforge.net/. Retrieved September 1, 2013.

Audioboo. https://audioboo.fm/.Retrieved September 1, 2013.

Baker, D. L., Stoolmiller, M., Good, R. & Baker, S. K. (2011). Effect of reading comprehension of passage fluency in Spanish and English for second-grade English learners. *School Psychology Review, 40*(3), 331–51.

Bruce, D. (2011). Framing the text: Using storyboards to engage students with reading. *English Journal, 100*(6), 78–85.

Carpo, B. H., & Orellana, A. (2011). Web 2.0 technologies for classroom instruction: High school teachers' perceptions and adoption factors. *Quarterly Review of Distance Education, 12*(4), 235–53.

Center for Applied Technology in Learning (CAST). http://www.cast.org/index.html. Retrieved September 2, 2013.

Coiro, J., Knobel, M., Lankshear, C., & Leu, D. J. (2010). *Handbook of research on new literacies*. New York.

Considine, D., Horton, J., & Moorman, G. (2009). Teaching and reading the millennial generation through media literacy. *Journal of Adolescent and Adult Literacy, 52*(6), 471–81.

Cuban, L. (2003). *Oversold and underused: Computers in the classroom*. Cambridge, MA: Harvard University Press.

Davis, A., & McGrail, E. (2009). "Proof-Revising" with podcasting: Keeping readers in mind as students listen to and rethink their writing. *Reading Teacher, 62*(6), 522–29.

Dole, J., Brown, K., & Trathen, W. (1996). The effects of strategy instruction on the comprehension performance of at-risk students. *Reading Research Quarterly, 31*(1), 63–88.

Draw.to. http://draw.to/new.Retrieved September 1, 2013.

Fleischman, P. (2004). *Joyful noise: Poems for two voices*. NY: Zolotow Books.

Foer, J. (2011). *Moonwalking with Einstein: The art and science of remembering everything*. NY: The Penguin Press.

Gambrell, L. B., & Jawitz, P. B. (1983). Mental imagery, text illustrations, and children's story comprehension and recall. *Reading Research Quarterly, 23*(3), 265–73.

Garageband. http://www.apple.com/ilife/garageband/. Retrieved September 1, 2013.

Glogster Edu. http://edu.glogster.com/. Retrieved September 2, 2013.

Gormley, K. & McDermott, P. (2014). "We don't go to computers anymore." Comparing urban and suburban children's experiences with the new literacies. *The Educational Forum, 78*, 1–15.

Griner, A. C., & Steward, M. L. (2013). Addressing the achievement gap and dissproportionality through the use of culturally responsive teaching practices. *Urban Education, 48*(4), 585–621.

Guthrie, J., & Fox, K. (2001). Classroom conditions for motivation and engagement in reading. *Educational Psychology Review, 13*(3), 283–302.

Guthrie, J. T., & Wigfield, A. (2000). Engagement and motivation in reading. In M. L. Kamil & P. B. Mosenthal (Eds.), *Handbook of reading research* (Vol. 3, pp. 403–22). Mahwah, NJ: Erlbaum.

Guthrie, J. T., Wigfield, A., & You, W. (2012). Instructional contexts for engagement and achievement in reading. In S. L. Christenson, A. L. Reschly, & C. Wylie (Eds.), *Handbook of research on student engagement* (pp. 601–34). New York: Springer. doi:10.1007/978-1-4614-2018-7_29.

Hennessy, S. (2011). The role of digital artifacts on the interactive whiteboard in supporting classroom dialogue. *Journal of Computer Assisted Learning, 27*(6), 463–89.

Hurston, Z. N. (1937). *Their eyes were watching God.* NY: J. B. Lippincott, Inc.

International Reading Association (IRA). www.reading.org. Retrieved August 25, 2013.

Jacobs, G. E. (2012). Rethinking common assumptions about adolescents' motivation to use technology in and out of school. *Journal of Adolescent & Adult Literacy, 56*(4), 271–74.

Jenkins, H. (2006). Confronting the challenges of participatory culture: Media education for the 21st century. White paper on digital media and learning from The MacArthur Foundation. Available from http://www.macfound.org/search/?q=jenkins.

Jing. http://www.techsmith.com/jing.html. Retrieved September 1, 2013.

Kauffman, G. (2006). Authoring ourselves as readers and writers. *Language Arts, 83*(6), 502–505.

Knovio. http://www.knovio.com/. Retrieved September 1, 2013.

Krashen, S. (2011). *Free voluntary reading.* Santa Barbara, CA: Libraries Unlimited.

Krashen, S. (2011). Access to books and time to read versus the Common Core State Standards and tests. *English Journal, 103*(2), 21–29.

Leigh, S. R. (2012). Writers draws visual hooks: Children's inquiry into writing. *Language Arts, 89*(6), 396–404.

Leu, D., McVerry, G., O'Byrne, W., Kiili, C., Zawillinger, L,, Everett-Cacopardo,, H., Kennedy, C., & Forzani, E. (2011). The new literacies of online reading comprehension: Expanding the literacy and learning curriculum. *Journal of Adolescent and Adult Literacy*, 55(11), 5–14.

Marcell, B. (2011). Putting fluency on a fitness plan: Building fluency's meaning-making muscles. *Reading Teacher, 65*(4), 242–49.

Margulies, N., & Maal, N. (2002). *Mapping inner space: Learning and teaching visual mapping.* Tucson, AZ: Zephyr Press.

McKenna, M., Conradi, K., Lawrence, C., Jang, B. G., & Meyer, J. P. (2013). Reading attitudes of middle school students: Results of a U.S. Survey. *Reading Research Quarterly,* 47(3), 283–306.

McKown, C. (2013). Social equity theory and racial-ethnic achievement gaps. *Child Development,* 84(4), 1120–36.

Millard, E. (2012). 5 reasons flipped classrooms work. *University Business,* 15(11), 26–29.

Miller, D. (2013). I can create images to retell and infer big ideas. *Reading Teacher,* 66(5), 360–64.

Moll, L., Amanti, C., Neff, D. and Gonzalez, N. (1992). Funds of knowledge for teaching: Using a qualitative approach to connect homes and classrooms. *Theory into Practice, XXXI,* 2, 132–41.

Narkon, D. E., & Wells, J. G. (2013). Improving reading comprehension for elementary students with learning disabilities: UDL enhanced story mapping. *Preventing School Failure,* 57(4), 231–39.

National Assessment of Educational Progress (NAEP). Available at http://nces.ed.gov/nationsreportcard/.

National Council of Teachers of English (2007). *21st Century literacies: A Policy Research Brief.* Urbana, IL: National Council of Teachers of English. Available at http://www.ncte.org/library/NCTEfiles/Resources/Magazine/Chron110721CentLitBrief.pdf.

National Governors Association (2010). *Common Core State Standards.* National Governors Association Center for Best Practices, Council of Chief State School Officers, Washington, D.C. Available at http://www.corestandards.org/.

National Reading Panel. (2000). *Report of the National Reading Panel: Teaching people to read.* Washington: National Institute of Child Health and Human Development.

New London Group. (1996). A pedagogy of multiliteracies: Designing social futures. *Harvard Educational Review, 66*(1), 60–92.

No Child Left Behind Act (2001). Available at http://www2.ed.gov/nclb/landing.jhtml.

O'Brien, D., Beach, R., & Scharber, C. (2007). "Struggling" middle schoolers: Engagement and literate competence in a reading writing intervention class. *Reading Psychology, 28,* 51–73.

O'Brien, D., & Scharber, C. (2008). Teaching old dogs new tricks: The luxury of digital abundance. *Journal of Adolescent & Adult Literacy, 52*(1), 66–68.

O'Brien, D., & Voss, S. (2011). Reading multimodally: What Is afforded? *Journal of Adolescent and Adult Literacy, 55*(1), 75–78.

Ogle, D. (1986). K-W-L: A teaching model that develops active reading of expository text. *The Reading Teacher, 39*(6), 564–70. doi:10.1598/RT.39.6.11.

Owen, D., & Sarles, P. (2012). Exit tickets: The reflective ticket to understanding. *Library Media Connection, 31*(3), 20–22.

Owens, R. (2013). Old time podcasts for new-time podcast. *English Journal 102*(6), 66–70.

Philip, T., & Garcia, A. (2013). The importance of still teaching the iGeneration: New technologies and the centrality of pedagogy. *Harvard Educational Review, 83*(2), 300–19.

Popplet. http://popplet.com/. Retrieved September 5, 2013.

Pressley, M., Levin, J. R., & Delaney, H. D. (1982). The mnemonic keyword method. *Review of Educational Research, 52*(1), 61–91.

Race to the Top. (2009). Available from http://www2.ed.gov/programs/racetothetop/index.html.

Rasinski, T. V. (2012). Why reading fluency should be hot. *Reading Teacher, 65*(8), 516–22.

Reif, L. (2007). Writing: Commonsense matters. In K. Beers, R. Probst, & L. Rief (Eds.), *Adolescent literacy: Turning promise into practice* (pp. 189–208). Portsmouth, NH: Heinemann.

Ring, J. I., Barefoot, L. C., Avrit, K., Brown, S. A., & Black, J. L. (2013). Reading fluency instruction for students at risk for reading failure. *Remedial and Special Education, 34*(2), 102–12.

Robb, L. (2000). *Teaching reading in middle school.* NY: Scholastic.

Sadoski, M.. & Paivio, A (2001). *Imagery and text: A dual coding theory of reading and writing.* Mahwah, NJ: Erlbaum.

Sams, A., & Bergmann, J. (2013). Flip your students' learning. *Educational Leadership, 70*(6), 16–20.

Screencast-o-matic. http://www.screencast-o-matic.com/. Retrieved September 1, 2013.

Short, K., Hartse, J., & Burke, C. (1996). *Creating classrooms for authors and inquirers.* Portsmouth, NH: Heinemann.

Slavin, R. E., Madden, N. A., Dolan, L. J., & Wasik, B. A. (1996). *Every child, every school: Success for all.* Thousand Oaks, CA: Corwin Press.

Smagorinsky, P., & O'Donnell-Allen, C. (1998). Reading as mediated and mediating action: Composing meaning for literature through multimedia interpretive texts. *Reading Research Quarterly, 33,* 198–226.

Smith, C. B. (1990). Story map: Setting, plot, mood, theme. *Reading Teacher, 44*(2), 178–79.

Stahl, S. A., Duffy-Hester, A., & Stahl, K. A. D. (1998). Everything you wanted to know about phonics (but were afraid to ask). *Reading Research Quarterly, 33,* 338–55.

Sundeen, T. H., & Sundeen, D. M. (2013). Instructional technology for rural schools: Access and acquisition. *Rural Special Education, 32*(2), 8–14.

Taylor, B. M., Hanson, B. E., Justice-Swanson, K., & Watts, S. M. (1997). Helping struggling readers: Linking small-group intervention with cross age tutoring. *Reading Teacher, 51*(3), 196–209.

Taylor, B. M., Pearson, P. D., Peterson, D. S., & Rodriquez, M. C. (2003). Reading growth in high-poverty classrooms: The influence of teacher practices that encourage cognitive engagement in literacy learning. *Elementary School Journal*, 104(1), 3–28.

Thompson, T. (2008). *Adventures in graphica*. Portland, ME: Stenhouse.

Turner, N. (2011). "Rap universal": Using multimodal media production to develop ICT literacies. Journal of *Adolescent and Adult Literacy, 54*(8), 613–24.

Tux Paint. http://tuxpaint.org/. Retrieved September 2, 2013.

Vasinda, S., & McLeod, J. (2011). Extending readers theatre: A powerful and purposeful match with podcasting. *Reading Teacher, 64*(7), 486–97.

Voki. http://www.voki.com/. Retrieved September 2, 2013.

Wilson, C., Chavez, K., & Anders, P. L. (2012). "From the *Koran* and *Family Guy*": Expressions of Identity in English learners' digital podcasts. *Journal of Adolescent & Adult Literacy, 55*(5), 374–84.

Wood, K. D. (2011). Bridging print literacies and digital literacies using strategy guides. *Journal of Adolescent & Adult Literacy, 55*(3), 248–52.

13

Concluding Thoughts

Francine Falk-Ross

As you read through the chapters in this book of frames for thought in the literacy education of all students, it is clear that there is overlap in the authors' messages. Each author, however, highlights a different view that changes/expands educators' orientation to teaching and draws us, as readers, to rethink the most appropriate, most socially just, next steps for teaching our own students. The common themes that seem to resonate most clearly focus on the following:

- *Students' strengths are individual,* and this knowledge requires teachers to value those features and elements with which they are familiar and those that require alternative thinking. Teachers can use flexibility in thought for finding and acknowledging students' strengths.
- *Linguistic and cultural practices have strong influences on students' learning,* and teachers can learn from students and their parents about alternative approaches to viewing the world and how our educational system fits within those lenses. Teachers can provide choices for students that allow for differences in learning styles and cultural practices.
- *Students and teachers interact and learn through language in the classroom,* and how teachers engage in pedagogic discourse to structure that learning requires critical thought and analysis to open teachers' self-awareness of the stance they bring to communicating an idea through the use of specific vocabulary, grammar, tone, and emphases on language elements. Teachers can be the ones to open access and equalize "voices" in classroom environments.
- *Knowledge of specific content, or academic language, provides a common ground for literacy development* for students as they strive to succeed in school and feel confident in their contributions. Teachers can use a balance of explicit instruction

and collaborative learning to support students' mastery of basic competencies for literacy development.

- *The form or format of learning influences engagement in learning.* Integrating multimodal approaches creates overlap in learning, and can be highly motivating. Building students' use of new literacies using technology and online formats expands their reach for information and their access to ways to share their understandings. Weaving elements of the arts into classroom events empowers students to participate and contribute in new and expanded ways using their own intelligences and insight. Teachers can be models for using a wide variety of format for literacy events.

As the student population in schools grows for a variety of reasons from economic to political issues, educators endeavor to find pedagogical approaches that are sensitive to all students' strengths and can build students' competencies. Students, at the same time, send teachers messages through their language and actions as they find their voices in the classroom, and teachers may miss the meaning. This text is full of ideas for rethinking the plethora of ways that teachers can reach out to students to support new learning using positive and effective approaches to empower all students and build teachers' pedagogical repertoires. These represent positive approaches to teaching and learning, all derived from new frames of reference.

Index

academic achievement, 160
academic agency, 147
academic vocabulary, 30, 58
access, 154–57
achievement gap, 143
adolescent ELLs, 144
Adolescent Motivation to Read Profile,
    Pitcher, S., 13, 39
affinity groups, 184
agency, 151–54
Alvermann, D. E., 11, 183,198, 199, 203
Animoto, 222
Aronson, E., 187
arts and professional development, 116
arts and reading comprehension, 118
arts and test scores, 124
arts infused pedagogy: learning with, 113;
    learning through, 113; learning about
    the arts, 113
arts integration, 114, 124
associationism, 146
Au, K., 200, 202
audacity, 215
Audioboo, 214

Bakhtin, M., 25, 26
Bandura, A., 147
bilingual, 72–73

Bloome, D., 25, 26
book clubs, 193
booktalks: for leadership development 188–
    90; and cross age literacy engagement,
    189. *See also* Common Core State
    Standards—English language arts anchor
    standards addressed through booktalks,
    Table 11.3, *191*
Bromley, K., 195
Bronfenbrenner, 68
Burnaford, G., 114

Cazden, Courtney, 25, 27, 29, 35, 38
Chang, C., 188
Chen, S. X., Benet-Martinez, V. & Bond,
    M. H., 182, 201
Christie, F., 30
Clark, E. G. & Justice, E. M., 183
Coiro, J., Knobel, M., Lankshear, C., Leu,
    D., 10
comics: *see* graphica
Comic Life, 230
Common Core Standards: adolescents'
    access, 144, 158; arts standards, 127,
    131–34; booktalks, Table 11.*3, 19*;
    critical literacy discussions and response
    journals, Table 11.1, *186*; discourse,
    92, 111–12; English language arts

anchor standards, 184; Jigsaw, Table
11.2, *189*; Language, Anchor Standard
5, 213; literacy circles, Table 11.4,
194–95; parenting and family, 81–83;
Reading, Anchor Standard 7, 220,
228, 229; Speaking and Listening,
Anchor Standard 1, 223; Speaking
and Listening, Anchor Standard 2,
211; Speaking and Listening, Anchor
Standard 5, 222; Writing, Anchor
Standard 2, 213; Writing, Anchor
Standard 6, 211; Writing, Anchor
Standard 8, 211
communicative competence, 53
comprehension strategies, 59
context of situation, 28
cooperative learning, 54, 91
Council of Chief State School Officers, 93
critical literacy 184–86
cross-age literacy experiences: and leadership
development 189; *see also* booktalks
cultural practices, 67, 76
cultural responsiveness, 200–2
Cummins, J., 30, 31, 36
curriculum genres/registers, 30

Daniels, H., 192
Delpit, L., 31
Desimone, L., 116
digital literacies, 209–12, 231; educational
reform, 210–12
Digital Media Production, 222–23
direct instruction, 92
Directed Inquiry Activity (DIA), 97, 111
discourse processes: definitions, 5, 25;
nature and purposes, 26; forms and
formats, 27
discourse strategies/interventions: Table
Talk, 37–39; Expanded Language
Routines, 5, 35, 43–44, 36–37; Online
Learning Communities, 39–40;
Modified Critical Analyses, 40–44
Dozier, C., Johnston, P. & Rodgers, R., 41
drawings, 219–21
draw to, 221
DREAM, 114–16

ecological systems, 68, 69
Edwards, M., 197

Edwards, D. & Mercer, N., 26, 28, 31
English as a Second Language, 70
English language learners (ELL), 93–94,
105
equity factors, 31, 32
Erikson, E., 183

Falk-Ross, F., 31, 32
Fairclough, N., 41
Faircloth, B. S. & Hamm, J. V., 183, 199
family literacy programs, 76–77
family routines, 71
family rules, 71
field, tenor, mode, 29
fluency, 213–14
Freire, P., 40
Freebody, P., Luke, A. & Gilbert, P., 31
freewriting, 99–100, 112f
funds of knowledge, Moll, 3
Furrer, C. & Skinner, E., 182
future-mindedness, 158

Galda, L. & Graves, M. F., 196
Gallas, K., 116
Gambrell, L., 116
Garageband, 216
Gee, J., 8, 26, 27, 31, 32, 41, 184
Glogster.edu, 222–23, 229
goals: mastery, 155; outcome, 155
Goldberg, M., 114–16
graphic organizers, 159, 217–19, 229
graphica, 230
Green, J. L., 26
guided reading, 96, 111
Gutierrez, K., 35

Hall, G. S., 187
Halliday, M.A.K. & Hasan, R., 25, 26, 31
Handford, M., 8
Hanze, M. & Berger, R.,187
Hetland, L., 114
hope theory, 147–48
Hymes, D., 27, 31

identity challenges: identity formation, 184,
186; identity construction, 183
immigrant, 70, 72, 73, 74, 79
individuation, 183
inference, 115

inspiration, 217
International Reading Association (IRA), 9, 210, 211
IRE/IRF (initiation, response, evaluation/ feedback) pattern, 30, 72

Jigsaw strategy: definition, 185; expert and home groups 187–88; *see also* Common Core State Standards—English language arts anchor standards addressed through Jigsaw, Table 11.2, *189*
Jing, 224
Jung, C. G., 183

Keane, N., 188
Kerpoof Studio, 230
Kirshner, B., O'Donoghue, J. L. & McLaughlin, M. W. (Eds.), 183, 202
Knovio, 225; Know—Want to Know— Learned Strategy (KWL), 96, 111
Kordalewski, J., 183

Ladson-Billings, G., 200
Latinos, 155, 158
learning coaches, 148
learning styles, 10
Leu, D., 10, 39
Lewis, J. & Jones, B., 181
Lewis, 181, 183, 192, 198, 199
Lewison, M., Flint, A. S. & Van Sluys, K. V., 40, 184
leisure reading, 71, 73, 82
literacy event, 76, 80, 82
literacy circles, 190; identity development, 193; roles, 192–93; *see also* Common Core State Standards—English language arts anchor standards addressed through literacy circles Table 11.4, 194–95
literacy opportunities: to build positive identities as community members, 196–97; to promote positive identities, 184; to promote personal agency, 187, 195
literacy supportive home environment, 70, 77

Mages W. K., 116
McIntosh, P., 185
McLaughlin, M. & DeVoogd, G. L., 185

Mario's literacy development: blog. *See* composing, 227–30; comprehension, 227–31; cultural resources identity, 200–2; multimedia composing, 230–31; out of school identities and literacy, 202–4; screencasting, 223; self-efficacy and identity, 198–200; spelling, 225–27; writing (see composing)
Mathematics as a Second Language (MSL), 105
mathematics autobiography, 100–1, 112
mathematics history, 101
mathematics journal, 100, 112
mathematics logs, 99–100, 112
Michaels, S., 30
Moeller, V.]. & Moeller, M. V., 192
Moje, E. B., 196, 201
Moje, E. B., Ciechanowski, K. M., Kramer, K., Ellis, L., Carrillo, R. & Collazo, T., 201, 202, 203 motivation, 147
multiple intelligences, 3
multiple representations, 91

NAEP scores, 143
narratives, 156
National Council of Supervisors of Mathematics (NCSM), 91
National Council of Teachers of Mathematics (NCTM), 91–92, 95
National Council of Teachers of English (NCTE), 210–11
National Governors Association Center for Best Practices, 10, 32, 93
National Literacy Panel, 52
National Research Council , 183, 202
new literacies, non-print literacies, 10, 60–63
Nieto, S. & Bode, P., 199, 200
numeracy, 94
Nystrand, M., 11, 32, 35

optimism, 155
oral language practice, 57
oral literacy practices, 72
out-of-school activity, 73

Padlet, 228
Papanastasiou, E. C., 182, 200
Pappas, C., 30

parent education programs, 76, 83
parent engagement: at home, 70–75; 82; at school, 75–77, 82; homework, 74–75, 82; resources for, 81; socialization practices, 76; strategies for, 78–80, 82–83; types of, 69–70; volunteering, 71, 83
parent involvement. *See* parent engagement
partnership with parents, 70, 77–78
participatory environments, 9
Patrick, H., Kaplan, A. & Ryan, A., 183, 199
Perkins, D. V. & Saris, R. N., 187
Phinney, J., Horenczyk, G., Liebking, K. & Vedder, P., 182
perspectives on identity: crosscultural perspective, 192; psychosocicial perspective, 183
podcasting, 212–7
Polya, G., 92, 104
Popplet, 217–9, 229
Pozzi, F., 188
problem solving, 91–92, 94–96, 104–5, 112

Rasinski, N. & Padak, T., 38
reading comprehension, 92–93, 96
response journals, 185–86
Rios-Aguilar, C., Marquez Kiyama, J., Gravitt, M. & Moll, L. C., 200, 201
Risko, V. J. & Walker-Dalhouse, D., 201
Rodger, R. & Wetzel, M., 41
Rosenblatt, L., 115

scaffolding, 96
school-based norms, 194
screencasting, 223–25
Screencast-O-Matic, 221, 224–25
self-assessment and goal setting, 195–96; *see also* literacy opportunities
self-efficacy, 147
self-regulation, 147, 150,
Shiflett, A., 189
Shor, I. , 184

Sky-McIlvain, E., 185
sociocultural, 67–68, 72, 183
Spelling City, 227
socio-cognitive theory, 147, 150
sociocultural theory, 67–68, 72, 94
Standards for Mathematical Practice, 93
structuralism, 146
Survey, Question, Read, Recite, and Review (SQ3R), 97, 111

tableau, 115
Tatum, A., 198
teacher preparation programs, 144
television, 71, 82
Tomlinson, C. M. & Lynch-Brown, C., 205
tools of literacy, 67
Tux Paint, 221
Think-Alouds, 96, 111

Verbal and Visual Word Association (VVWA) strategy, 97, 111
visualizations: *see* drawings
vocabulary, 159
Vocabulary Self-Collection Strategy (VSS), 96, 111
VoiceThread, 214–15, 228
Voki, 215
Vygotsky, L., 68, 94, 96

Wells, G., 37
Winner, E., 116
Word Knowledge Check (WKC), 96, 111
word problems, 92, 97, 102–4, 112
Word Wall, 97, 111

Young, R., 32

Xu, S. H., 199, 203

Zeldin, S., Camino, L., & Mook, C., 183, 202

About the Contributors

Brian R. Evans is an associate professor in mathematics education and the department chairperson in the School of Education at Pace University in New York. His research interests are social justice in urban and international mathematics education, alternative teacher certification, and pre-service teacher preparation. Dr. Evans primarily teaches pedagogical and content courses in mathematics to both pre-service and in-service teachers at the adolescent and childhood levels. He is currently the managing editor for the peer-reviewed *Journal of the National Association for Alternative Certification.*

Michelle Flory is a doctoral candidate and adjunct faculty member for multiple universities including Utah State University, Ottawa University, and Utah Valley University. She teaches courses in literacy, curriculum, and elementary teaching methods. At the undergraduate level, she has taught methods courses in the language arts, science, social studies, as well as courses in educational assessment. Her research interests include children's literature, intermediate students' reading processes, reading motivation, and effective teaching practices in literacy.

Lenwood Gibson Jr. is an assistant professor of special education at Queens College (City University of New York). Dr. Gibson's area of expertise is in the identification and treatment of behavioral deficits for high risk student populations. His current research interests include: (a) the use and effectiveness of computer-assisted instruction as a supplemental tool for students at-risk for academic failure, particularly in urban schools; (b) closing the academic achievement between minority students and their non-minority peers; (c) closing the research to practice gap between effective, research-based strategies and the degree to which special education teachers use them with their daily instruction.

Merryl Goldberg is a professor of visual and performing arts at California State University San Marcos in California and Executive Director of Center ARTES. She teaches classes related to music and learning through the arts. Her multiple publications and national grants relate to her work with arts in the schools. Merryl is also a professional saxophonist and recording artist. Currently, Dr. Goldberg is co-principal investigator on a million-dollar Department of Education Model Arts Grant, DREAM (Developing Reading Education through Arts Methods).

Kathleen A. Gormley is an associate professor in the Department of Teaching and Inclusive Learning Department in the Esteves School of Education at The Sage Colleges in Troy, NY. She teaches a number of advanced literacy courses in hybrid, online, and face-to-face formats. She received a Teaching Certificate in Online Tool and Techniques in Teaching from the Sloan Consortium, an organization dedicated to developing excellence in online teaching. She edited the NYSRA journal, *Language and Literacy Spectrum*, with Dr. McDermott for five years. Her current research interests center around digital literacy and equity issues of literacy acquisition as well as the high-quality preparation of teachers and literacy specialists.

Lois Ann Knezek is a doctoral student in teacher education and administration at the University of North Texas in Denton, Texas. She teaches courses on curriculum and assessment for bilingual/ESL education and a course focused on linguistically diverse students. Her research interests are in dyslexia, English as a second language, reading, and special education.

Jill Lewis-Spector, a former middle and high school teacher in the United States and professor of literacy education at New Jersey City University, will become president of the International Reading Association in May 2014. She is the author of seven texts as well as numerous book chapters and articles on academic literacy, adolescent literacy, and literacy advocacy and has keynoted at state, national, and international conferences. Her current research focuses on literacy policy and teacher advocacy, critical literacy, teacher preparation, literacy leadership, and adolescent literacy.

Roberta Linder is an associate professor of education at the Wittenberg University Education Department in Springfield, Ohio. She is presently teaching courses in early childhood and adolescent literacy, reading assessment and strategies, and content area literacy. Her rich background in special education supports her instruction in literacy courses. Her recent research, publications, and presentations have addressed teacher professional development, adolescent literature, adolescents' in-school and out-of-school literacies, and intervention for struggling readers.

Elena Lyutykh is an assistant professor of research at Concordia University Chicago. Dr. Lyutykh studies literacy and concept development in bilingual children and adolescents. Informed by sociocultural theory, her work has focused on heritage language and literacy development of immigrant learners and contributions of heritage language literacy to their academic success in U.S. schools. Dr. Lyutykh's interests also include immigrant families' experiences and their involvement with their children's schooling in search of better ways to build school—family relationships across cultures and languages.

Peter McDermott is a professor of education at Pace University in New York City where he teaches graduate courses in literacy education and coordinates its adolescent education program. He has taught internationally as a Fulbright Scholar in Sarajevo, Bosnia, as a volunteer with the International Reading Association's (IRA) Reading, Writing and Critical Thinking project in Kazakhstan, IRA's Diagnostic Teaching Project in Tanzania, Africa, and currently with the same project in Sierra Leone. His research interests are in urban education, the new digital literacies, and international education.

Mary McGriff serves as an assistant professor in the College of Education at New Jersey City University. She is currently using design research to investigate faculty/instructor development within college-based literacy support programs. Dr. McGriff is a Literacy Research Association *Scholars of Color Transitioning into Academic Research* (STAR) fellow, and she serves as co-chair of the Association of Literacy Educators Researchers Legislative and Social Issues Committee. Her research interests focus on inquiry-based modes of teacher education, particularly those related to adolescent and post-secondary literacy instruction.

Kathleen A. J. Mohr, currently an associate professor of language and literacy, was an elementary school teacher in California and Texas for fifteen years. She now works to challenge prospective teachers to be more effective and efficient educators. Her research agenda has focused on accelerating the social and academic progress of English language learners. She uses a cognitive perspective and mixed methodologies to explore integrating and stacking research-recommended practices in sophisticated ways to support student achievement.

Shobana Musti-Rao is an associate professor in special education at Pace University's School of Education. Her research interests include academic and behavioral interventions for students with mild to moderate disabilities, use of technology in the classroom, and teaching students from culturally and linguistically diverse backgrounds. Her research focus is to help teachers in the classroom find effective ways to work with students in inclusive settings.

Lee Shumow is a distinguished teaching professor at Northern Illinois University. After working as a classroom teacher and serving as a parent educator, Dr. Shumow pursued a doctorate in educational psychology and became a professor. She applies her knowledge about parents, learning, and student development in her work as a teacher educator and in her research and writing about fostering students' school adjustment through building partnerships.

Laurie Stowell is a professor of literacy in the School of Education at California State University-San Marcos. Her primary responsibilities are teaching language and literacy courses in the middle level and multiple subjects (elementary) credential program, children's literature at the introductory and advanced level as well as other courses in the master's program. Dr. Stowell also founded and directs the San Marcos Writing Project. Her research interests are children's literature, writing, middle-level literacy, and assessment. She has also worked with elementary, middle, and high school teachers in San Diego and Riverside County to plan and implement reading strategies and the teaching of writing.

About the Editor

Francine Falk-Ross, Ph.D., is a professor and coordinator of the Literacy Education and Childhood Education programs at Pace University in Pleasantville, New York, where she teaches courses on literacy topics to preservice and practicing teachers. As an active member of the Literacy Research Association, International Reading Association, and American Educational Reading Association, she has been active in publishing studies focused on language and literacy issues, such as the integration of media into literacy lessons and discourse modifications for struggling readers, language factors in literacy achievement, and middle level teacher education. Her articles, book, and book chapters on literacy education issues have been published in peer-reviewed publications such as *Research in the Teaching of English, Language Arts, Reading and Writing Quarterly, Journal of Early Childhood Teacher Education,* and *Journal of Adolescent and Adult Literacy,* among others. Her text, *Classroom-based Language and Literacy Intervention: A Programs and Case Studies Approach,* focuses on inclusive strategies for struggling readers. Dr. Falk-Ross has served on several university-school partnership projects, sharing in the research, presentations, and publications from those collaborations